entaur's Life

19

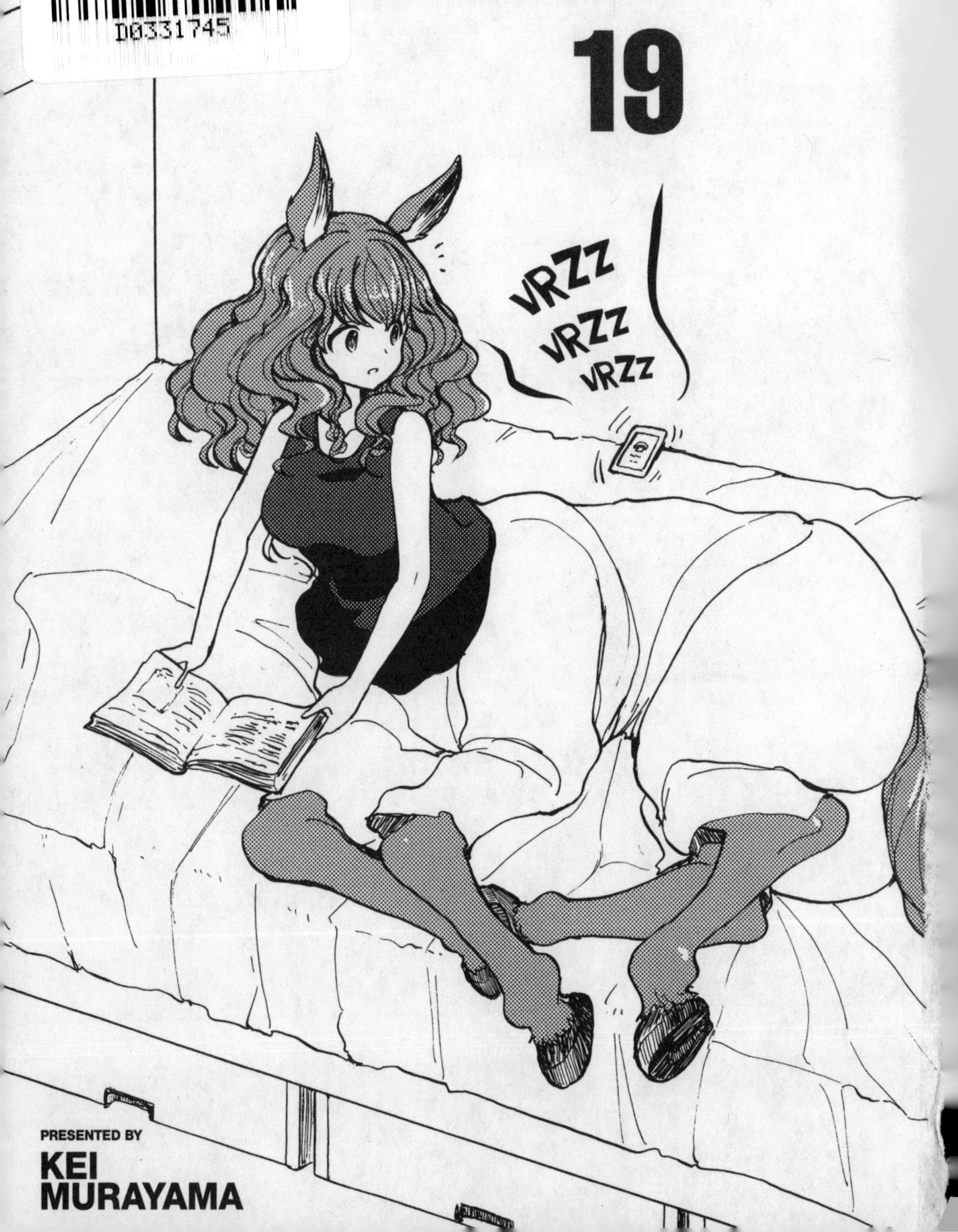
VRZZ
VRZZ
VRZZ

PRESENTED BY

KEI MURAYAMA

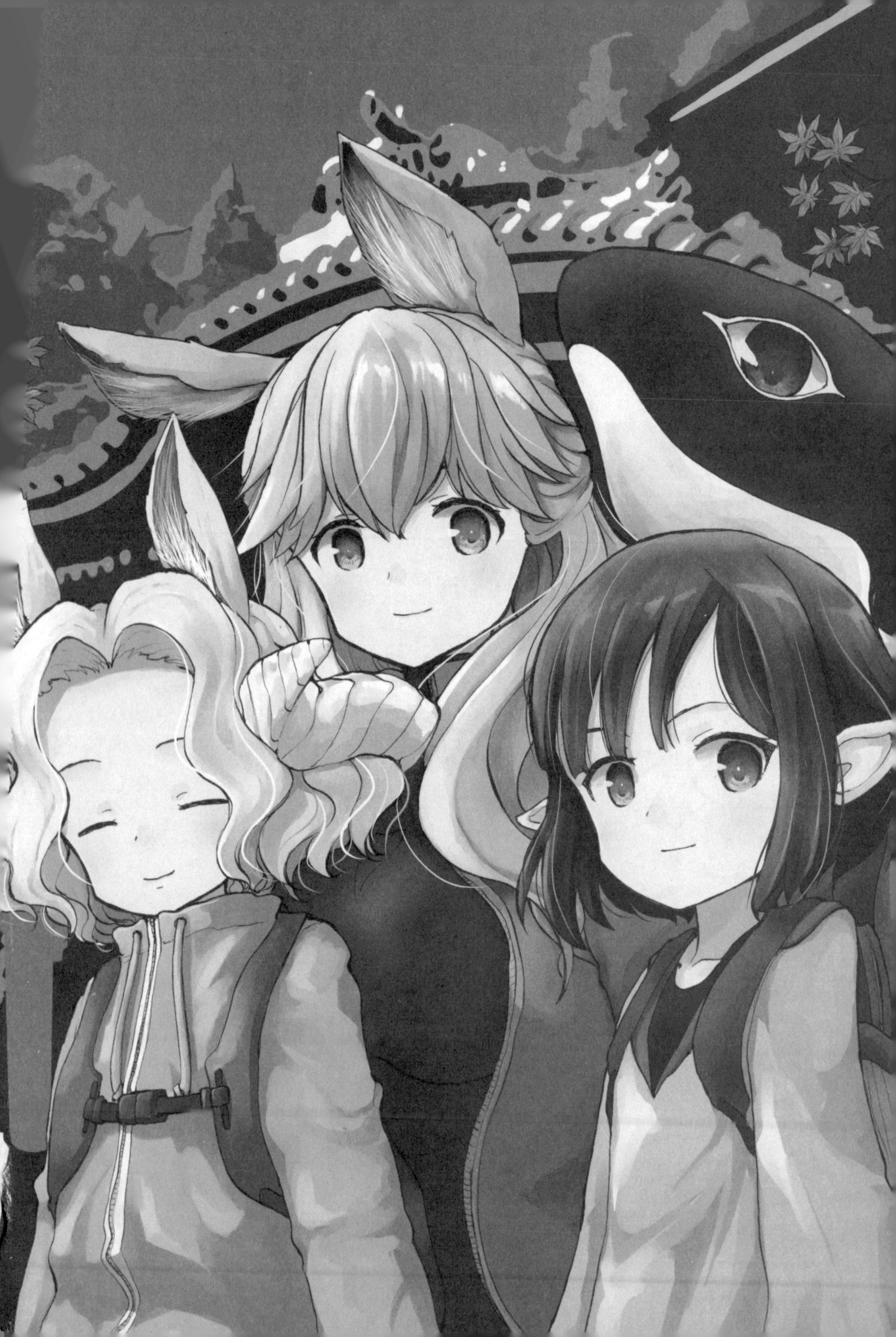

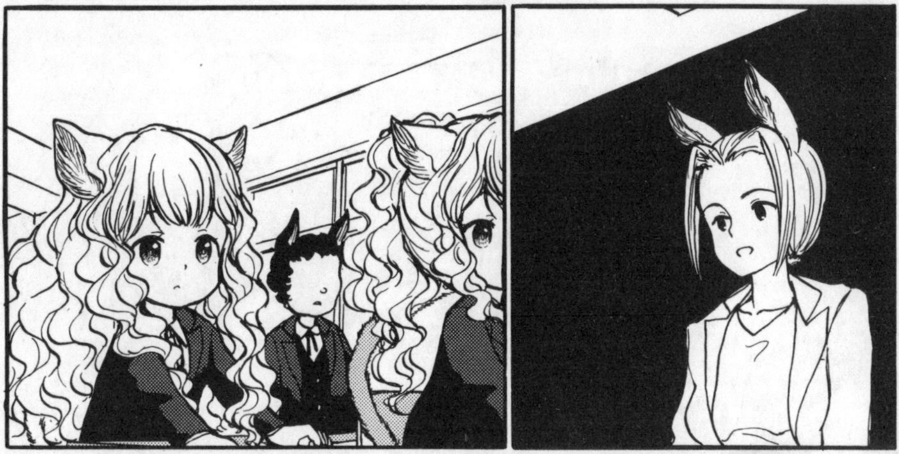

CHAPTER 151

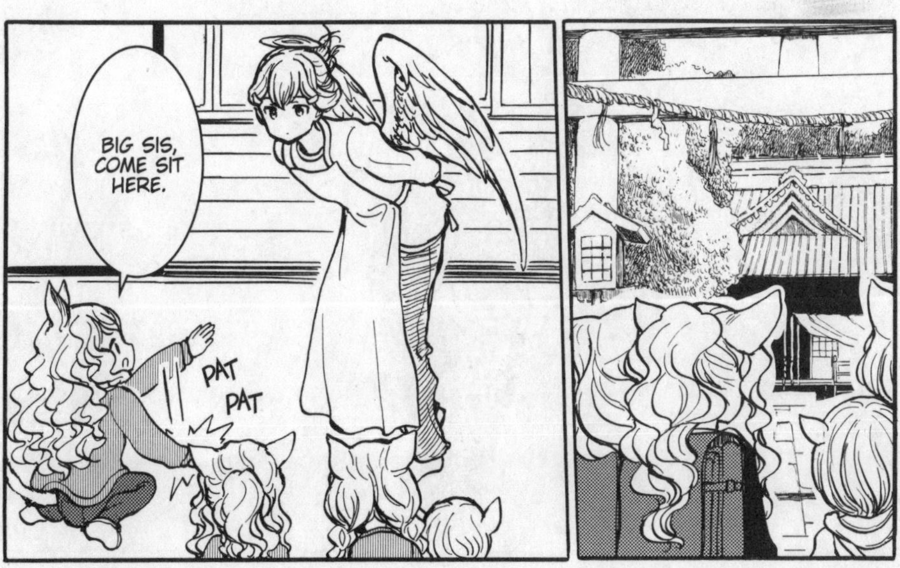
BIG SIS, COME SIT HERE.
PAT PAT

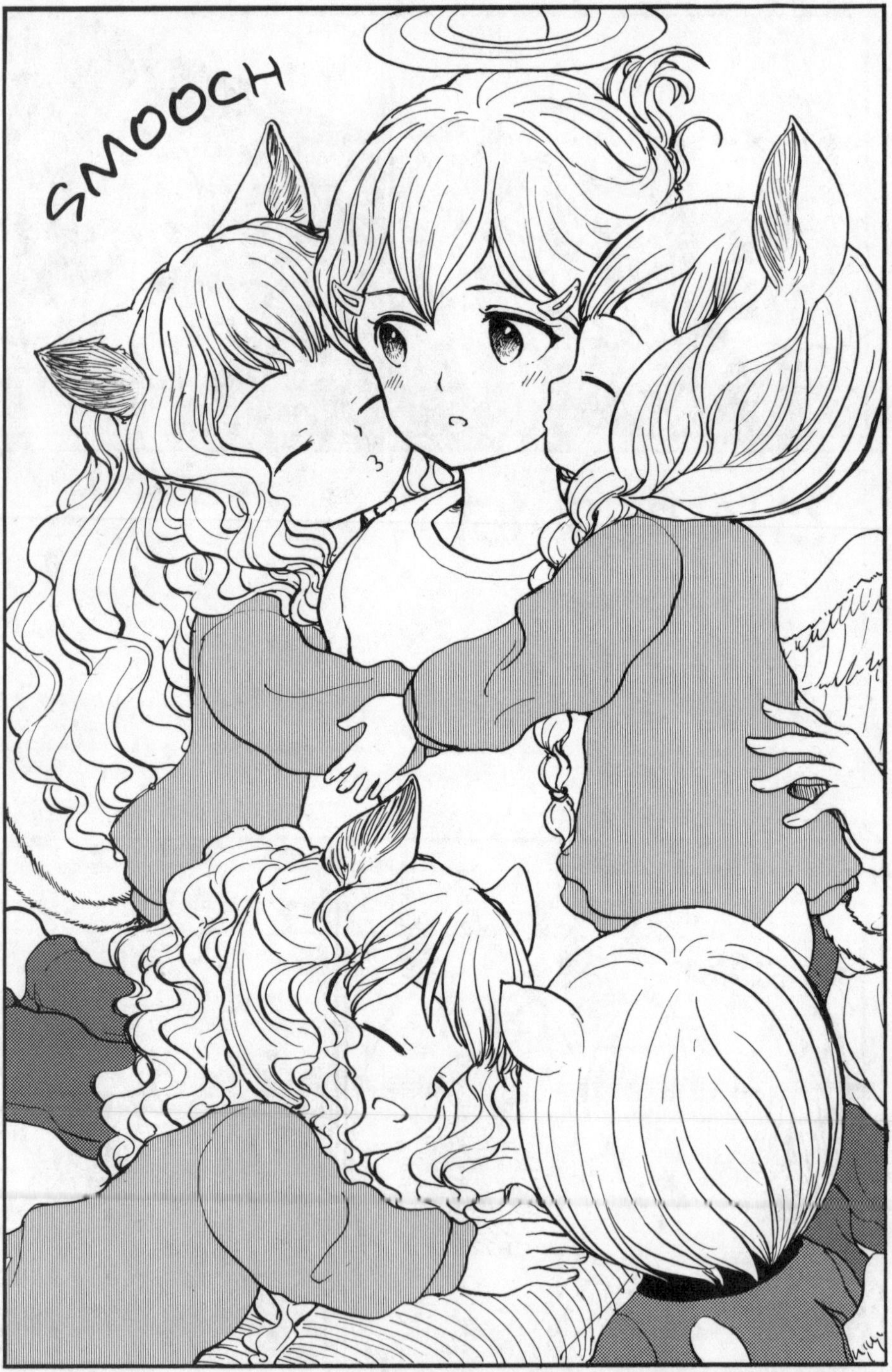
SMOOCH

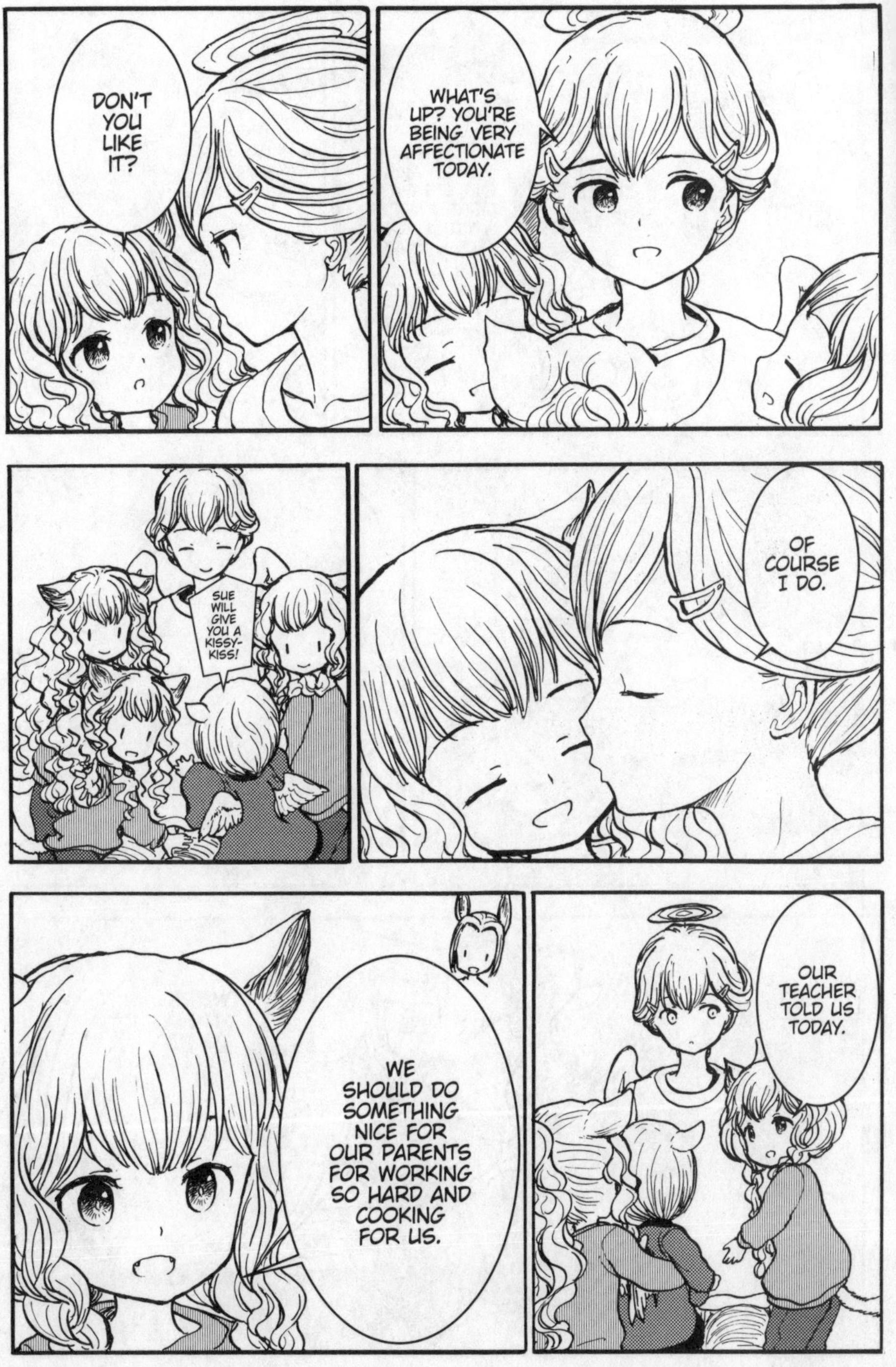
WHAT'S UP? YOU'RE BEING VERY AFFECTIONATE TODAY.
DON'T YOU LIKE IT?
OF COURSE I DO.
SUE WILL GIVE YOU A KISSY-KISS!
OUR TEACHER TOLD US TODAY.
WE SHOULD DO SOMETHING NICE FOR OUR PARENTS FOR WORKING SO HARD AND COOKING FOR US.

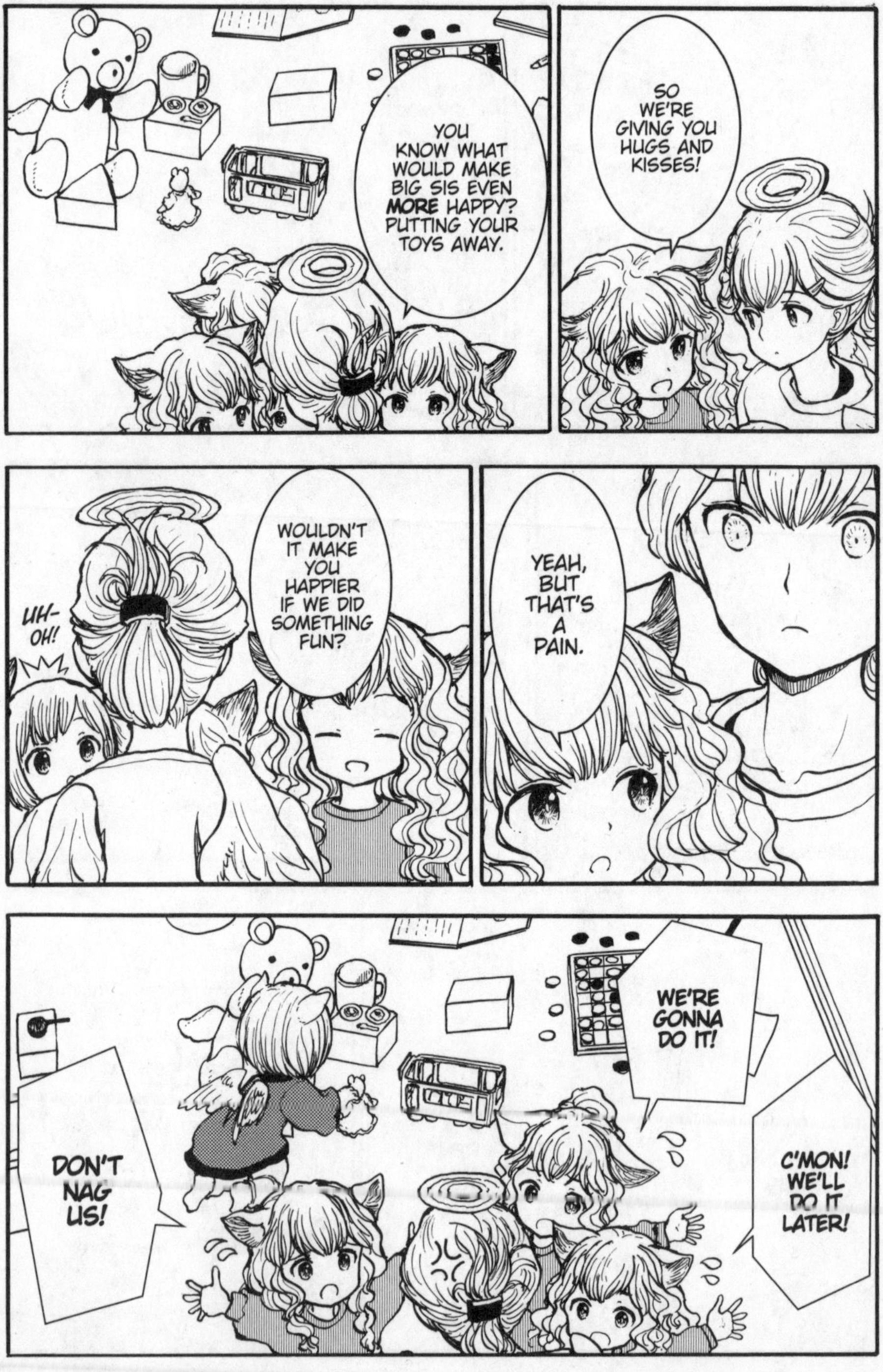
SO WE'RE GIVING YOU HUGS AND KISSES!
YOU KNOW WHAT WOULD MAKE BIG SIS EVEN **MORE** HAPPY? PUTTING YOUR TOYS AWAY.
YEAH, BUT THAT'S A PAIN.
WOULDN'T IT MAKE YOU HAPPIER IF WE DID SOMETHING FUN?
UH-OH!
C'MON! WE'LL DO IT LATER!
WE'RE GONNA DO IT!
DON'T NAG US!

A CentaUr's Life

GREAT SCHOLARS OF THE WORLD:
<1> CONFUCIUS

CONFUCIUS IS KNOWN AS THE FATHER OF CONFUCIANISM. HE AND HIS DISCIPLES CREATED A DOCTRINE, KNOWN AS LITERATI, WHICH SPREAD CONFUCIANISM ACROSS EAST ASIA. CONFUCIANISM ADVOCATED FOR STRONG MORALS BUT WAS CRITICIZED FOR DISCOURAGING THE GROWTH AND DEVELOPMENT OF SOCIETY. FOR MANY YEARS, THIS WAS A BARRIER TO ITS PRACTICE. TODAY, HOWEVER, SYSTEMS OF LAW HAVE TAKEN THE PLACE OF DICTATORSHIPS, LEAVING THEM AND THEIR CRITICISMS OF CONFUCIANISM IN THE PAST.

CONFUCIUS WAS BORN IN THE STATE OF LU DURING CHINA'S SPRING AND AUTUMN PERIOD. DURING THIS PERIOD, THE ZHOU DYNASTY WAS IN DECLINE AND MANY VASSAL STATES HAD BEGUN TO FIGHT FOR SUPREMACY. THE STATE OF LU WAS CONSTANTLY THREATENED BY THE LARGER SURROUNDING STATES: QI, JIN, AND CHU. THE DUKE OF LU HAD GROWN WEAK, AND THE STATE WAS DOMINATED BY MINISTERIAL FAMILIES CALLED THE THREE HUANS. THEIR RETAINERS STAGED A COUP D'ETAT AGAINST THE DUKE.

IT WAS DURING THIS TIME THAT CONFUCIUS WAS BORN TO A FAMILY OF FUNERAL CONDUCTORS. AT THE TIME, FUNERAL RITUALS WERE LED BY SPIRITUAL MEDIUMS WHO ENSHRINED THE SPIRITS OF THE DEAD BY DIGGING OUT THEIR SKULLS AND PLACING THEM ON THEIR HEADS. THIS ARCHAIC RITE INFORMED CONFUCIUS' TEACHINGS AND BELIEFS. FROM IT, HE DEVELOPED "FILIAL PIETY"--THE IDEA OF RESPECT NOT ONLY FOR ONE'S PARENTS AND ANCESTORS, BUT FOR THOSE OUTSIDE OF ONE'S LINEAGE BY VIRTUE OF LOYALTY, BENEVOLENCE, AND RIGHTEOUSNESS. THIS CONCEPT ALLOWED CONFUCIUS TO BETTER UNDERSTAND BOTH DEATH AND SOCIETY.

DURING CONFUCIUS'S LIFETIME, THE BUREAUCRATIC SYSTEM WAS STILL IN ITS EARLY STAGES OF DEVELOPMENT, WHICH MEANT THAT THE STATE TOOK TO MORE TRADITIONAL RULES AND NORMS. CHIEFS CHOSE TO FOLLOW OLD RULES AND ACT IN ACCORDANCE WITH THE MANDATES CREATED BY THEIR ANCIENT PREDECESSORS. THIS ALLOWED FOR THE SOCIAL STABILITY OF THE TIME, WHICH THEN GAVE WAY TO CUSTOMS AND RITUALS SUCH AS MUSIC, PRAYER, AND THE PURSUIT OF KNOWLEDGE WHICH REFLECTED THE PRINCIPLES OF CONFUCIANISM.

HOWEVER, DESPITE THESE PEACEFUL TEACHINGS, THE QIN DYNASTY DESTROYED THE STATES OF THE SPRING, AUTUMN, AND WARRING STATES PERIODS, SOLIDIFYING LEGALISM AS THE NEW FOUNDATION OF GOVERNMENTAL POWER. UNDER THIS NEW REGIME, THE BURNING OF BOOKS AND OPPRESSION OF SCHOLARS TOOK PLACE, LEADING TO THE SUPPRESSION OF CONFUCIANISM. IT WAS ONLY AFTER THE HAN DYNASTY DESTROYED THE QIN DYNASTY THAT CONFUCIANISM WAS REINSTATED WHEN THE NEW EMPEROR SOUGHT A NEW BINDING RITUAL UNDER HIS REIGN. HOWEVER, UNDER THE HAN DYNASTY, THE SURVIVING CONFUCIAN TEXTS WERE COMBINED WITH MODERN TEXTS TO MAINTAIN THEIR RELEVANCE. AS A RESULT, OUR CURRENT PARTIAL UNDERSTANDING OF CONFUCIANISM IS ALL THAT REMAINS.

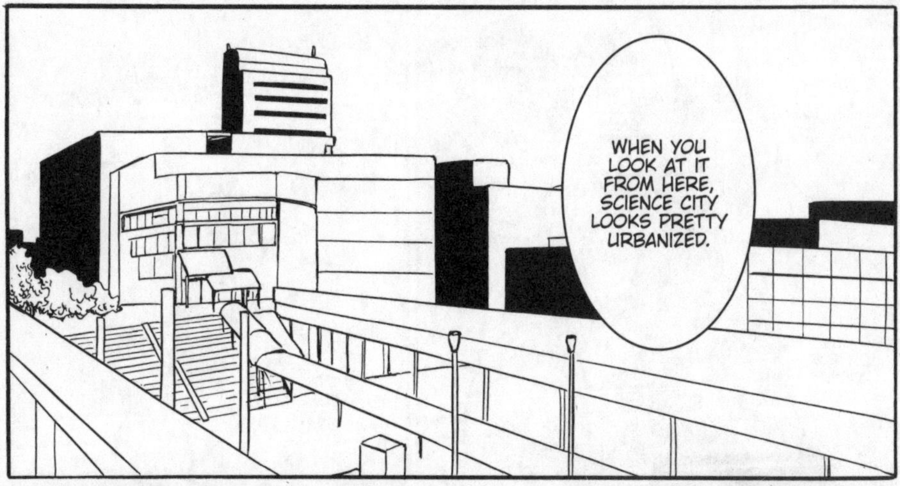
WHEN YOU LOOK AT IT FROM HERE, SCIENCE CITY LOOKS PRETTY URBANIZED.

CHAPTER 152

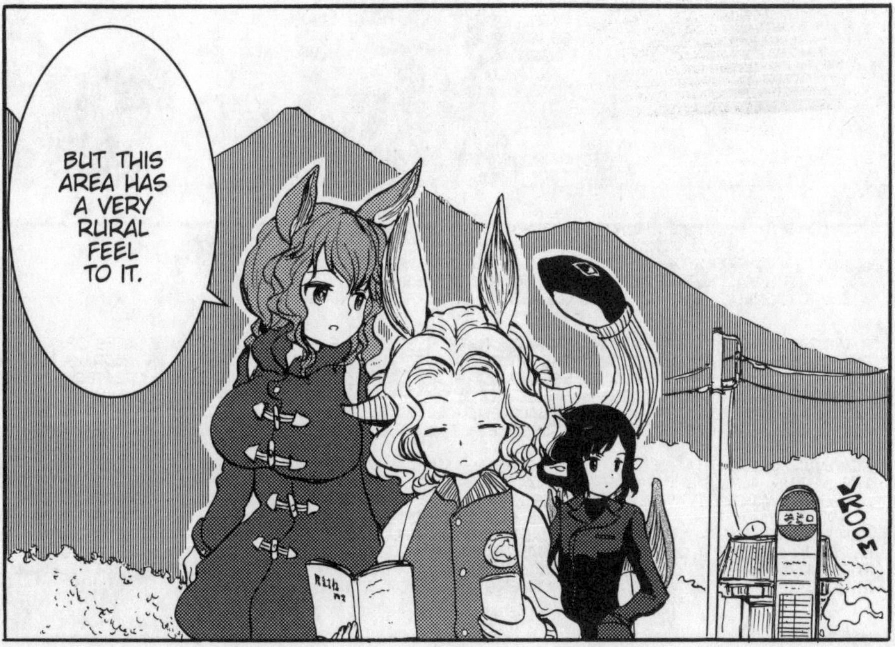
BUT THIS AREA HAS A VERY RURAL FEEL TO IT.
VROOM

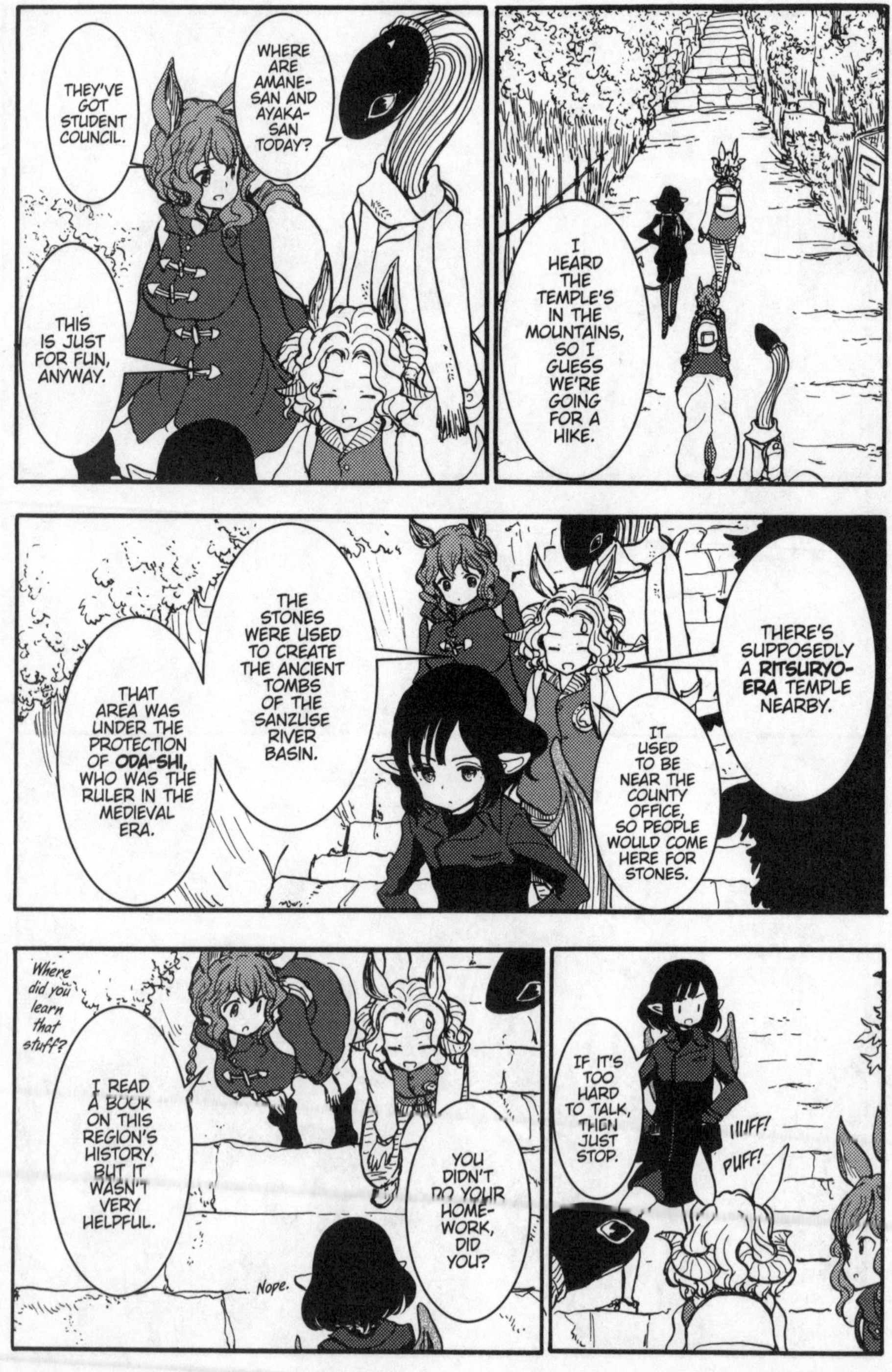
I HEARD THE TEMPLE'S IN THE MOUNTAINS, SO I GUESS WE'RE GOING FOR A HIKE.
WHERE ARE AMANE-SAN AND AYAKA-SAN TODAY?
THEY'VE GOT STUDENT COUNCIL.
THIS IS JUST FOR FUN, ANYWAY.
THERE'S SUPPOSEDLY A **RITSURYO-ERA** TEMPLE NEARBY.
IT USED TO BE NEAR THE COUNTY OFFICE, SO PEOPLE WOULD COME HERE FOR STONES.
THE STONES WERE USED TO CREATE THE ANCIENT TOMBS OF THE SANZUSE RIVER BASIN.
THAT AREA WAS UNDER THE PROTECTION OF **ODA-SHI,** WHO WAS THE RULER IN THE MEDIEVAL ERA.
IF IT'S TOO HARD TO TALK, THEN JUST STOP.
HUFF!
PUFF!
YOU DIDN'T DO YOUR HOMEWORK, DID YOU?
Where did you learn that stuff?
I READ A BOOK ON THIS REGION'S HISTORY, BUT IT WASN'T VERY HELPFUL.
Nope.

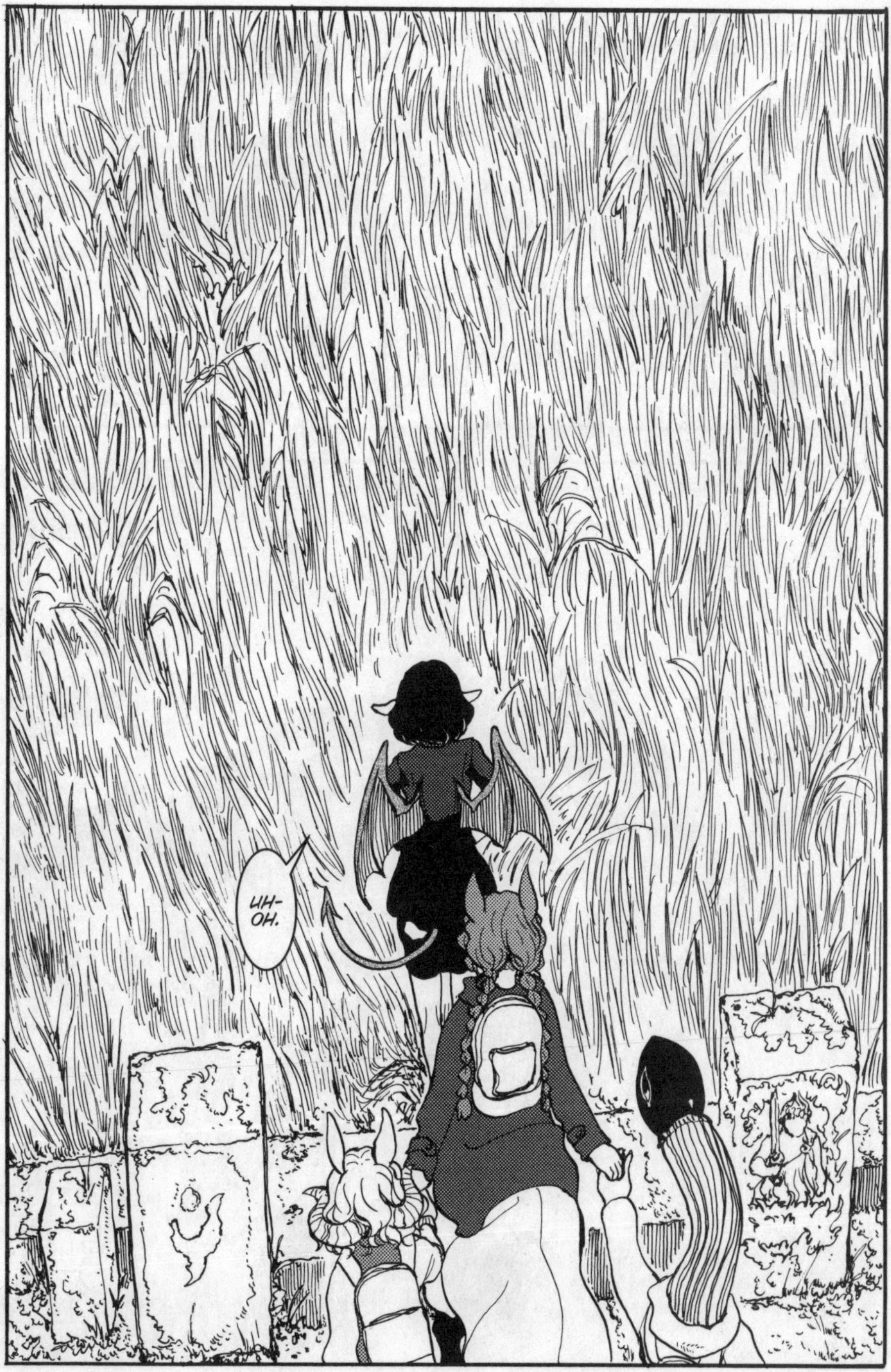
UH-OH.

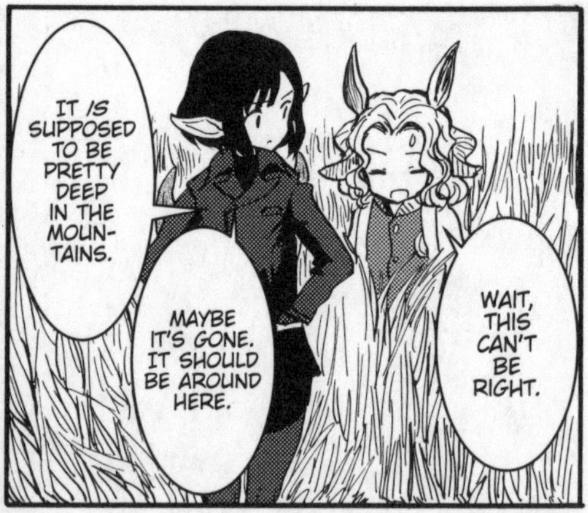
WAIT, THIS CAN'T BE RIGHT.
MAYBE IT'S GONE. IT SHOULD BE AROUND HERE.
IT IS SUPPOSED TO BE PRETTY DEEP IN THE MOUN-TAINS.

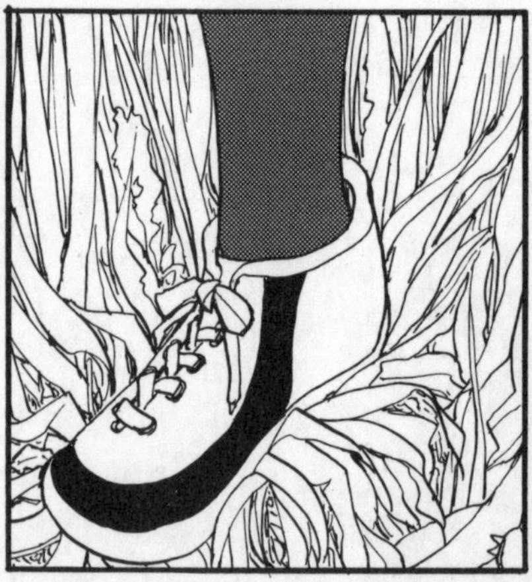

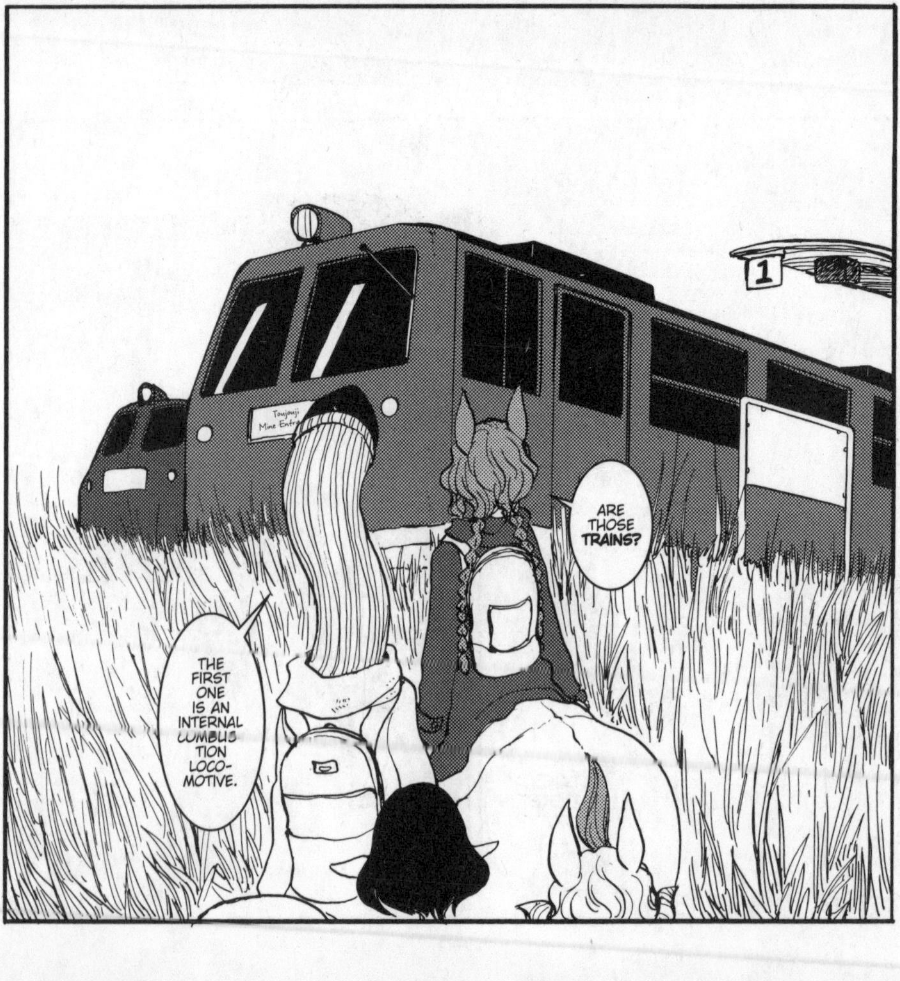
1
ARE THOSE TRAINS?
THE FIRST ONE IS AN INTERNAL COMBUS-TION LOCO-MOTIVE.

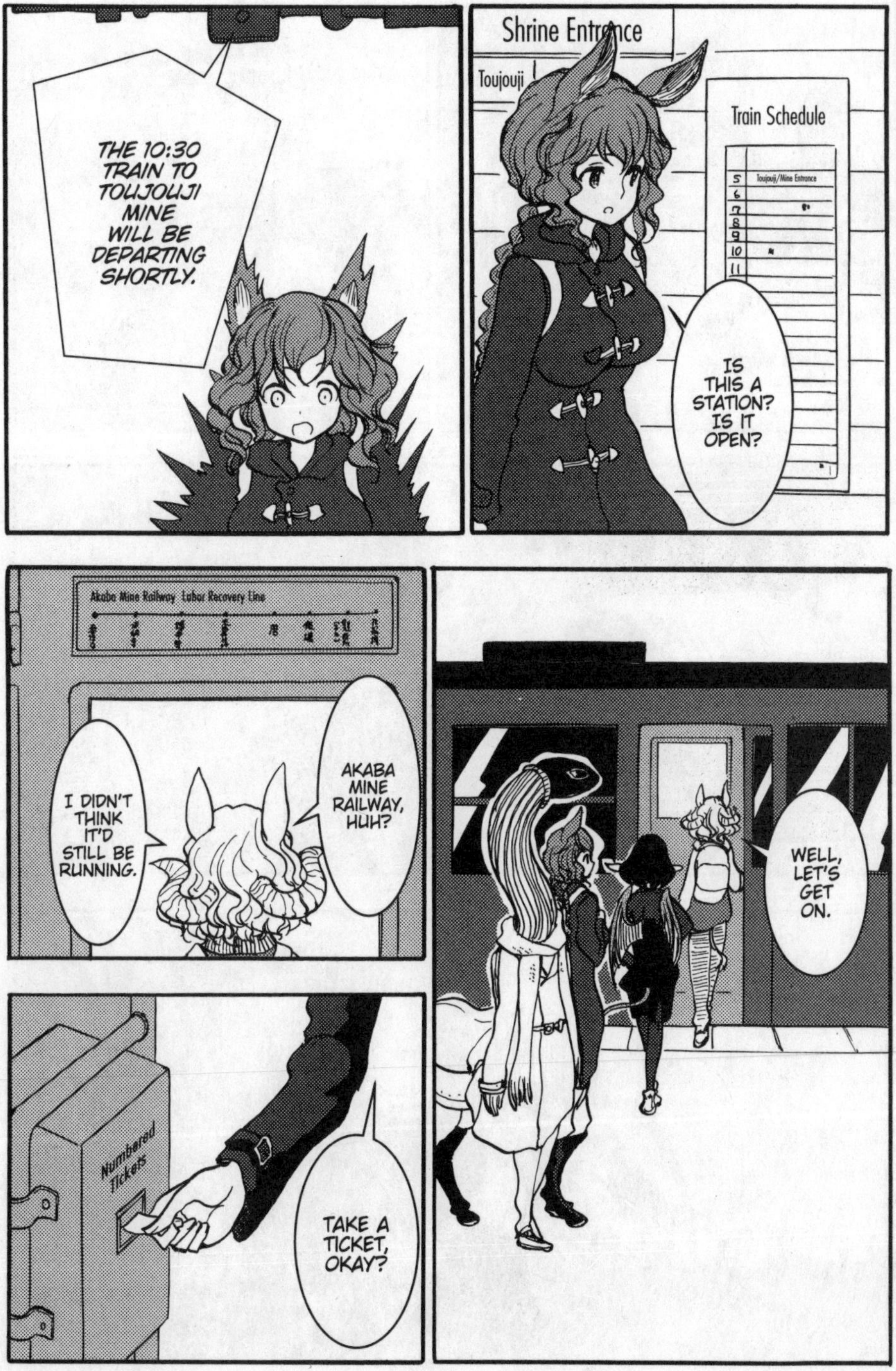
Shrine Entrance
Toujouji
Train Schedule
Toujouji/Mine Entrance
IS THIS A STATION? IS IT OPEN?
THE 10:30 TRAIN TO TOUJOUJI MINE WILL BE DEPARTING SHORTLY.
WELL, LET'S GET ON.
Akaba Mine Railway Labor Recovery Line
AKABA MINE RAILWAY, HUH?
I DIDN'T THINK IT'D STILL BE RUNNING.
Numbered Tickets
TAKE A TICKET, OKAY?

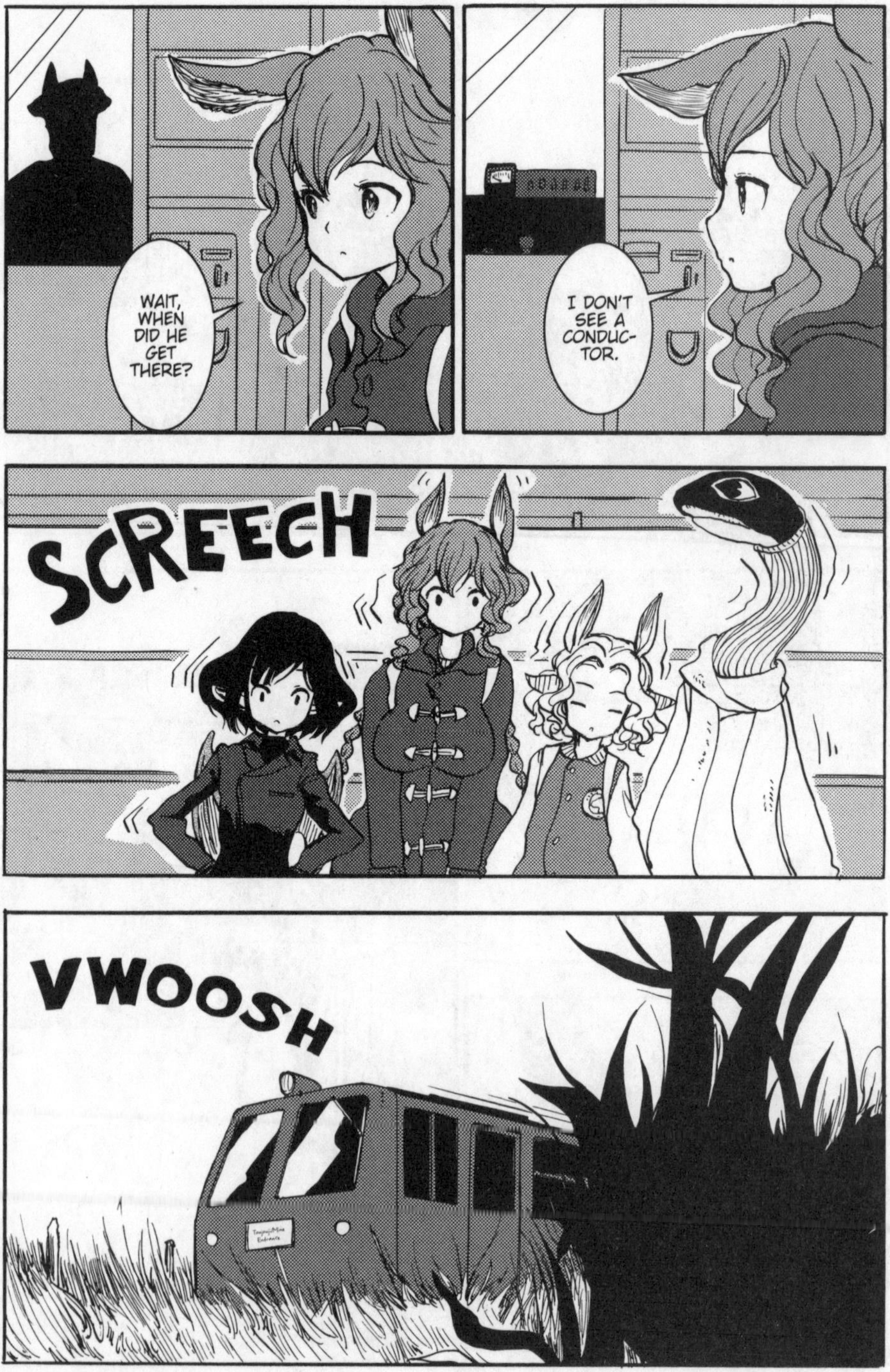
I DON'T SEE A CONDUCTOR.
WAIT, WHEN DID HE GET THERE?
SCREECH
VWOOSH

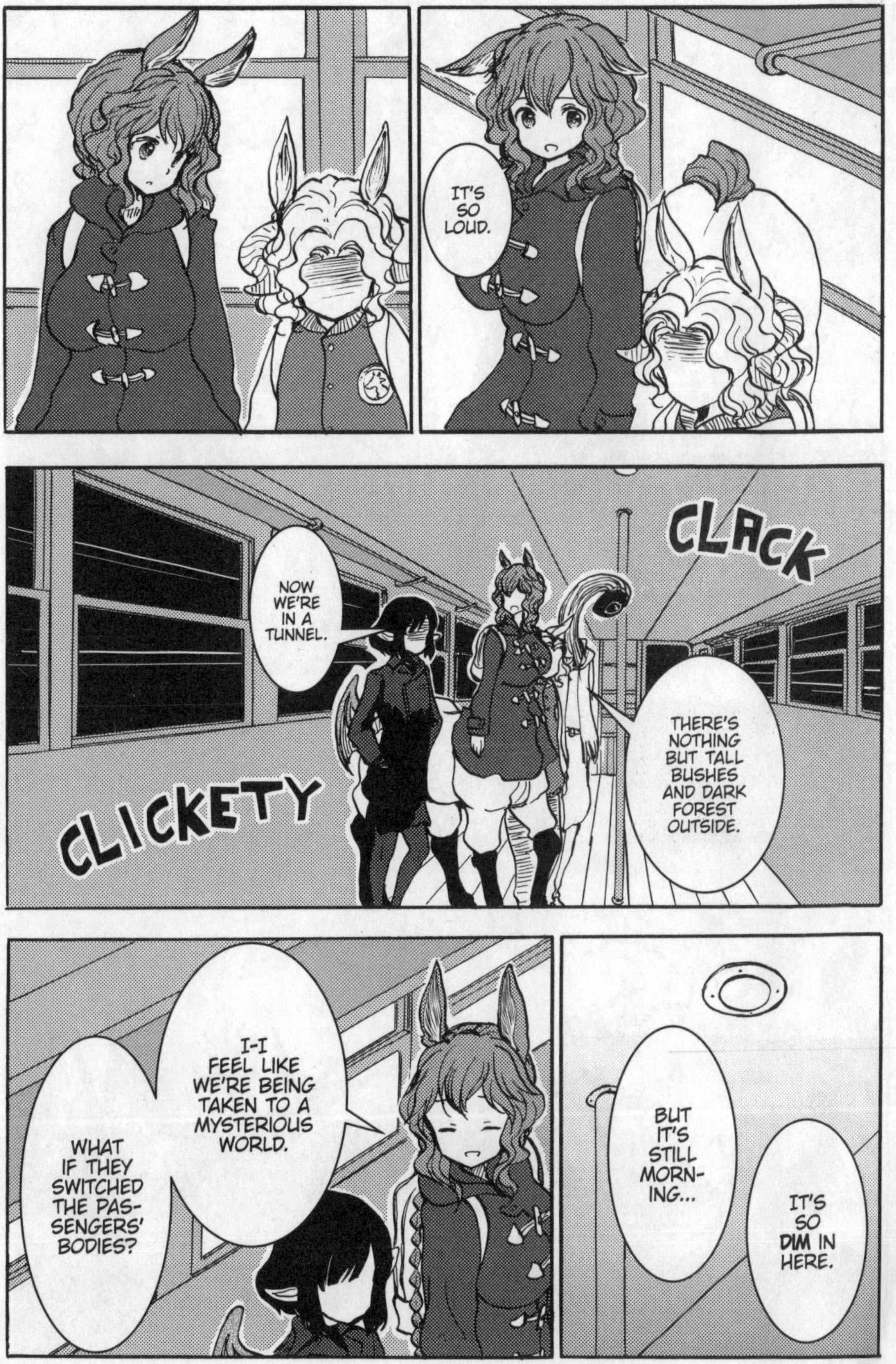
IT'S SO LOUD.
CLACK
NOW WE'RE IN A TUNNEL.
THERE'S NOTHING BUT TALL BUSHES AND DARK FOREST OUTSIDE.
CLICKETY
IT'S SO **DIM** IN HERE.
BUT IT'S STILL MORN-ING...
I-I FEEL LIKE WE'RE BEING TAKEN TO A MYSTERIOUS WORLD.
WHAT IF THEY SWITCHED THE PAS-SENGERS' BODIES?

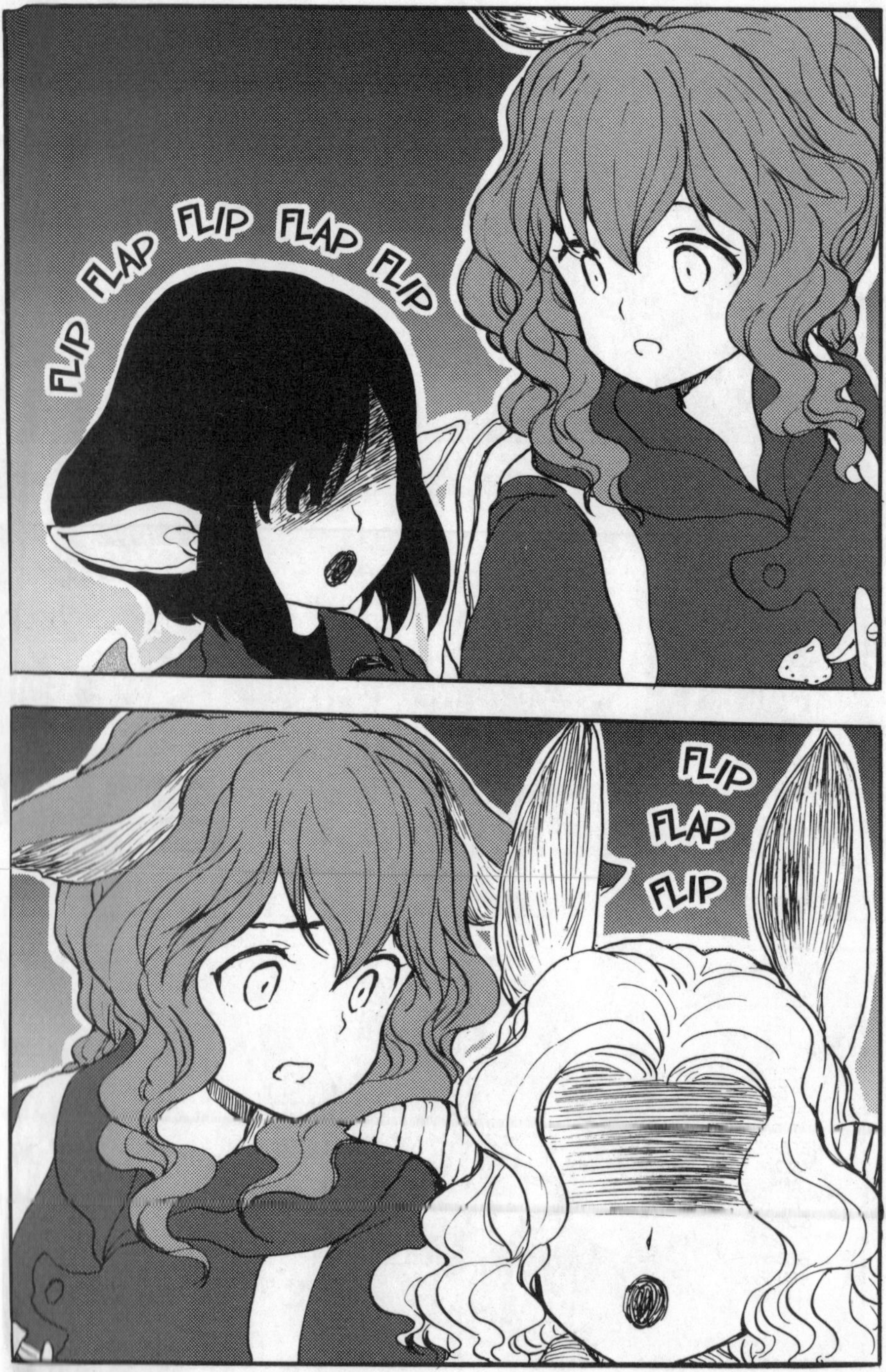
FLIP FLAP FLIP FLAP FLIP
FLIP
FLAP
FLIP

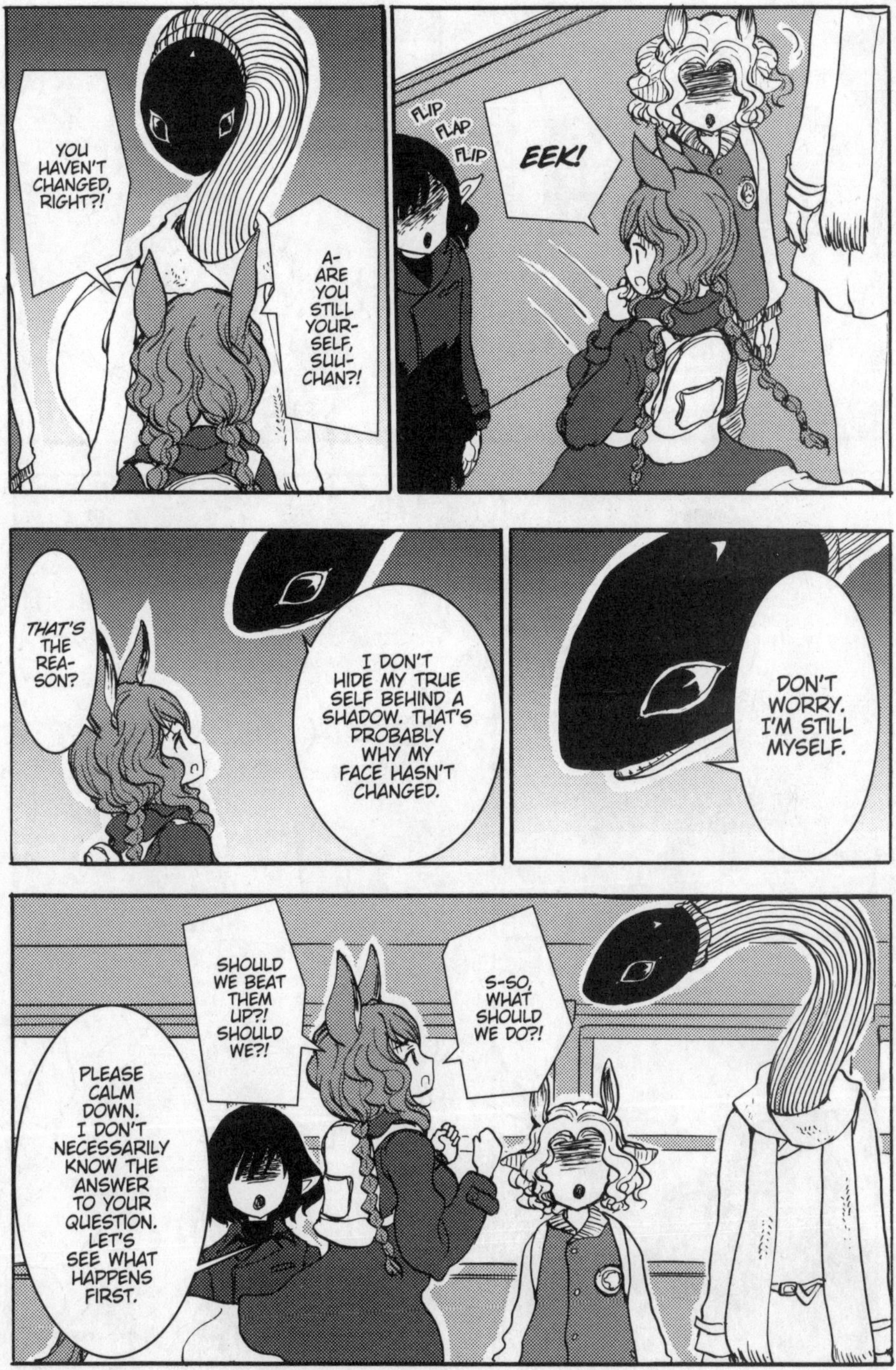
FLIP
FLAP
FLIP
EEK!
A- ARE YOU STILL YOURSELF, SUU-CHAN?!
YOU HAVEN'T CHANGED, RIGHT?!
DON'T WORRY. I'M STILL MYSELF.
I DON'T HIDE MY TRUE SELF BEHIND A SHADOW. THAT'S PROBABLY WHY MY FACE HASN'T CHANGED.
THAT'S THE REASON?
S-SO, WHAT SHOULD WE DO?!
SHOULD WE BEAT THEM UP?! SHOULD WE?!
PLEASE CALM DOWN. I DON'T NECESSARILY KNOW THE ANSWER TO YOUR QUESTION. LET'S SEE WHAT HAPPENS FIRST.

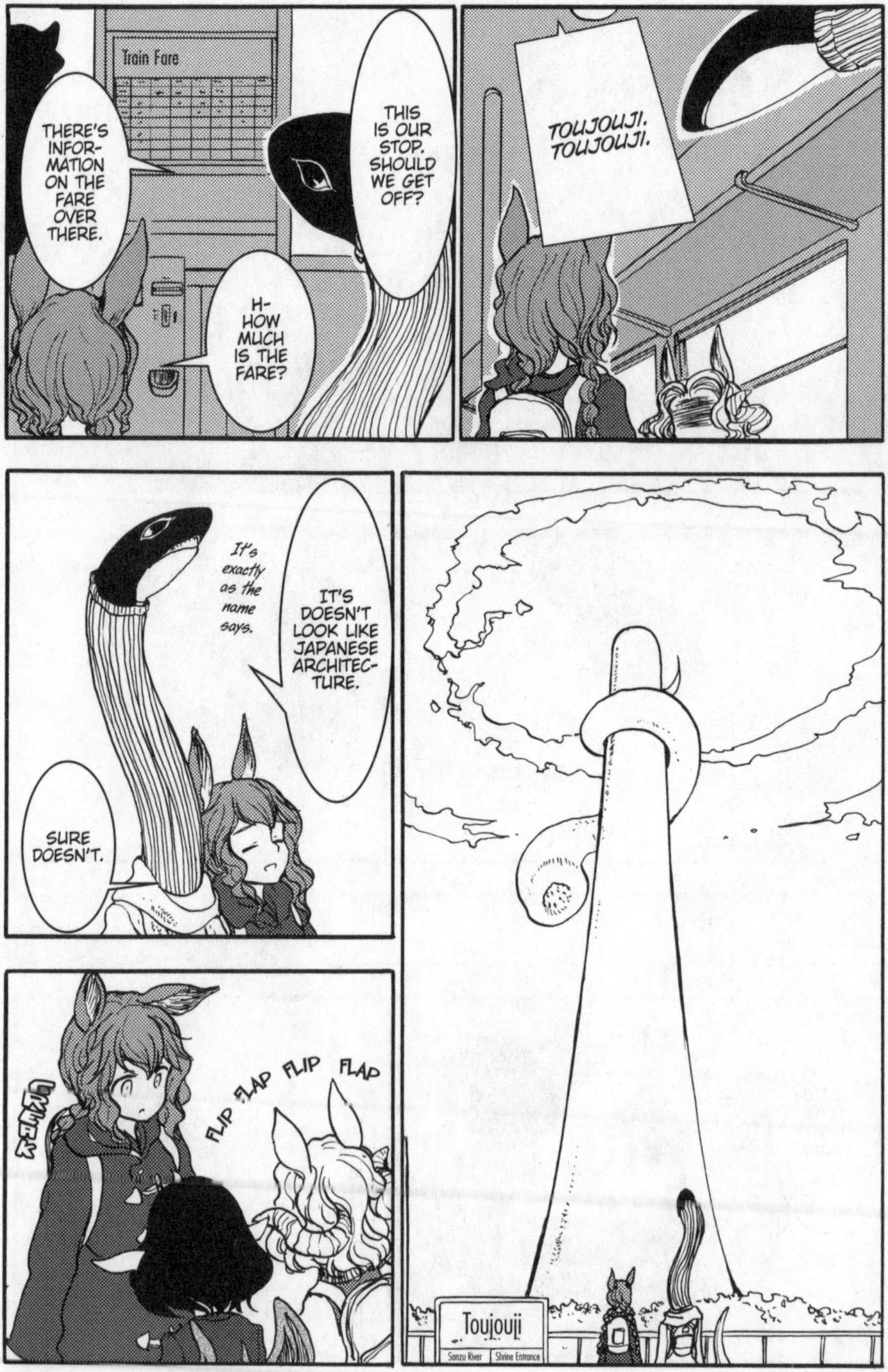
TOUJOUJI. TOUJOUJI.
Train Fare
THIS IS OUR STOP. SHOULD WE GET OFF?
THERE'S INFORMATION ON THE FARE OVER THERE.
H-HOW MUCH IS THE FARE?
Toujouji
Sanzu River
Shrine Entrance
IT'S DOESN'T LOOK LIKE JAPANESE ARCHITECTURE.
It's exactly as the name says.
SURE DOESN'T.
FLIP FLAP FLIP FLAP

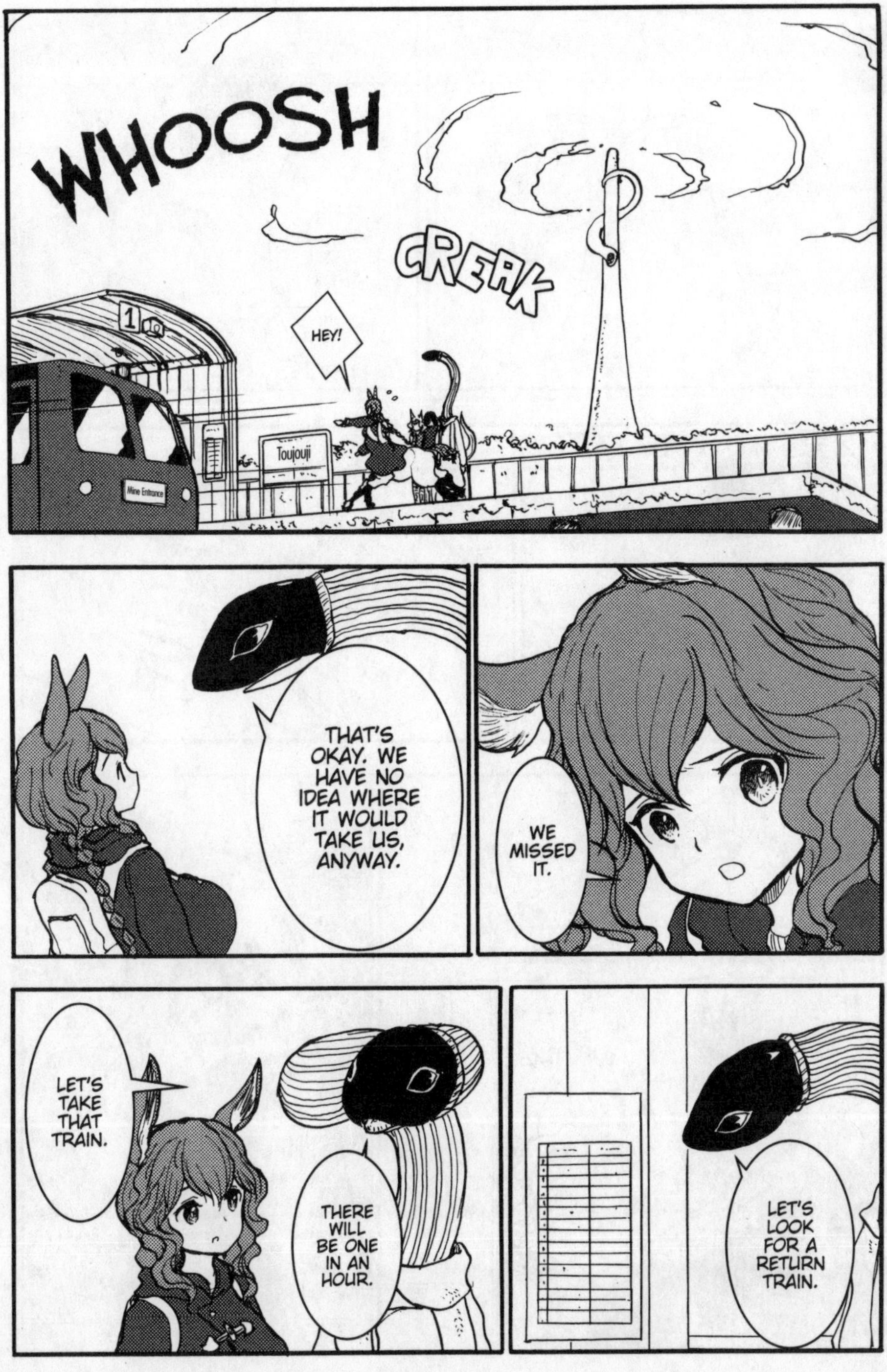
WHOOSH
CREAK
HEY!
1
Toujouji
Mine Entrance
WE MISSED IT.
THAT'S OKAY. WE HAVE NO IDEA WHERE IT WOULD TAKE US, ANYWAY.
LET'S LOOK FOR A RETURN TRAIN.
THERE WILL BE ONE IN AN HOUR.
LET'S TAKE THAT TRAIN.

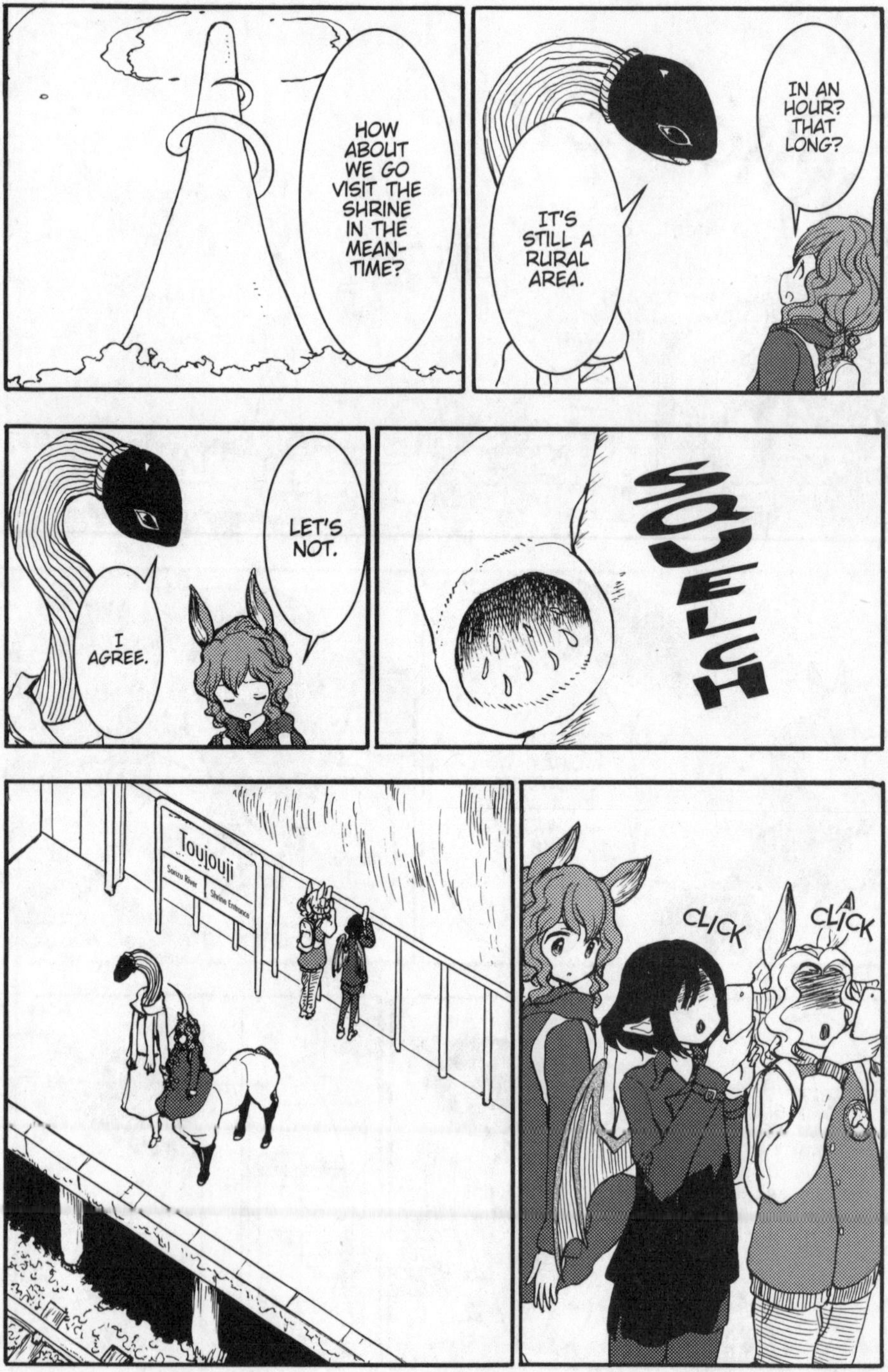
IN AN HOUR? THAT LONG?
IT'S STILL A RURAL AREA.
HOW ABOUT WE GO VISIT THE SHRINE IN THE MEAN-TIME?
SQUELCH
LET'S NOT.
I AGREE.
CLICK
CLICK
Toujouji
Sonzu River
Shrine Entrance

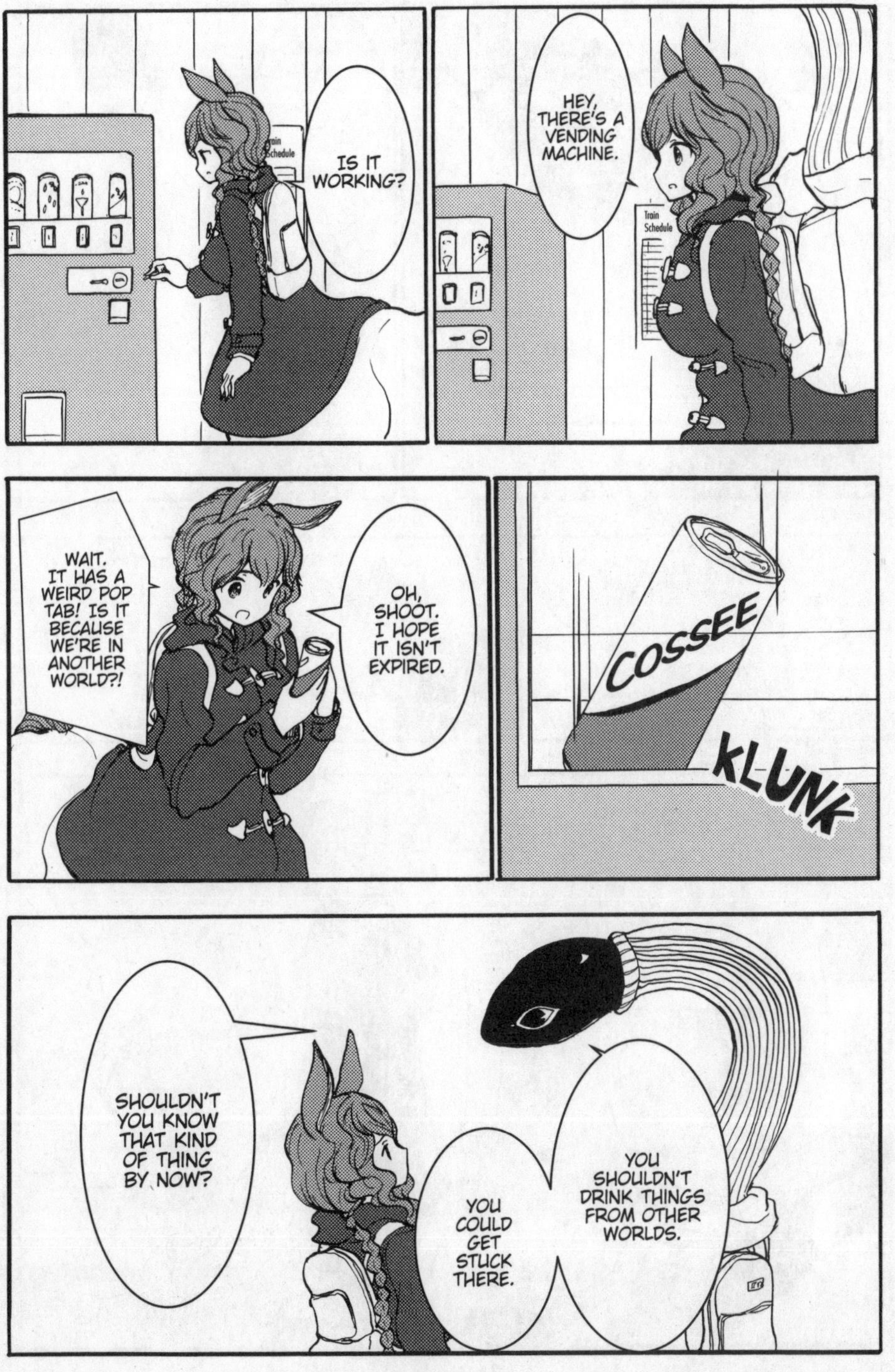
HEY, THERE'S A VENDING MACHINE.
Train Schedule
IS IT WORKING?
Train Schedule
COSSEE
KLUNK
OH, SHOOT. I HOPE IT ISN'T EXPIRED.
WAIT. IT HAS A WEIRD POP TAB! IS IT BECAUSE WE'RE IN ANOTHER WORLD?!
YOU SHOULDN'T DRINK THINGS FROM OTHER WORLDS.
YOU COULD GET STUCK THERE.
SHOULDN'T YOU KNOW THAT KIND OF THING BY NOW?

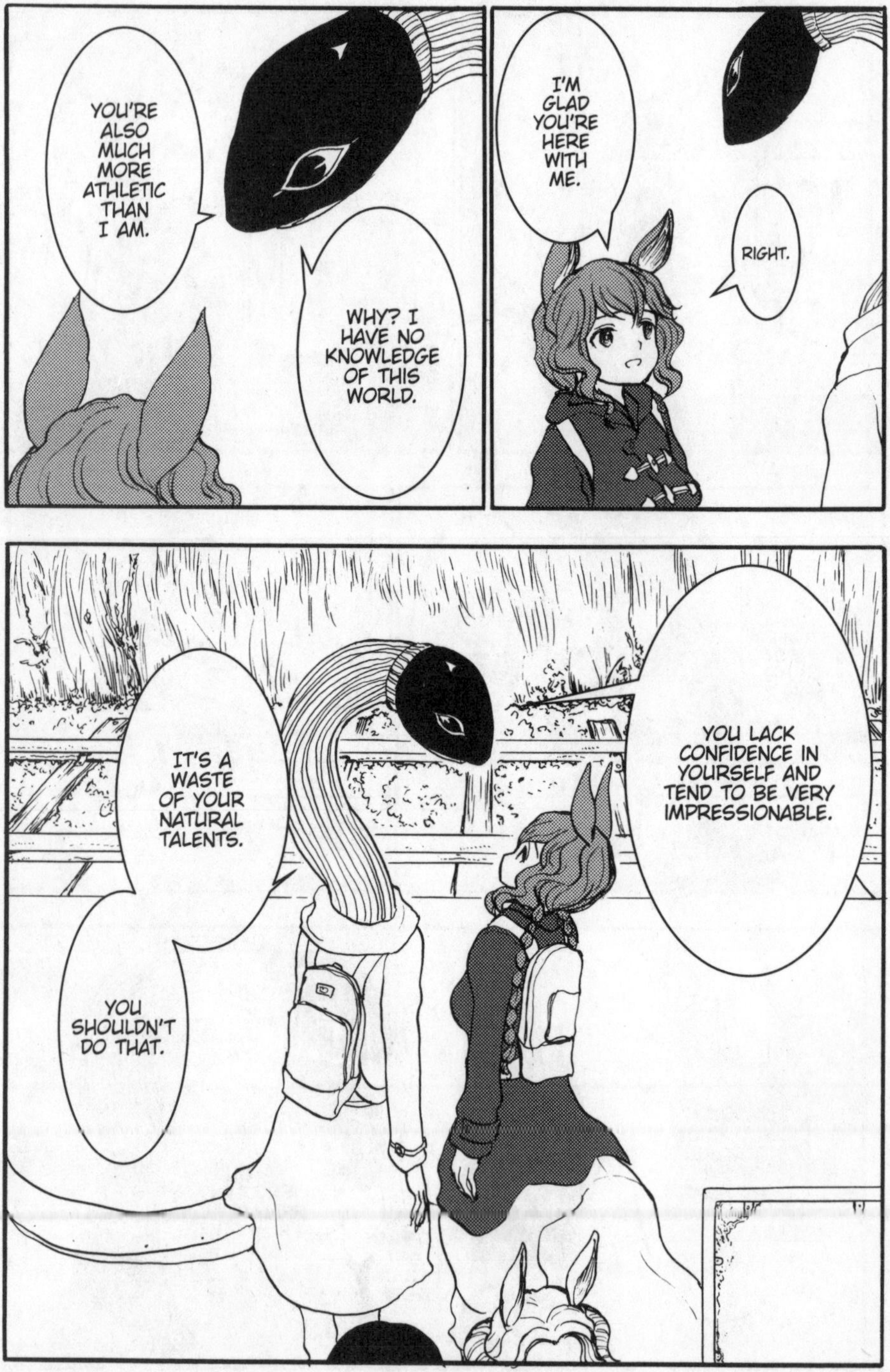
I'M GLAD YOU'RE HERE WITH ME.
RIGHT.
YOU'RE ALSO MUCH MORE ATHLETIC THAN I AM.
WHY? I HAVE NO KNOWLEDGE OF THIS WORLD.
YOU LACK CONFIDENCE IN YOURSELF AND TEND TO BE VERY IMPRESSIONABLE.
IT'S A WASTE OF YOUR NATURAL TALENTS.
YOU SHOULDN'T DO THAT.

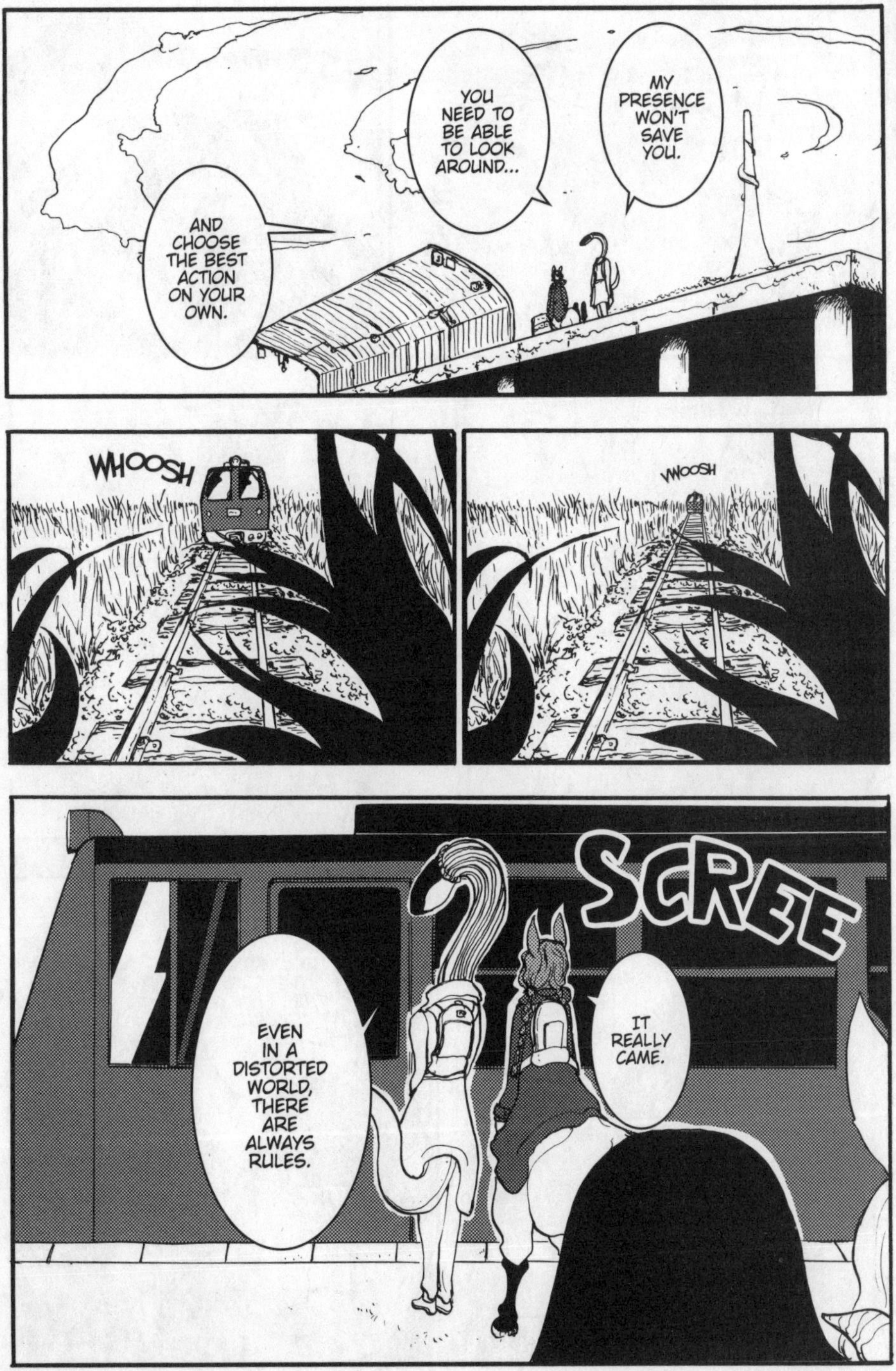
MY PRESENCE WON'T SAVE YOU.
YOU NEED TO BE ABLE TO LOOK AROUND...
AND CHOOSE THE BEST ACTION ON YOUR OWN.
WHOOSH
WHOOSH
SCREE
IT REALLY CAME.
EVEN IN A DISTORTED WORLD, THERE ARE ALWAYS RULES.

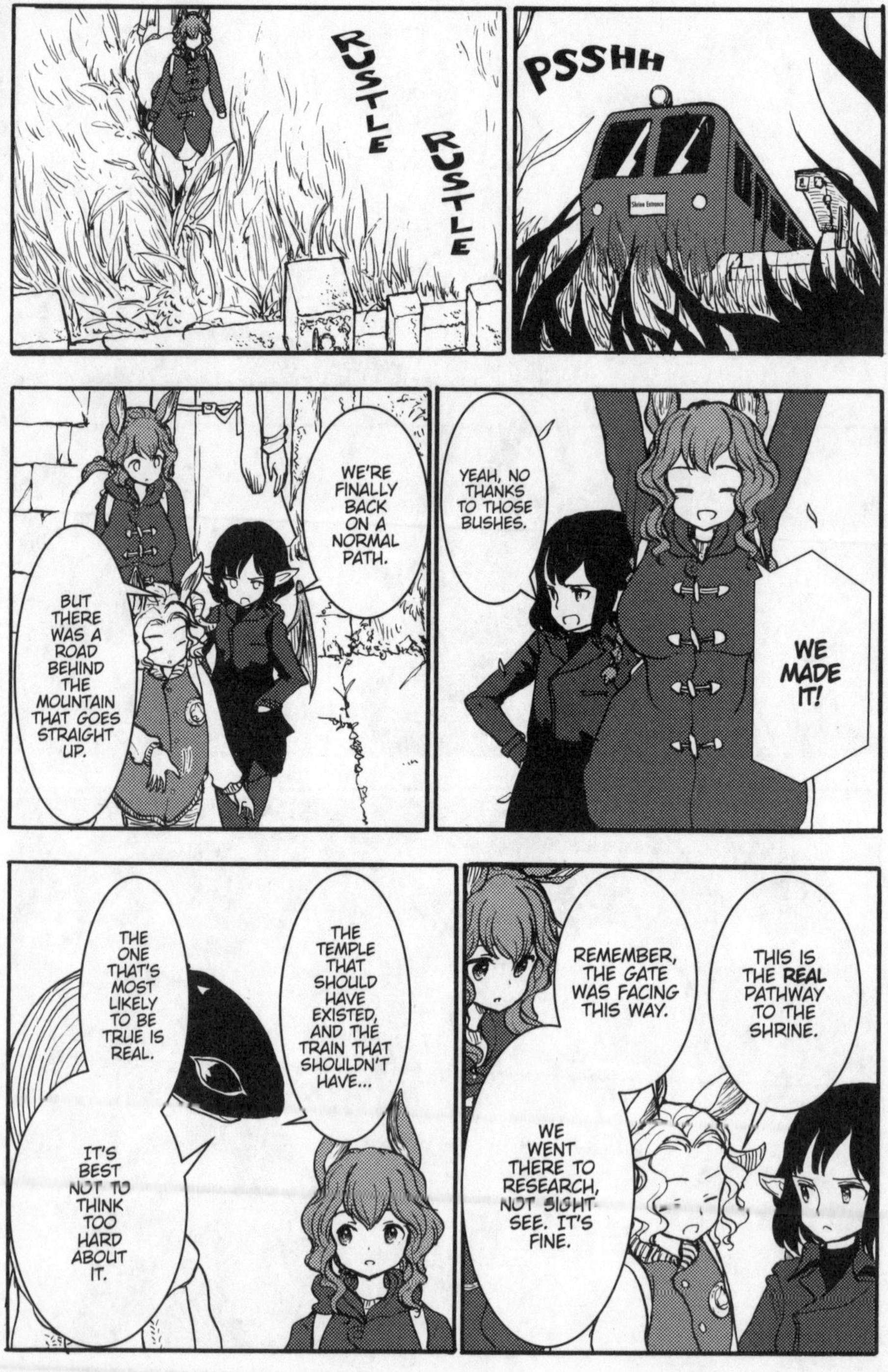
PSSHH
Shrine Entrance
RUSTLE
RUSTLE
WE MADE IT!
YEAH, NO THANKS TO THOSE BUSHES.
WE'RE FINALLY BACK ON A NORMAL PATH.
BUT THERE WAS A ROAD BEHIND THE MOUNTAIN THAT GOES STRAIGHT UP.
THIS IS THE REAL PATHWAY TO THE SHRINE.
REMEMBER, THE GATE WAS FACING THIS WAY.
WE WENT THERE TO RESEARCH, NOT SIGHT SEE. IT'S FINE.
THE TEMPLE THAT SHOULD HAVE EXISTED, AND THE TRAIN THAT SHOULDN'T HAVE...
THE ONE THAT'S MOST LIKELY TO BE TRUE IS REAL.
IT'S BEST NOT TO THINK TOO HARD ABOUT IT.

A CentaUr's Life

GREAT SCHOLARS OF THE WORLD:
<2> PLATO

PLATO IS ONE OF THE MOST FAMOUS ANCIENT GREEK
PHILOSOPHERS. HE WAS THE STUDENT OF SOCRATES AND THE
TEACHER OF ARISTOTLE--TWO OTHER GREAT ANCIENT GREEK
PHILOSOPHERS. MANY OF HIS WORKS, WHICH WERE WRITTEN AS
DIALOGUES BETWEEN SOCRATES AND VARIOUS INDIVIDUALS, WERE
PUBLISHED IN MULTIPLE LANGUAGES AND CIRCULATED ALL OVER THE
WORLD. SOCRATES, PLATO'S MENTOR, IS POPULARLY SEEN AS BEING
ARGUMENTATIVE IN MANY OF PLATO'S WORKS. HOWEVER, BY LOOKING
FURTHER INTO THE HISTORICAL BACKGROUND OF BOTH SOCRATES
AND PLATO, WE MAY GAIN A BETTER UNDERSTANDING OF BOTH
PHILOSOPHERS AND THEIR WAYS OF THINKING.

ANCIENT GREECE WAS DIVIDED INTO MANY CITY-STATES CALLED
POLEIS. WHEN THE PERSIAN EMPIRE FIRST INVADED GREECE, THEY
WERE DEFEATED BY A COALITION OF THESE CITY-STATES, LED BY THE
DEMOCRATIC STATE OF ATHENS AND THE STRATOCRATIC STATE OF
LACEDAEMON, NOW COMMONLY REFERRED TO AS SPARTA. HOWEVER,
PEACE DID NOT LAST LONG FOR THE GREEKS. AFTER THE THREAT OF
THE PERSIAN EMPIRE HAD SUBSIDED, TENSIONS AROSE BETWEEN
ATHENS AND LACEDAEMON. THIS LED TO THE PELOPONNESIAN WAR.

LACEDAEMON HAD POWERFUL INFANTRIES AND WAS CONSTANTLY
ENGAGED IN MILITARY TRAINING. HOWEVER, THEY DID NOT HAVE NAVAL
UNITS OR SIEGE ENGINES AND WERE AT RISK FROM INTERNAL REVOLTS.
ATHENS, ON THE OTHER HAND, HAD PORTS, AND THEY BUILT MASSIVE
WALLS TO ENCLOSE THEIR CITY AS WELL AS CONNECTING PASSAGES.
THEY HAD A POWERFUL NAVY AND, AT THE TIME, SEEMED INVINCIBLE.

IT WAS LACEDAEMON, HOWEVER, WHO WON THE PELOPONNESIAN WAR. WITH THE
SUPPORT OF THE PERSIAN EMPIRE, LACEDAEMON CRUSHED ATHENS AND IMPOSED AN
ABSOLUTE OLIGARCHY. THIS RESULTED IN A STATE OF DISORDER FOR DEMOCRATIC ATHENS;
INTERNAL CONFLICT BETWEEN THE OLIGARCHS AND THE DEMOCRATS ENSUED, WHICH WOULD
CONTINUE TO PLAGUE THE CITY-STATE EVEN AFTER DEMOCRACY'S EVENTUAL VICTORY. IT
WOULD BE SOME TIME BEFORE THE CITY-STATE WOULD ACHIEVE TRUE PEACE AND HARMONY.

THIS CONFLICT, AND THE GOVERNMENT'S CONDUCT DURING IT, LEFT A HUGE IMPACT ON PLATO.
IN ONE OF PLATO'S DIALOGUES, SOCRATES SAID, "NO MAN, NOT EVEN THE TOUGHEST OF MEN,
UNDERTAKES A TRADE HE HAS NOT LEARNED; YET EVERYONE THINKS HIMSELF SUFFICIENTLY
QUALIFIED FOR THE HARDEST OF TRADES--THAT WHICH IS THE TRADE OF GOVERNMENT."

TODAY, PLATO'S WORDS STILL RING TRUE. THOSE WHO ARE MOST IGNORANT TEND TO BE
MOST VOCAL ABOUT THE GOVERNMENT AND, UNDER A DEMOCRATIC SYSTEM, THESE INDIVIDUALS
OFTEN GAIN THE MAJORITY AND THE ABILITY TO STEER THE NATION'S ACTIONS AND INTENTIONS.
THE QUESTION REMAINS, HOWEVER, WHETHER THEY STEER THE NATION'S COURSE IN THE
RIGHT DIRECTION. THIS IS SOMETHING PLATO PONDERED AFTER WITNESSING SICILY'S POLITICAL
CONFLICTS. THUS, PLATO CREATED THE THEORY OF FORMS TO ASSERT HOW HE BELIEVED
GOVERNMENT SHOULD BE.

AS TO THE FATE OF ATHENS, IT FELL UNDER THE CONTROL OF ALEXANDER THE GREAT OF
MACEDON. ALEXANDER WAS A PUPIL OF ARISTOTLE, WHO HIMSELF WAS A STUDENT OF PLATO.
FOLLOWING ALEXANDER'S REIGN, ATHENS BECAME A PROVINCE OF THE ROMAN EMPIRE.

CHAPTER 153

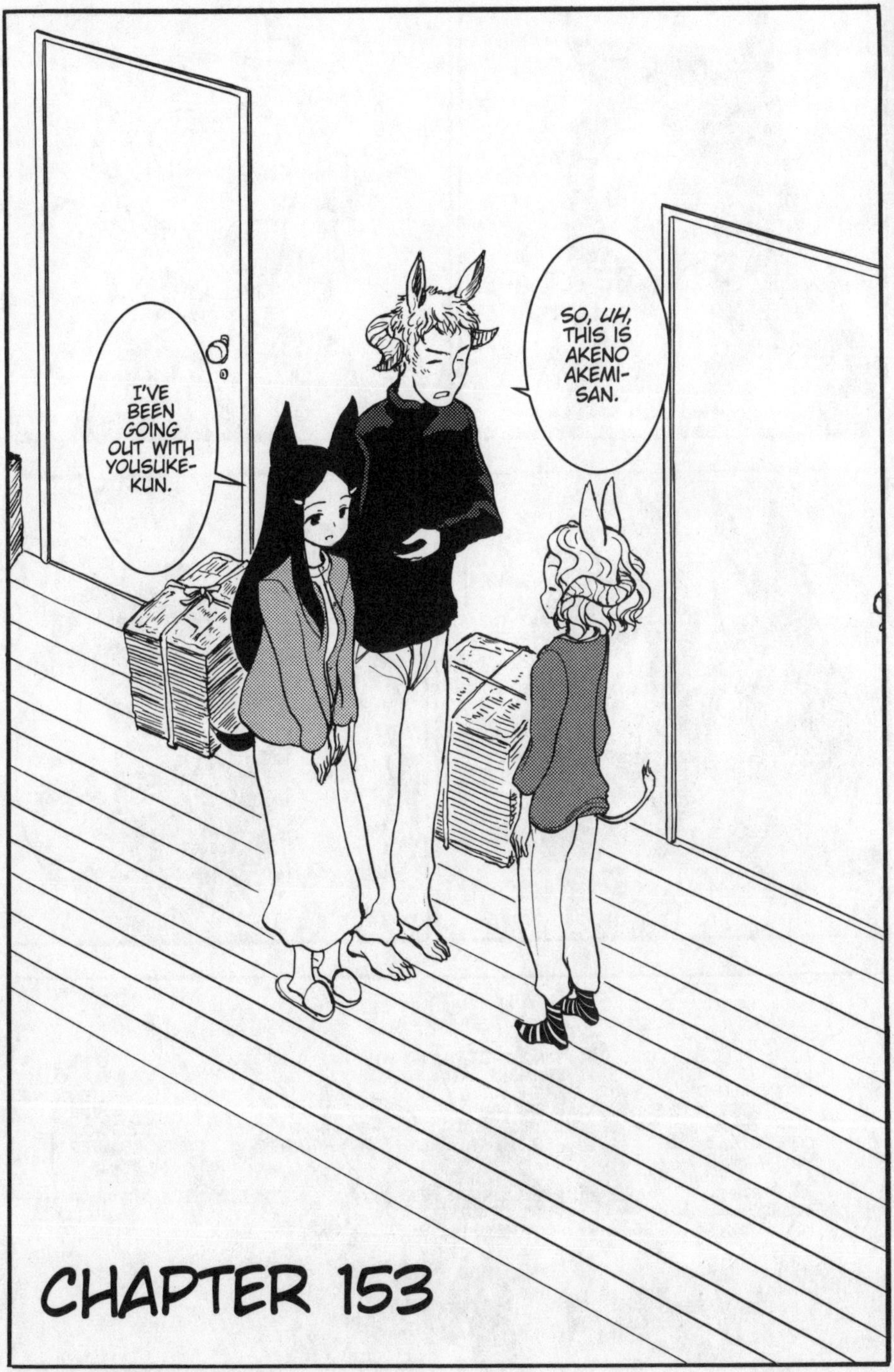
SO, UH, THIS IS AKENO AKEMI-SAN.
I'VE BEEN GOING OUT WITH YOUSUKE-KUN.

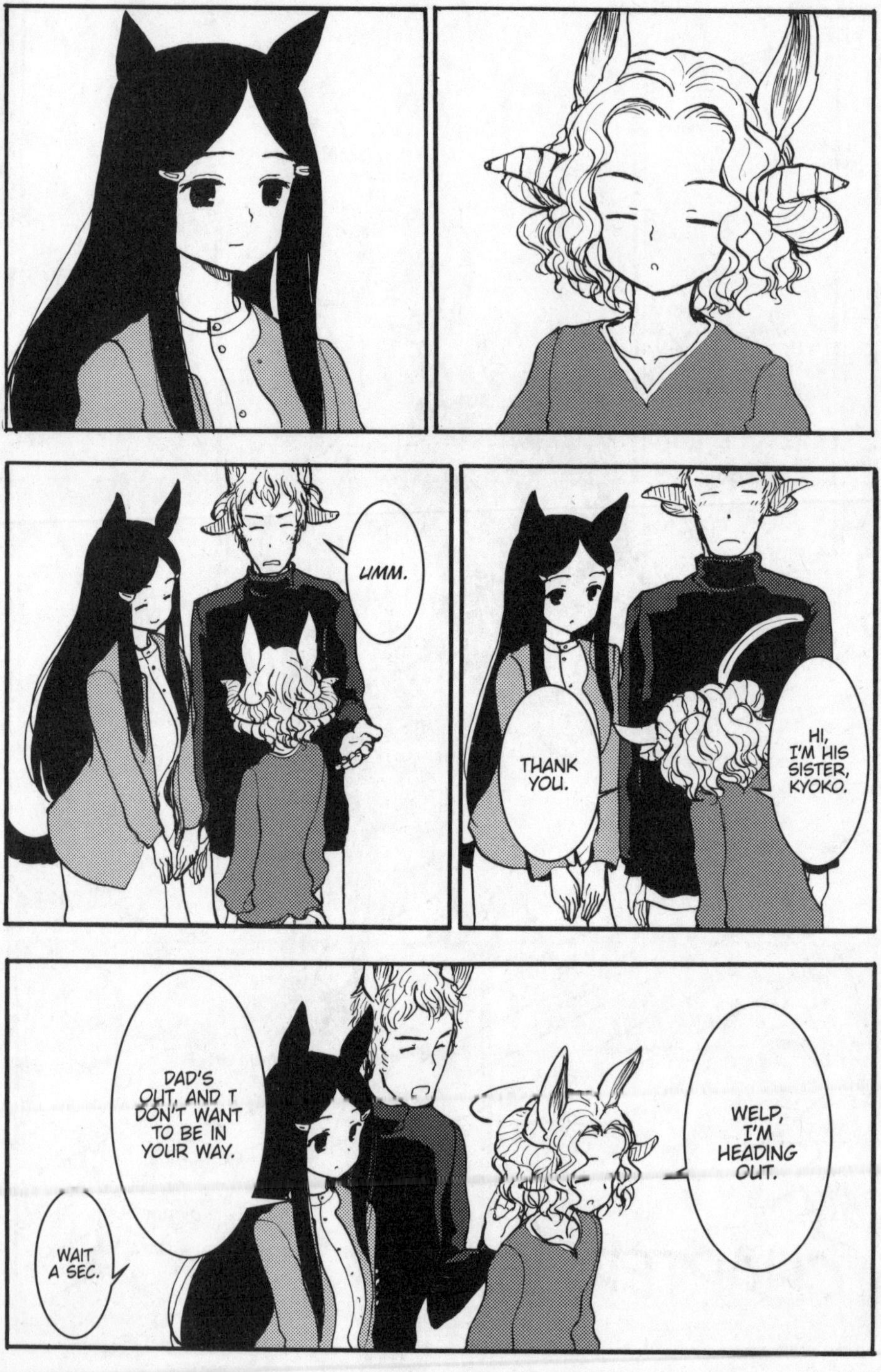
HI, I'M HIS SISTER, KYOKO.
THANK YOU.
UMM.
WELP, I'M HEADING OUT.
DAD'S OUT, AND I DON'T WANT TO BE IN YOUR WAY.
WAIT A SEC.

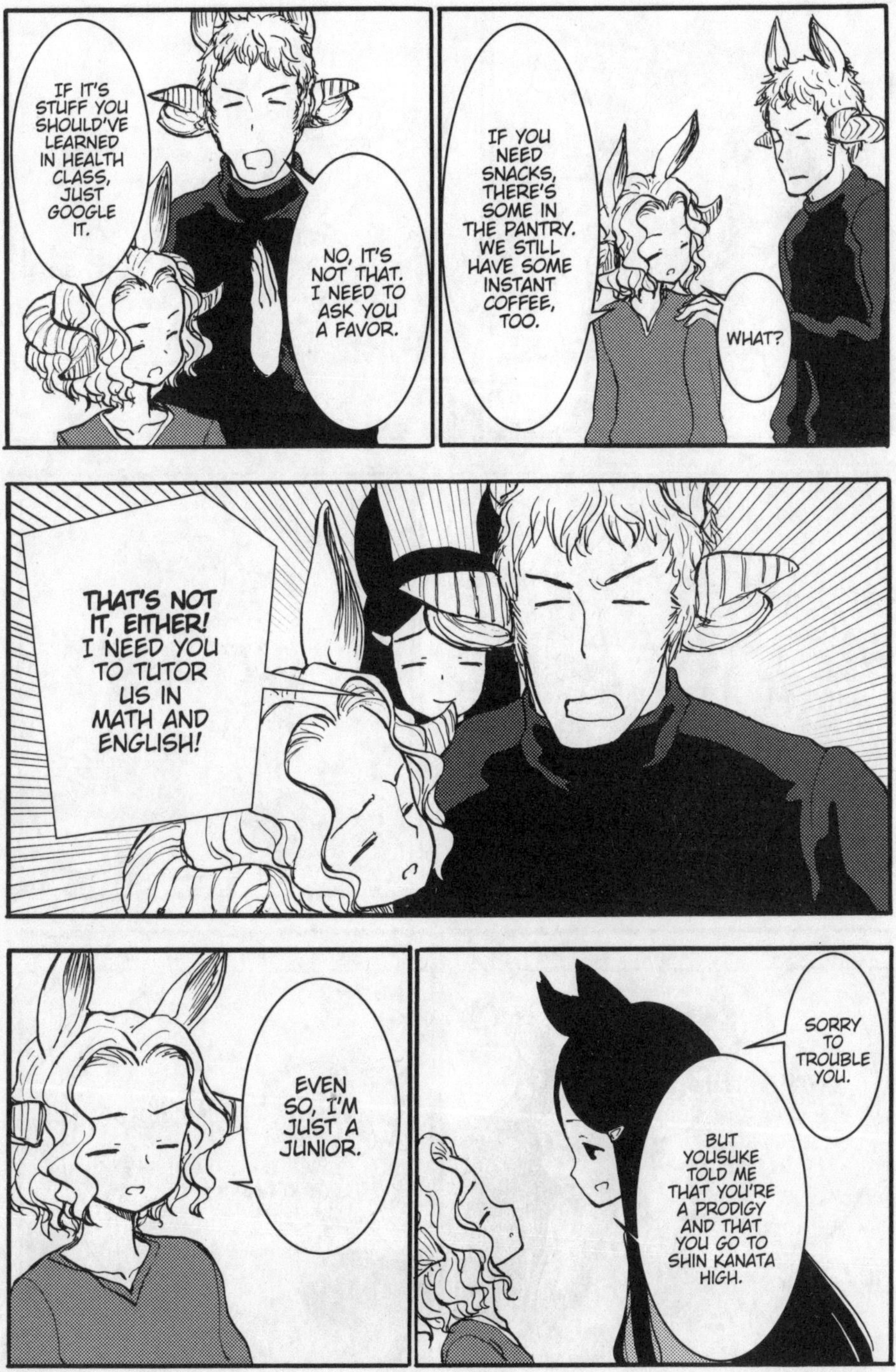
WHAT?
IF YOU NEED SNACKS, THERE'S SOME IN THE PANTRY. WE STILL HAVE SOME INSTANT COFFEE, TOO.
IF IT'S STUFF YOU SHOULD'VE LEARNED IN HEALTH CLASS, JUST GOOGLE IT.
NO, IT'S NOT THAT. I NEED TO ASK YOU A FAVOR.
THAT'S NOT IT, EITHER! I NEED YOU TO TUTOR US IN MATH AND ENGLISH!
SORRY TO TROUBLE YOU.
BUT YOUSUKE TOLD ME THAT YOU'RE A PRODIGY AND THAT YOU GO TO SHIN KANATA HIGH.
EVEN SO, I'M JUST A JUNIOR.

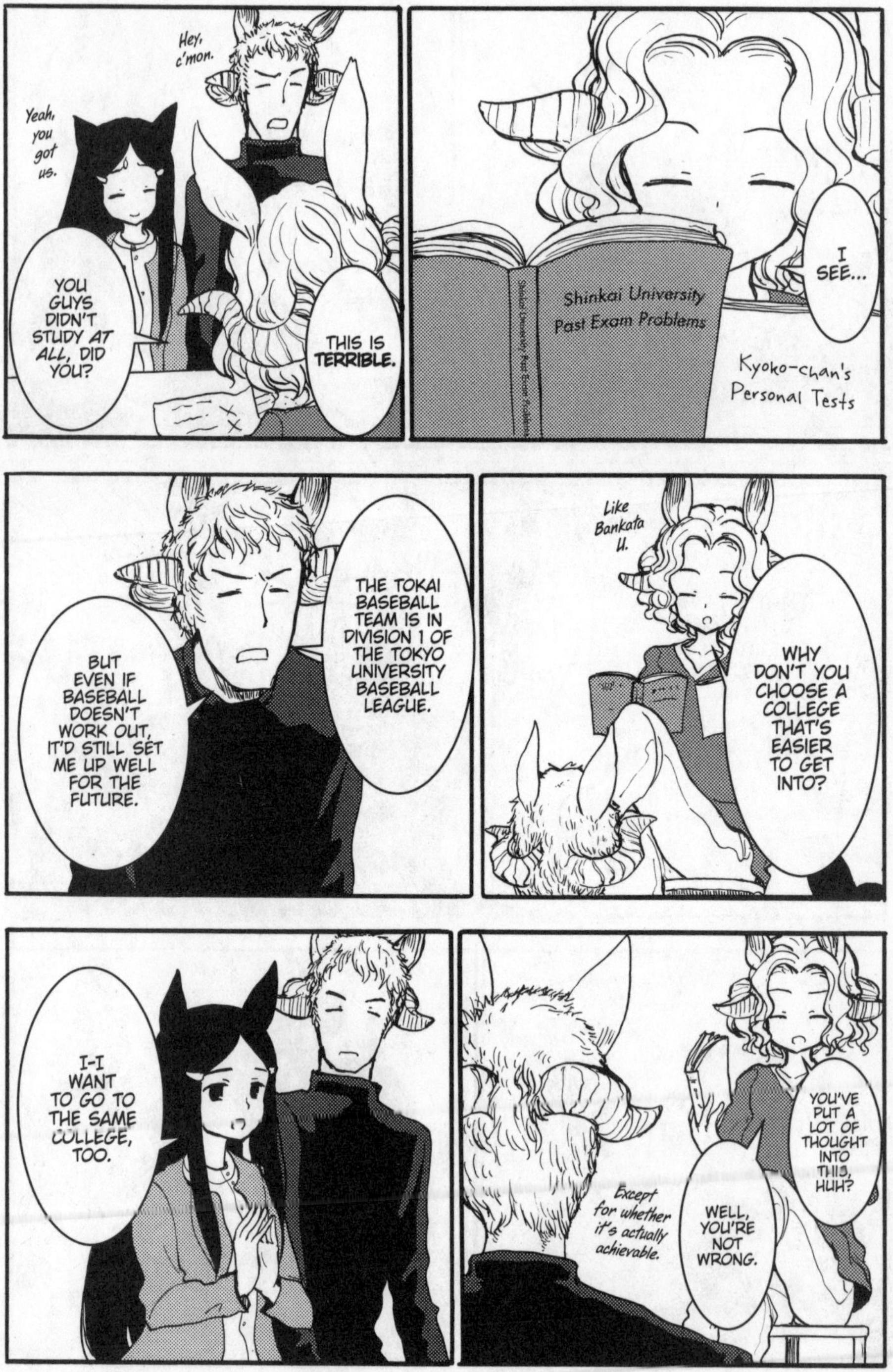
Shinkai University Past Exam Problems
I SEE...
Kyoko-chan's Personal Tests
Hey, c'mon.
THIS IS TERRIBLE.
Yeah, you got us.
YOU GUYS DIDN'T STUDY AT ALL, DID YOU?
Like Bankata U.
WHY DON'T YOU CHOOSE A COLLEGE THAT'S EASIER TO GET INTO?
THE TOKAI BASEBALL TEAM IS IN DIVISION 1 OF THE TOKYO UNIVERSITY BASEBALL LEAGUE.
BUT EVEN IF BASEBALL DOESN'T WORK OUT, IT'D STILL SET ME UP WELL FOR THE FUTURE.
YOU'VE PUT A LOT OF THOUGHT INTO THIS, HUH?
WELL, YOU'RE NOT WRONG.
Except for whether it's actually achievable.
I-I WANT TO GO TO THE SAME COLLEGE, TOO.

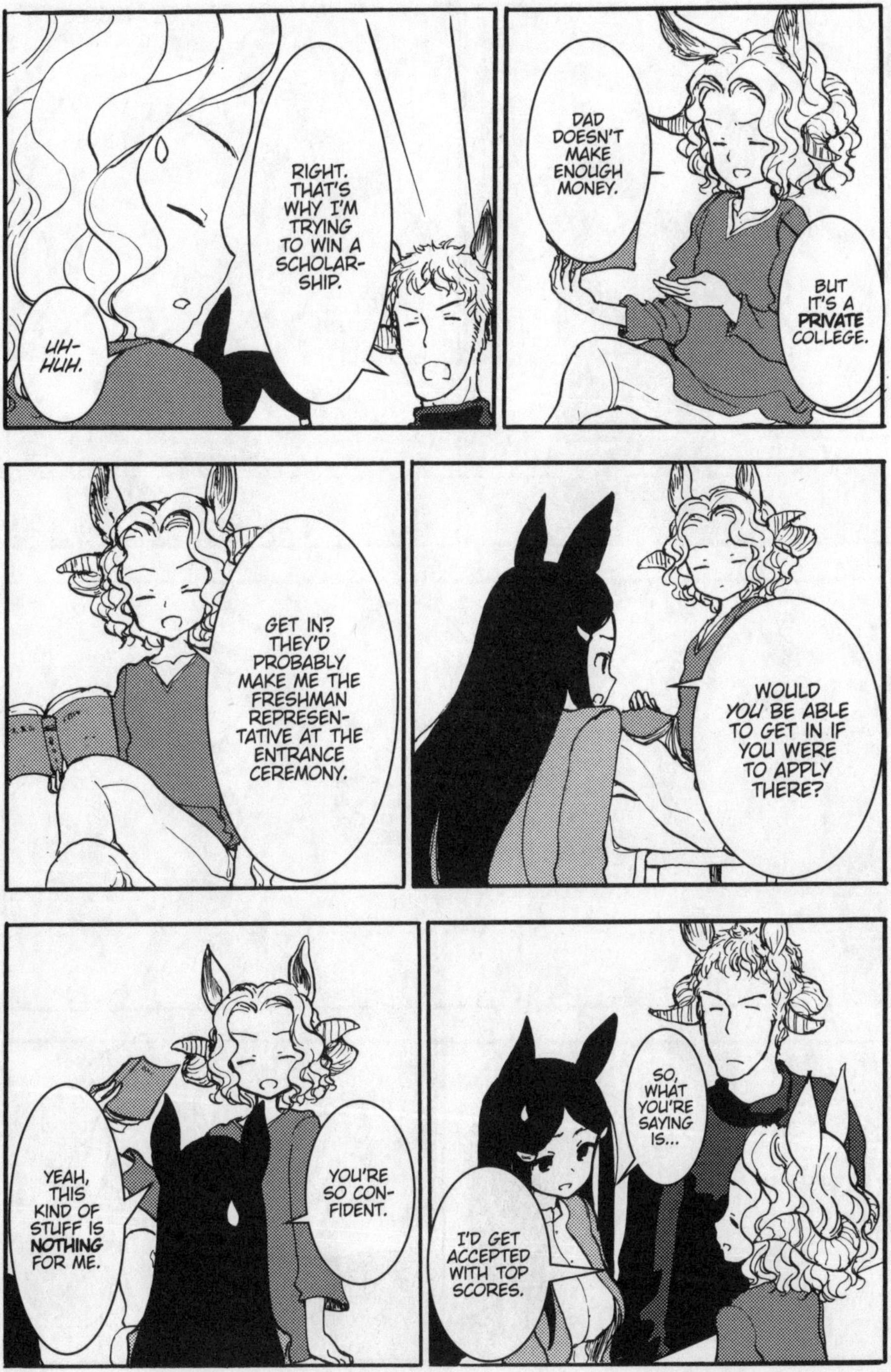
DAD DOESN'T MAKE ENOUGH MONEY.
BUT IT'S A PRIVATE COLLEGE.
RIGHT. THAT'S WHY I'M TRYING TO WIN A SCHOLAR-SHIP.
UH-HUH.
WOULD YOU BE ABLE TO GET IN IF YOU WERE TO APPLY THERE?
GET IN? THEY'D PROBABLY MAKE ME THE FRESHMAN REPRESEN-TATIVE AT THE ENTRANCE CEREMONY.
SO, WHAT YOU'RE SAYING IS...
I'D GET ACCEPTED WITH TOP SCORES.
YOU'RE SO CON-FIDENT.
YEAH, THIS KIND OF STUFF IS NOTHING FOR ME.

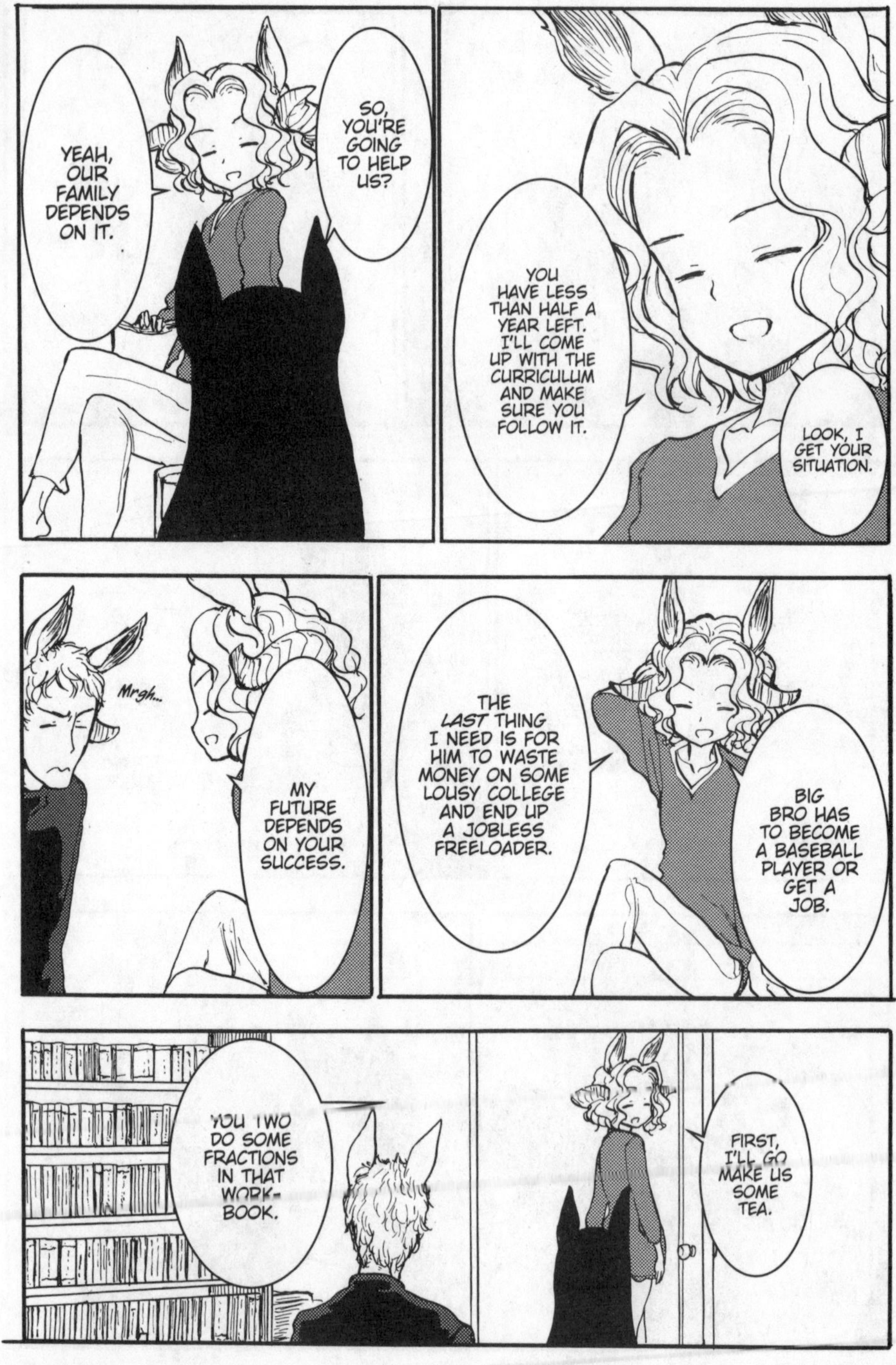
LOOK, I GET YOUR SITUATION.
YOU HAVE LESS THAN HALF A YEAR LEFT. I'LL COME UP WITH THE CURRICULUM AND MAKE SURE YOU FOLLOW IT.
SO, YOU'RE GOING TO HELP US?
YEAH, OUR FAMILY DEPENDS ON IT.
BIG BRO HAS TO BECOME A BASEBALL PLAYER OR GET A JOB.
THE *LAST* THING I NEED IS FOR HIM TO WASTE MONEY ON SOME LOUSY COLLEGE AND END UP A JOBLESS FREELOADER.
MY FUTURE DEPENDS ON YOUR SUCCESS.
Mrgh...
FIRST, I'LL GO MAKE US SOME TEA.
YOU TWO DO SOME FRACTIONS IN THAT WORK-BOOK.

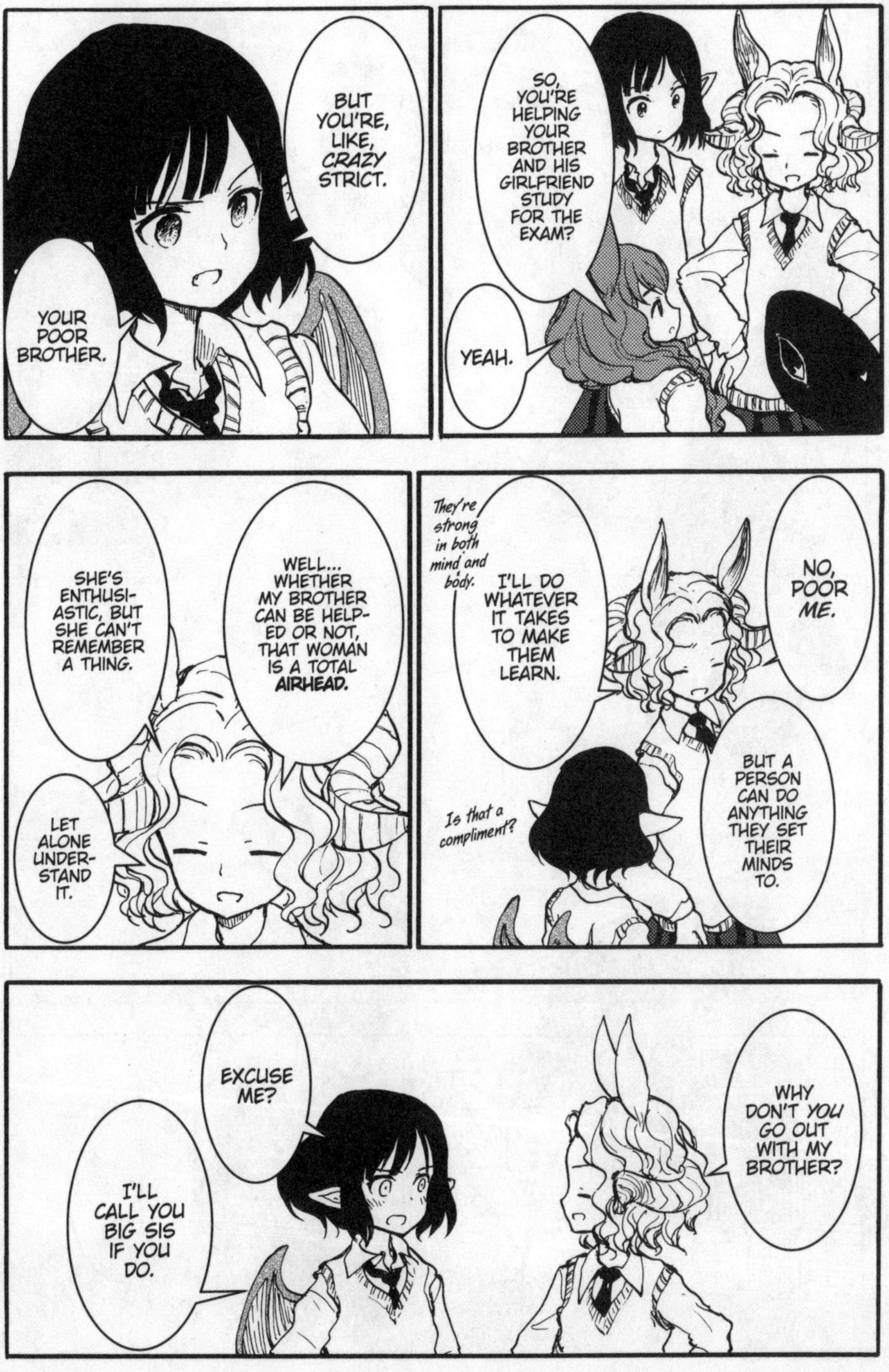
SO, YOU'RE HELPING YOUR BROTHER AND HIS GIRLFRIEND STUDY FOR THE EXAM?
YEAH.
BUT YOU'RE, LIKE, *CRAZY* STRICT.
YOUR POOR BROTHER.
NO, POOR *ME.*
I'LL DO WHATEVER IT TAKES TO MAKE THEM LEARN.
They're strong in both mind and body.
BUT A PERSON CAN DO ANYTHING THEY SET THEIR MINDS TO.
Is that a compliment?
WELL... WHETHER MY BROTHER CAN BE HELPED OR NOT, THAT WOMAN IS A TOTAL **AIRHEAD.**
SHE'S ENTHUSIASTIC, BUT SHE CAN'T REMEMBER A THING.
LET ALONE UNDERSTAND IT.
WHY DON'T *YOU* GO OUT WITH MY BROTHER?
EXCUSE ME?
I'LL CALL YOU BIG SIS IF YOU DO.

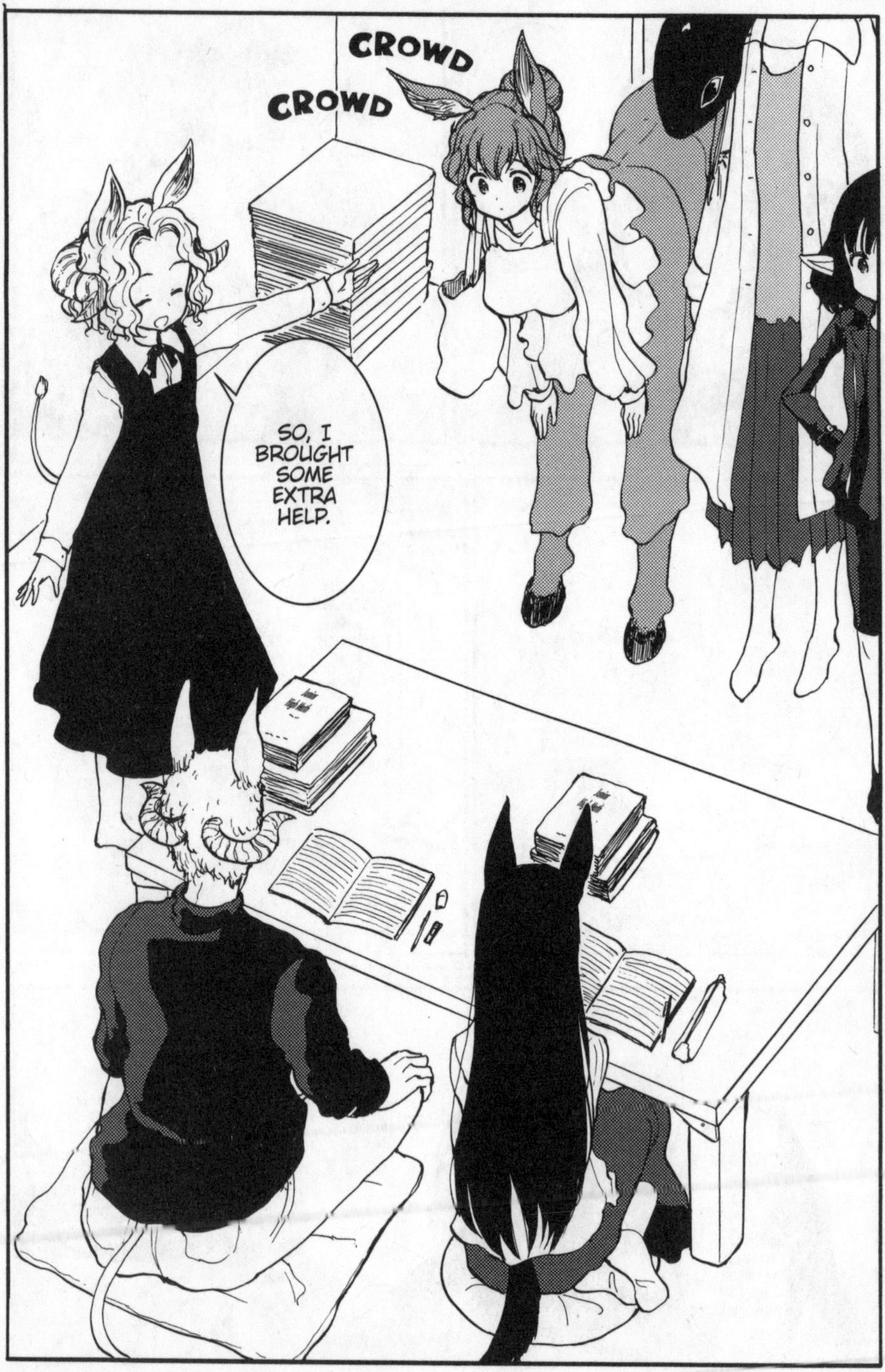
CROWD
CROWD
SO, I BROUGHT SOME EXTRA HELP.

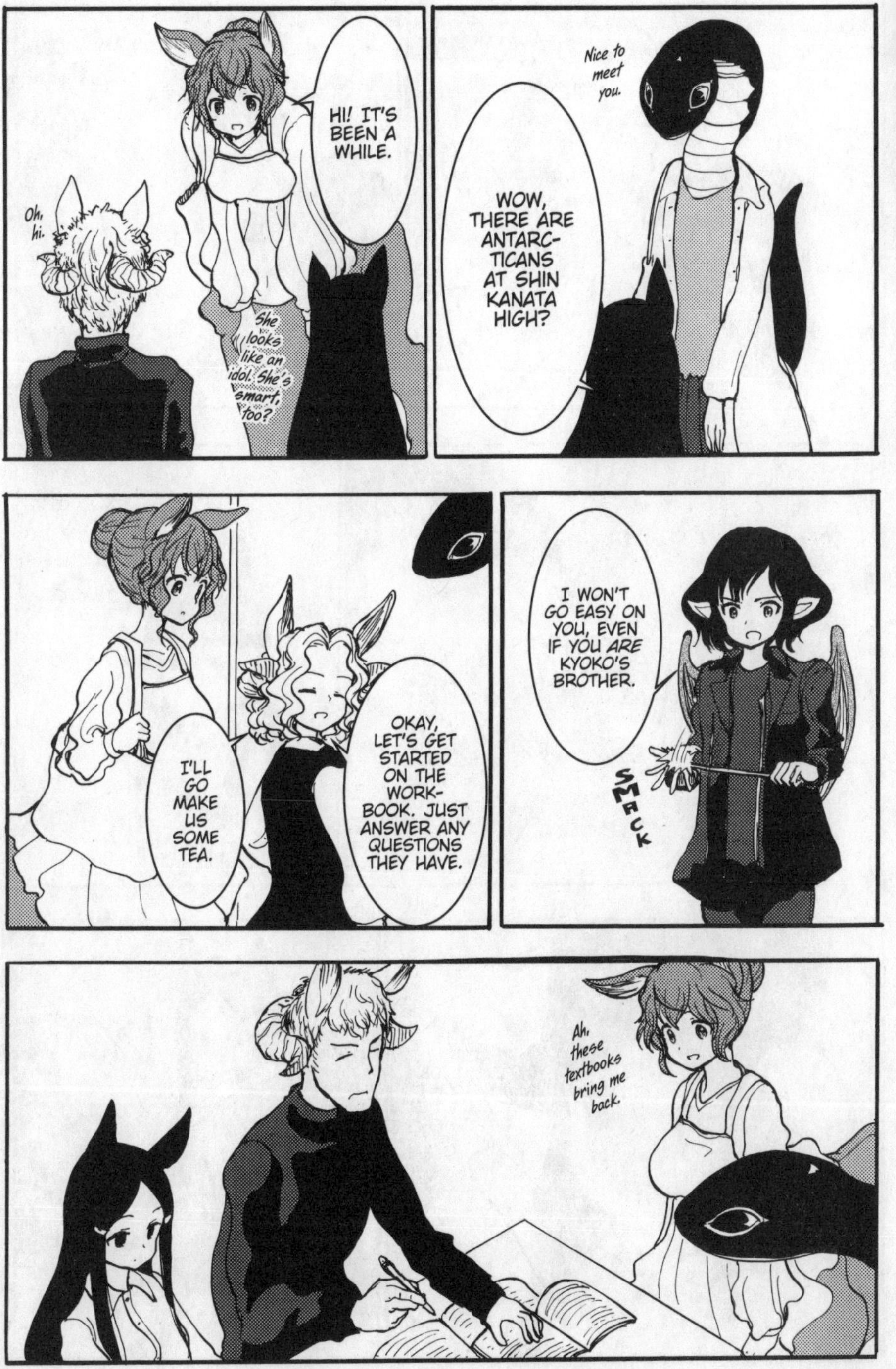
Nice to meet you.
WOW, THERE ARE ANTARCTICANS AT SHIN KANATA HIGH?
HI! IT'S BEEN A WHILE.
Oh, hi.
She looks like an idol. She's smart, too?
I WON'T GO EASY ON YOU, EVEN IF YOU *ARE* KYOKO'S BROTHER.
SMACK
OKAY, LET'S GET STARTED ON THE WORKBOOK. JUST ANSWER ANY QUESTIONS THEY HAVE.
I'LL GO MAKE US SOME TEA.
Ah, these textbooks bring me back.

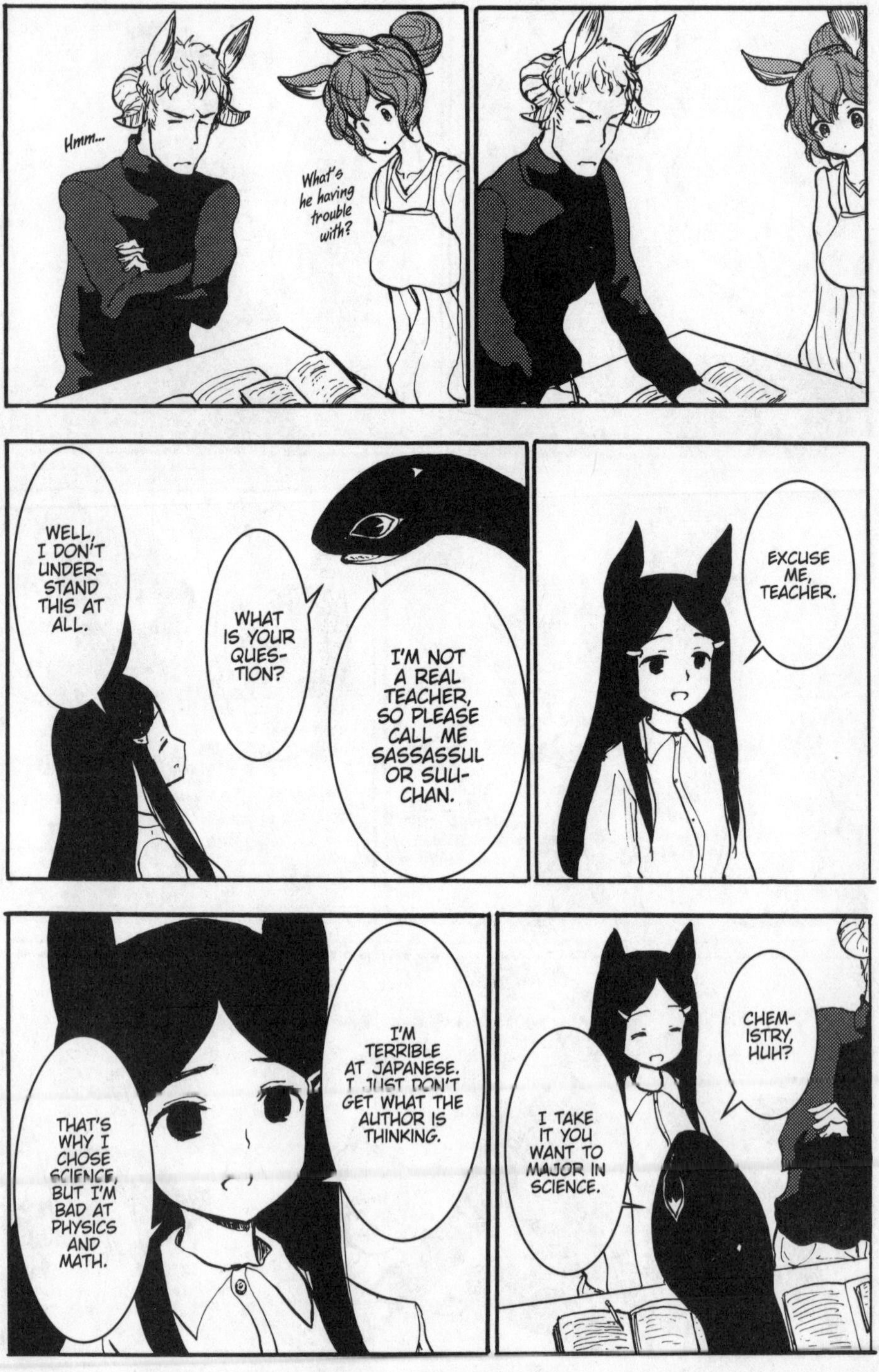
Hmm...
What's he having trouble with?
EXCUSE ME, TEACHER.
I'M NOT A REAL TEACHER, SO PLEASE CALL ME SASSASSUL OR SUU-CHAN.
WHAT IS YOUR QUESTION?
WELL, I DON'T UNDER-STAND THIS AT ALL.
CHEM-ISTRY, HUH?
I TAKE IT YOU WANT TO MAJOR IN SCIENCE.
I'M TERRIBLE AT JAPANESE. I JUST DON'T GET WHAT THE AUTHOR IS THINKING.
THAT'S WHY I CHOSE SCIENCE, BUT I'M BAD AT PHYSICS AND MATH.

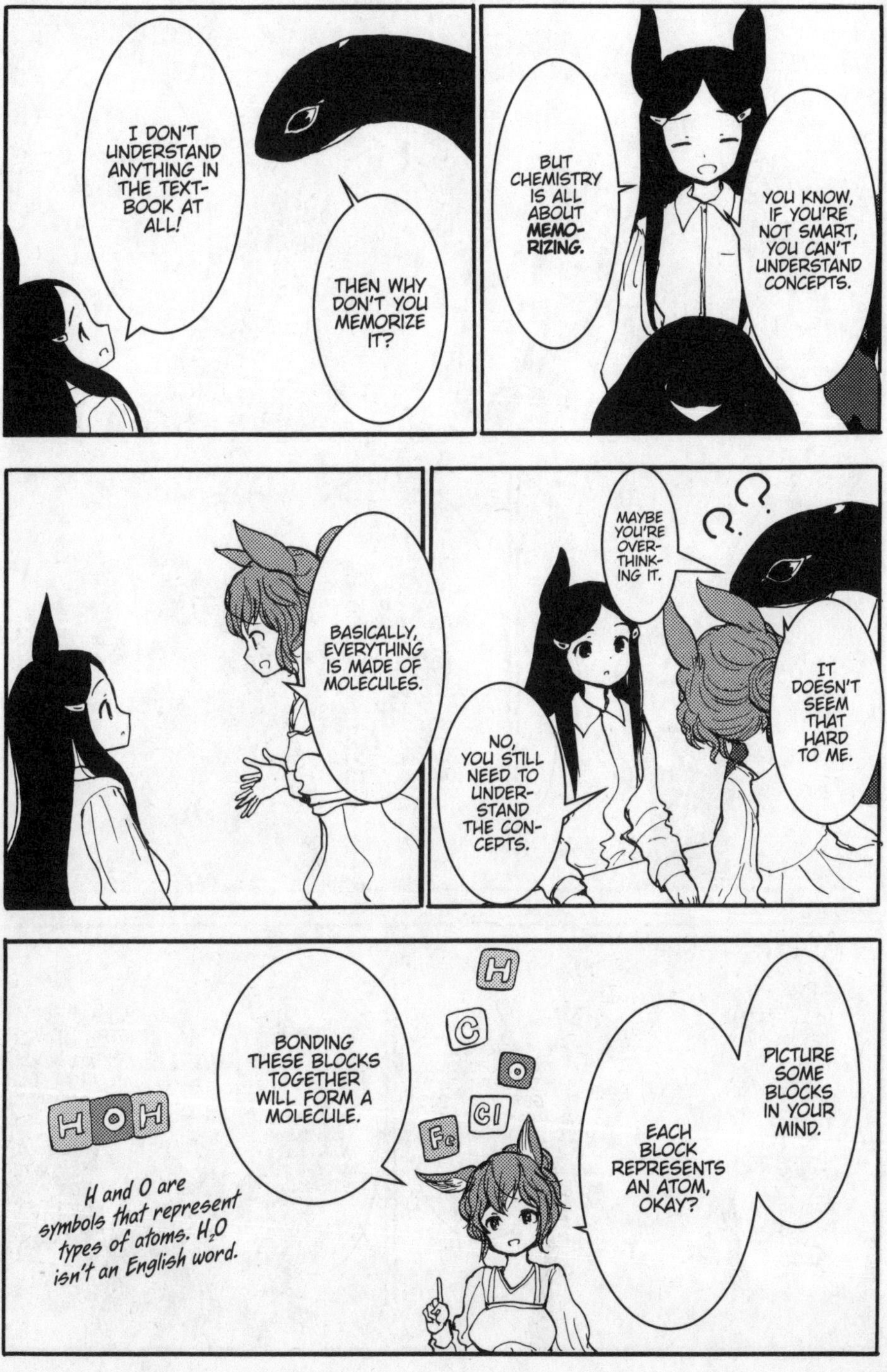
YOU KNOW, IF YOU'RE NOT SMART, YOU CAN'T UNDERSTAND CONCEPTS.
BUT CHEMISTRY IS ALL ABOUT **MEMORIZING.**
I DON'T UNDERSTAND ANYTHING IN THE TEXTBOOK AT ALL!
THEN WHY DON'T YOU MEMORIZE IT?
MAYBE YOU'RE OVERTHINKING IT.
IT DOESN'T SEEM THAT HARD TO ME.
NO, YOU STILL NEED TO UNDERSTAND THE CONCEPTS.
BASICALLY, EVERYTHING IS MADE OF MOLECULES.
PICTURE SOME BLOCKS IN YOUR MIND.
EACH BLOCK REPRESENTS AN ATOM, OKAY?
BONDING THESE BLOCKS TOGETHER WILL FORM A MOLECULE.
H
C
O
Cl
Fe
H O H
H and O are symbols that represent types of atoms. H_2O isn't an English word.

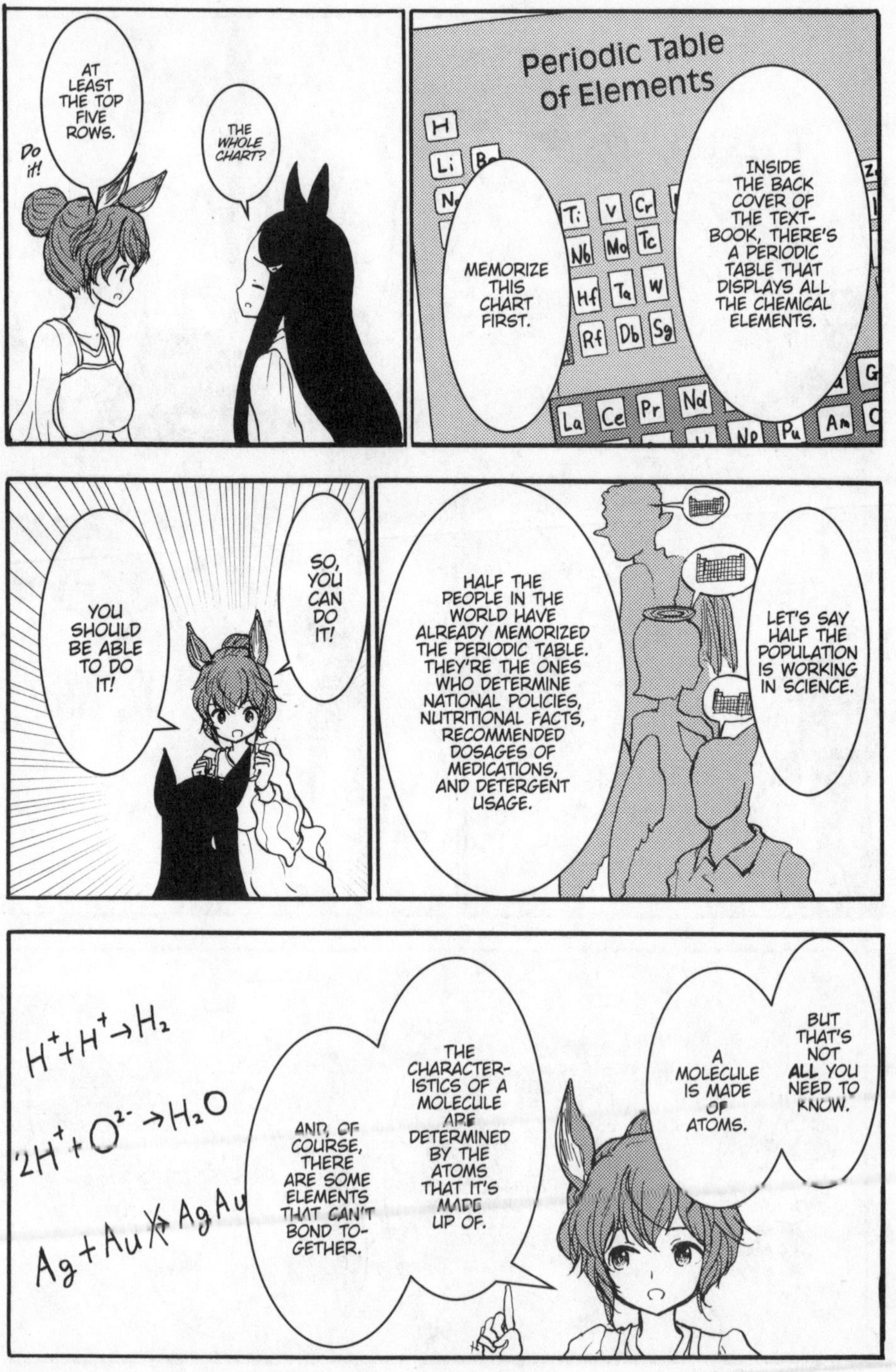
Periodic Table of Elements
H
Li
Ti V Cr
Nb Mo Tc
Hf Ta W
Rf Db Sg
La Ce Pr Nd
Np Pu Am
INSIDE THE BACK COVER OF THE TEXTBOOK, THERE'S A PERIODIC TABLE THAT DISPLAYS ALL THE CHEMICAL ELEMENTS.
MEMORIZE THIS CHART FIRST.
THE WHOLE CHART?
AT LEAST THE TOP FIVE ROWS.
Do it!
LET'S SAY HALF THE POPULATION IS WORKING IN SCIENCE.
HALF THE PEOPLE IN THE WORLD HAVE ALREADY MEMORIZED THE PERIODIC TABLE. THEY'RE THE ONES WHO DETERMINE NATIONAL POLICIES, NUTRITIONAL FACTS, RECOMMENDED DOSAGES OF MEDICATIONS, AND DETERGENT USAGE.
SO, YOU CAN DO IT!
YOU SHOULD BE ABLE TO DO IT!
BUT THAT'S NOT ALL YOU NEED TO KNOW.
A MOLECULE IS MADE OF ATOMS.
THE CHARACTERISTICS OF A MOLECULE ARE DETERMINED BY THE ATOMS THAT IT'S MADE UP OF.
AND, OF COURSE, THERE ARE SOME ELEMENTS THAT CAN'T BOND TOGETHER.
H+ + H+ → H2
2H+ + O2- → H2O
Ag + Au ↛ AgAu

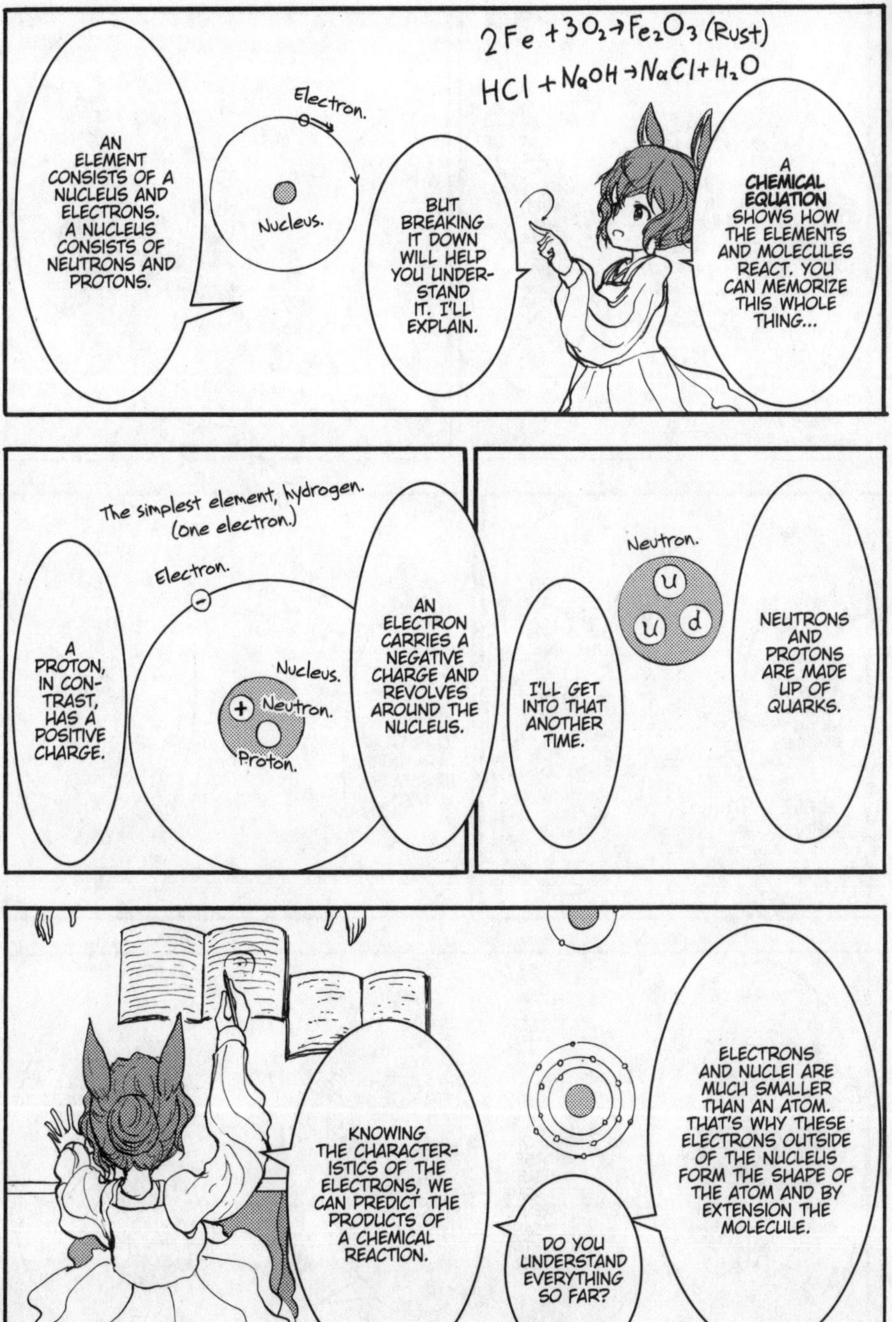
$2Fe + 3O_2 \rightarrow Fe_2O_3$ (Rust)
$HCl + NaOH \rightarrow NaCl + H_2O$
A **CHEMICAL EQUATION** SHOWS HOW THE ELEMENTS AND MOLECULES REACT. YOU CAN MEMORIZE THIS WHOLE THING...
BUT BREAKING IT DOWN WILL HELP YOU UNDERSTAND IT. I'LL EXPLAIN.
Electron.
Nucleus.
AN ELEMENT CONSISTS OF A NUCLEUS AND ELECTRONS. A NUCLEUS CONSISTS OF NEUTRONS AND PROTONS.
NEUTRONS AND PROTONS ARE MADE UP OF QUARKS.
Neutron.
u
u
d
I'LL GET INTO THAT ANOTHER TIME.
The simplest element, hydrogen. (one electron.)
AN ELECTRON CARRIES A NEGATIVE CHARGE AND REVOLVES AROUND THE NUCLEUS.
Electron.
Nucleus.
Neutron.
Proton.
A PROTON, IN CONTRAST, HAS A POSITIVE CHARGE.
ELECTRONS AND NUCLEI ARE MUCH SMALLER THAN AN ATOM. THAT'S WHY THESE ELECTRONS OUTSIDE OF THE NUCLEUS FORM THE SHAPE OF THE ATOM AND BY EXTENSION THE MOLECULE.
DO YOU UNDERSTAND EVERYTHING SO FAR?
KNOWING THE CHARACTERISTICS OF THE ELECTRONS, WE CAN PREDICT THE PRODUCTS OF A CHEMICAL REACTION.

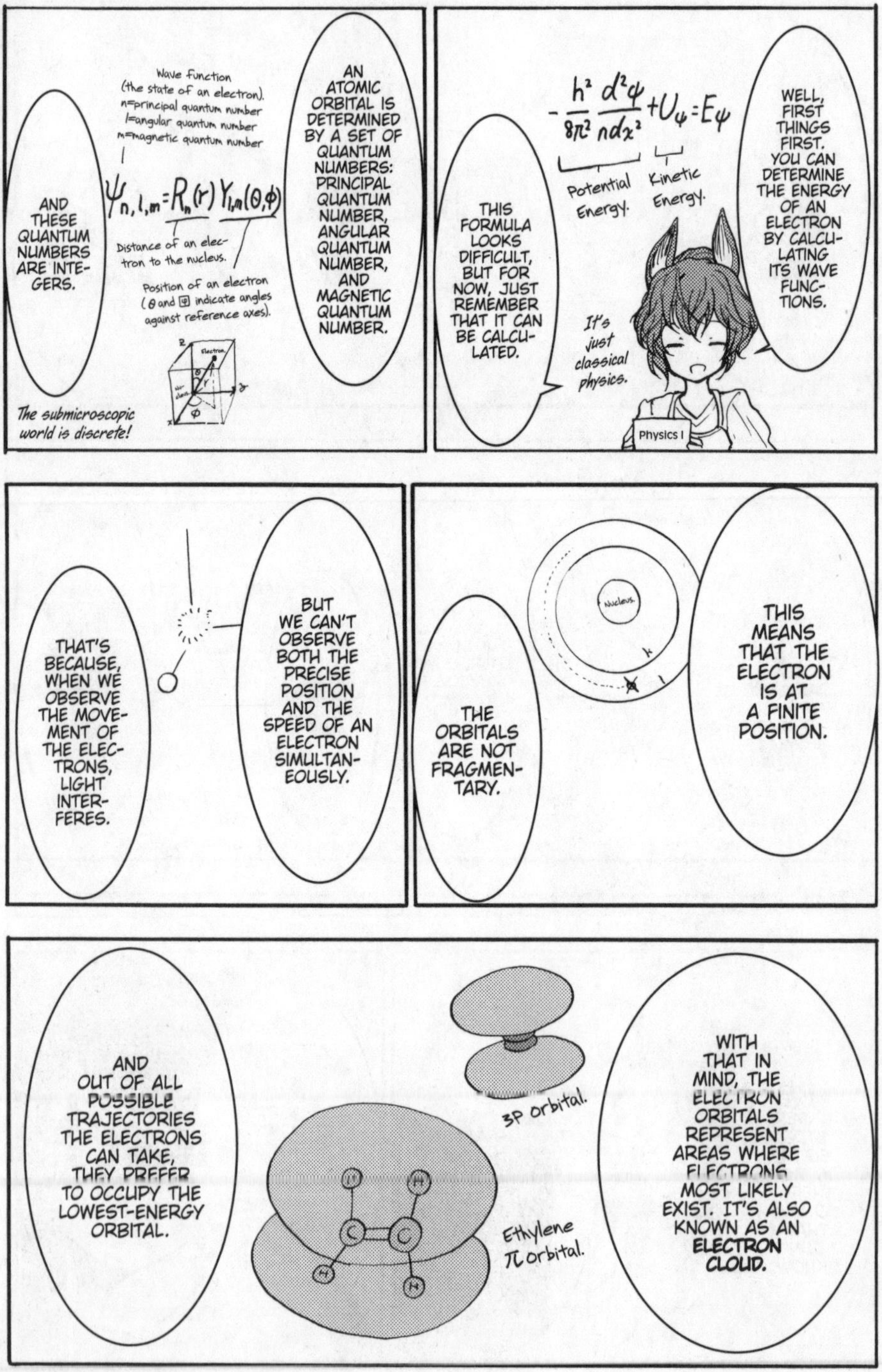

WELL, FIRST THINGS FIRST. YOU CAN DETERMINE THE ENERGY OF AN ELECTRON BY CALCULATING ITS WAVE FUNCTIONS.
$-\frac{h^2}{8\pi^2}\frac{d^2\psi}{ndx^2}+U_\psi=E\psi$
Potential Energy.
Kinetic Energy.
It's just classical physics.
Physics I
THIS FORMULA LOOKS DIFFICULT, BUT FOR NOW, JUST REMEMBER THAT IT CAN BE CALCULATED.
AN ATOMIC ORBITAL IS DETERMINED BY A SET OF QUANTUM NUMBERS: PRINCIPAL QUANTUM NUMBER, ANGULAR QUANTUM NUMBER, AND MAGNETIC QUANTUM NUMBER.
Wave function (the state of an electron). n=principal quantum number l=angular quantum number m=magnetic quantum number
$\psi_{n,l,m}=R_n(r)Y_{l,m}(\theta,\phi)$
Distance of an electron to the nucleus.
Position of an electron (θ and φ indicate angles against reference axes).
AND THESE QUANTUM NUMBERS ARE INTEGERS.
The submicroscopic world is discrete!
THIS MEANS THAT THE ELECTRON IS AT A FINITE POSITION.
Nucleus.
THE ORBITALS ARE NOT FRAGMENTARY.
BUT WE CAN'T OBSERVE BOTH THE PRECISE POSITION AND THE SPEED OF AN ELECTRON SIMULTANEOUSLY.
THAT'S BECAUSE, WHEN WE OBSERVE THE MOVEMENT OF THE ELECTRONS, LIGHT INTERFERES.
WITH THAT IN MIND, THE ELECTRON ORBITALS REPRESENT AREAS WHERE ELECTRONS MOST LIKELY EXIST. IT'S ALSO KNOWN AS AN **ELECTRON CLOUD.**
3P Orbital.
Ethylene π Orbital.
AND OUT OF ALL POSSIBLE TRAJECTORIES THE ELECTRONS CAN TAKE, THEY PREFER TO OCCUPY THE LOWEST-ENERGY ORBITAL.

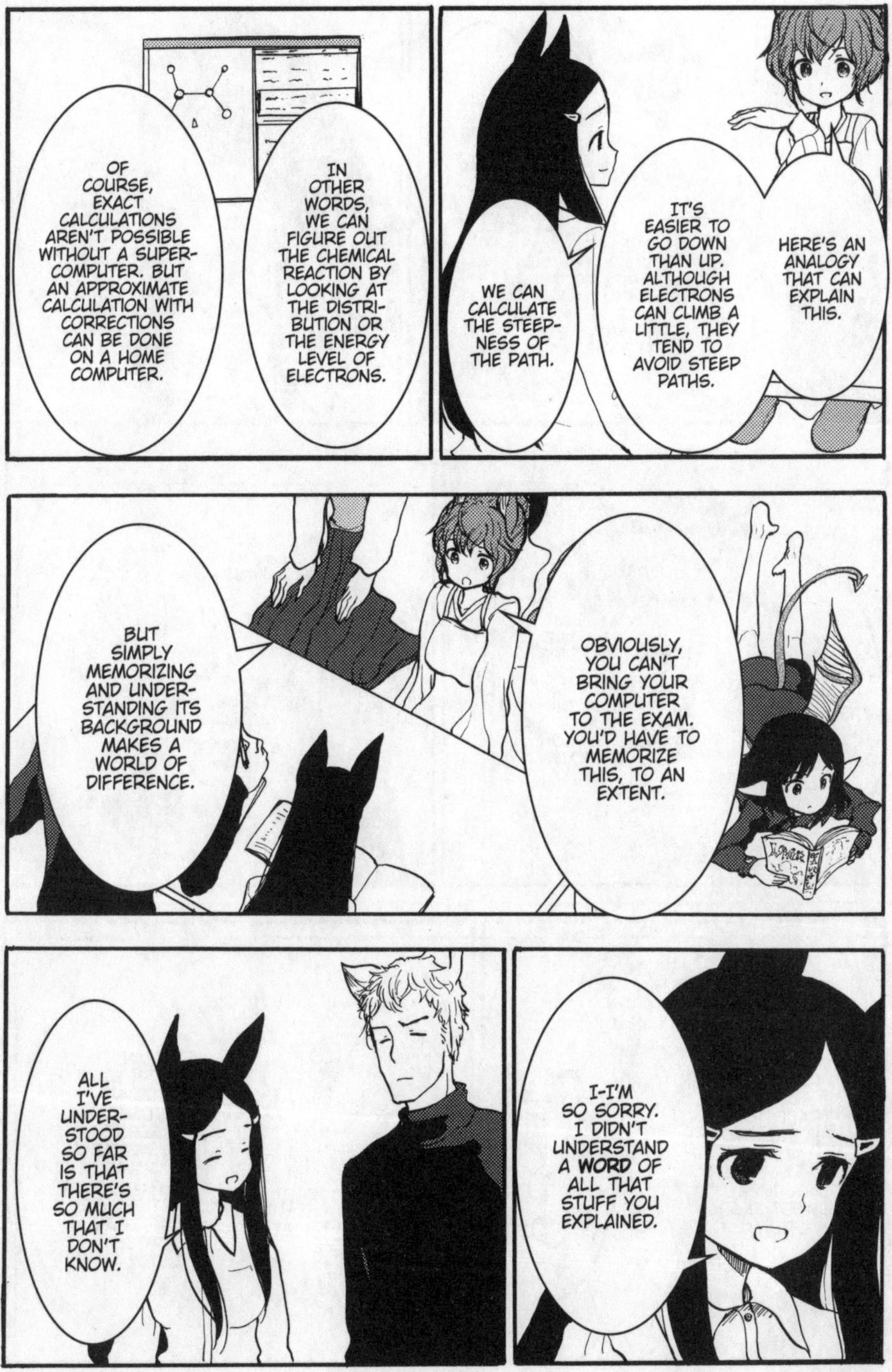
HERE'S AN ANALOGY THAT CAN EXPLAIN THIS.
IT'S EASIER TO GO DOWN THAN UP. ALTHOUGH ELECTRONS CAN CLIMB A LITTLE, THEY TEND TO AVOID STEEP PATHS.
WE CAN CALCULATE THE STEEPNESS OF THE PATH.
IN OTHER WORDS, WE CAN FIGURE OUT THE CHEMICAL REACTION BY LOOKING AT THE DISTRIBUTION OR THE ENERGY LEVEL OF ELECTRONS.
OF COURSE, EXACT CALCULATIONS AREN'T POSSIBLE WITHOUT A SUPER-COMPUTER. BUT AN APPROXIMATE CALCULATION WITH CORRECTIONS CAN BE DONE ON A HOME COMPUTER.
OBVIOUSLY, YOU CAN'T BRING YOUR COMPUTER TO THE EXAM. YOU'D HAVE TO MEMORIZE THIS, TO AN EXTENT.
BUT SIMPLY MEMORIZING AND UNDERSTANDING ITS BACKGROUND MAKES A WORLD OF DIFFERENCE.
I-I'M SO SORRY. I DIDN'T UNDERSTAND A **WORD** OF ALL THAT STUFF YOU EXPLAINED.
ALL I'VE UNDERSTOOD SO FAR IS THAT THERE'S SO MUCH THAT I DON'T KNOW.

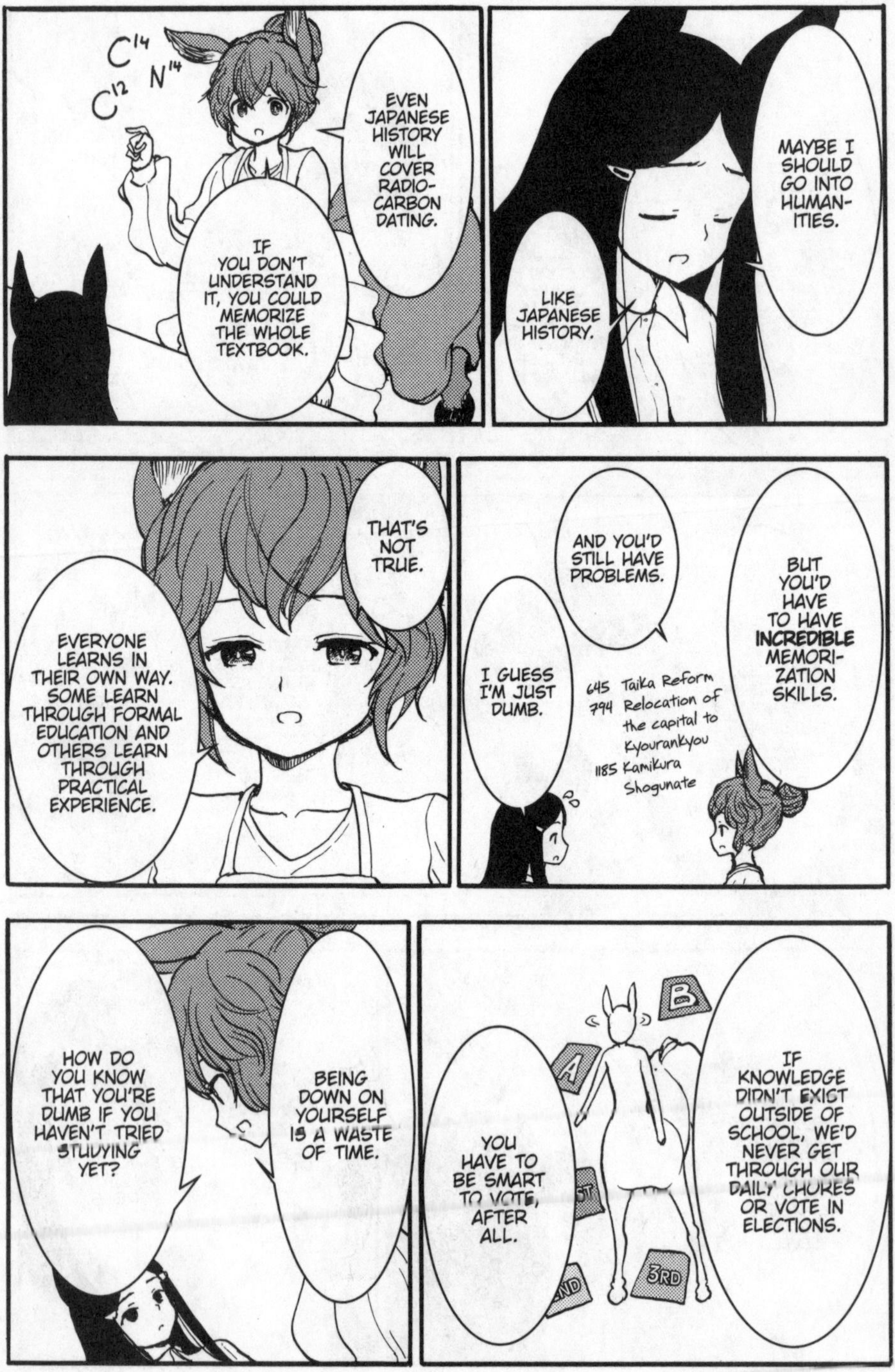

MAYBE I SHOULD GO INTO HUMANITIES.
LIKE JAPANESE HISTORY.
EVEN JAPANESE HISTORY WILL COVER RADIOCARBON DATING.
C14 C12 N14
IF YOU DON'T UNDERSTAND IT, YOU COULD MEMORIZE THE WHOLE TEXTBOOK.
BUT YOU'D HAVE TO HAVE **INCREDIBLE** MEMORIZATION SKILLS.
AND YOU'D STILL HAVE PROBLEMS.
645 Taika Reform
794 Relocation of the capital to Kyouränkyou
1185 Kamikura Shogunate
I GUESS I'M JUST DUMB.
THAT'S NOT TRUE.
EVERYONE LEARNS IN THEIR OWN WAY. SOME LEARN THROUGH FORMAL EDUCATION AND OTHERS LEARN THROUGH PRACTICAL EXPERIENCE.
IF KNOWLEDGE DIDN'T EXIST OUTSIDE OF SCHOOL, WE'D NEVER GET THROUGH OUR DAILY CHORES OR VOTE IN ELECTIONS.
YOU HAVE TO BE SMART TO VOTE, AFTER ALL.
B
A
3RD
BEING DOWN ON YOURSELF IS A WASTE OF TIME.
HOW DO YOU KNOW THAT YOU'RE DUMB IF YOU HAVEN'T TRIED STUDYING YET?

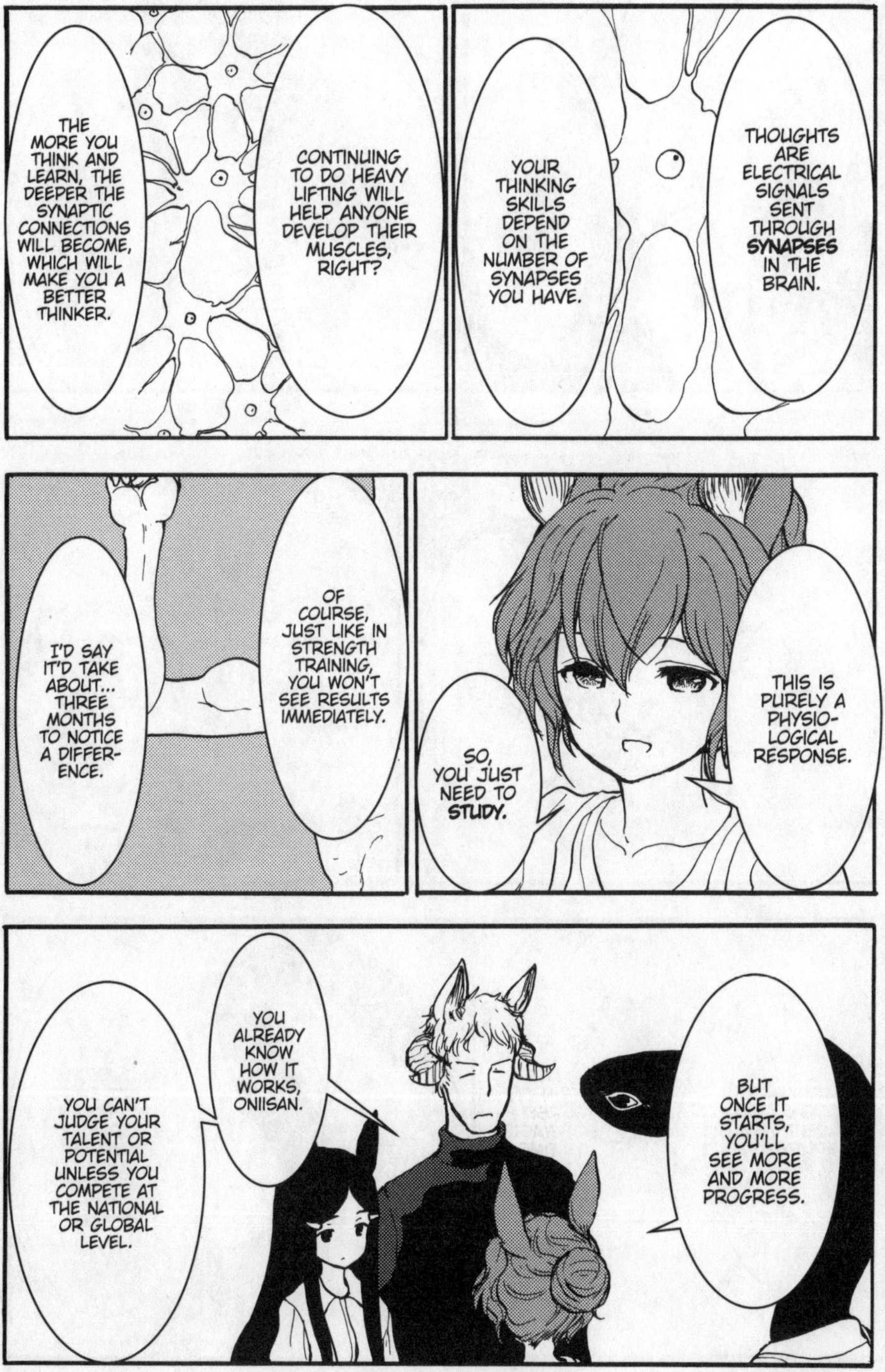
THOUGHTS ARE ELECTRICAL SIGNALS SENT THROUGH **SYNAPSES** IN THE BRAIN.
YOUR THINKING SKILLS DEPEND ON THE NUMBER OF SYNAPSES YOU HAVE.
CONTINUING TO DO HEAVY LIFTING WILL HELP ANYONE DEVELOP THEIR MUSCLES, RIGHT?
THE MORE YOU THINK AND LEARN, THE DEEPER THE SYNAPTIC CONNECTIONS WILL BECOME, WHICH WILL MAKE YOU A BETTER THINKER.
THIS IS PURELY A PHYSIOLOGICAL RESPONSE.
SO, YOU JUST NEED TO **STUDY.**
OF COURSE, JUST LIKE IN STRENGTH TRAINING, YOU WON'T SEE RESULTS IMMEDIATELY.
I'D SAY IT'D TAKE ABOUT... THREE MONTHS TO NOTICE A DIFFERENCE.
BUT ONCE IT STARTS, YOU'LL SEE MORE AND MORE PROGRESS.
YOU ALREADY KNOW HOW IT WORKS, ONIISAN.
YOU CAN'T JUDGE YOUR TALENT OR POTENTIAL UNLESS YOU COMPETE AT THE NATIONAL OR GLOBAL LEVEL.

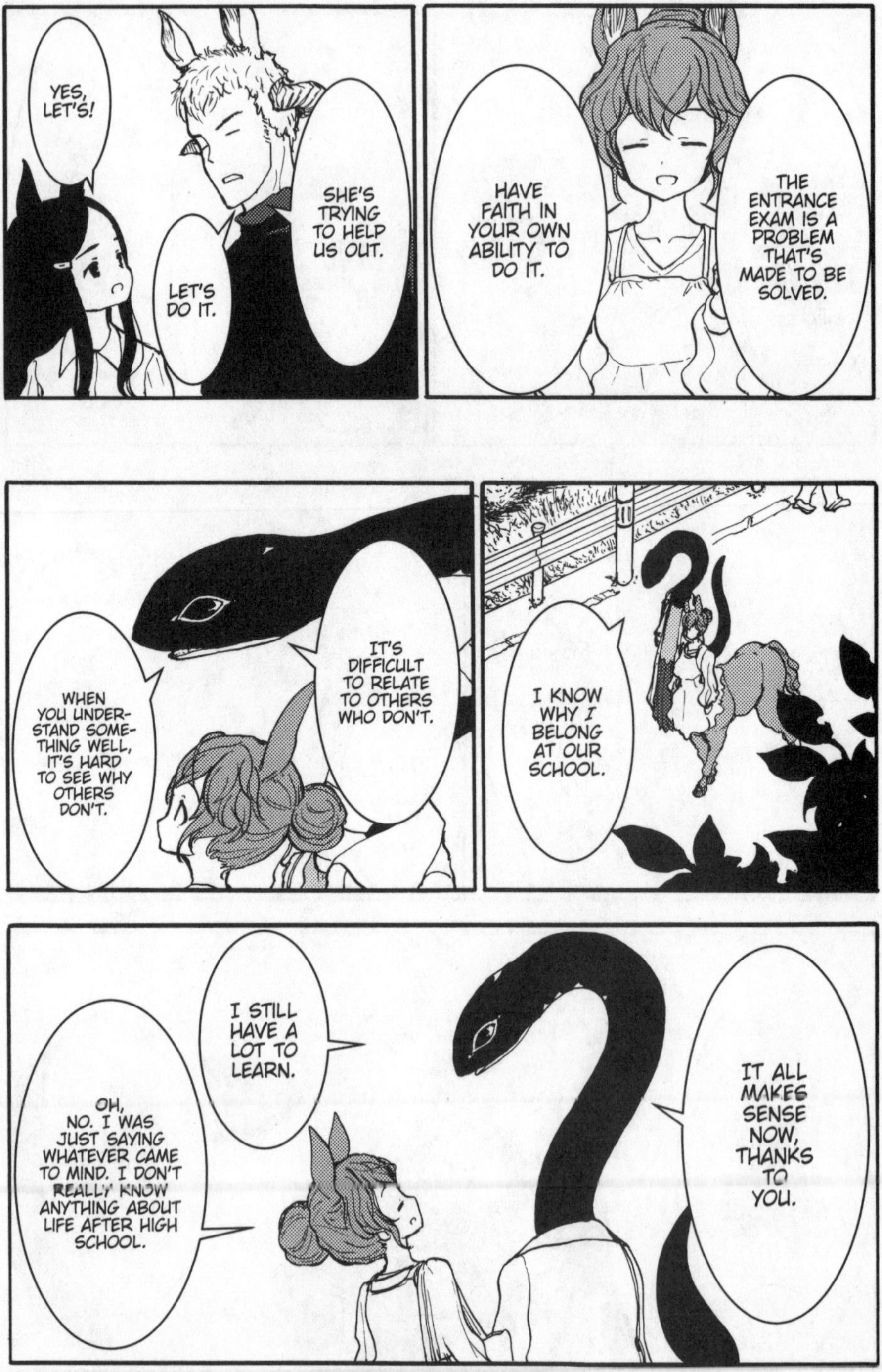
THE ENTRANCE EXAM IS A PROBLEM THAT'S MADE TO BE SOLVED.
HAVE FAITH IN YOUR OWN ABILITY TO DO IT.
SHE'S TRYING TO HELP US OUT.
LET'S DO IT.
YES, LET'S!
I KNOW WHY *I* BELONG AT OUR SCHOOL.
IT'S DIFFICULT TO RELATE TO OTHERS WHO DON'T.
WHEN YOU UNDER-STAND SOME-THING WELL, IT'S HARD TO SEE WHY OTHERS DON'T.
IT ALL MAKES SENSE NOW, THANKS TO YOU.
I STILL HAVE A LOT TO LEARN.
OH, NO. I WAS JUST SAYING WHATEVER CAME TO MIND. I DON'T REALLY KNOW ANYTHING ABOUT LIFE AFTER HIGH SCHOOL.

A Centaur's Life

GREAT SCHOLARS OF THE WORLD:
<3> OMAR KHAYYAM

ALTHOUGH OMAR KHAYYAM IS BEST KNOWN FOR HIS
COLLECTION OF QUATRAINS--THE *RUBAIYAT*--HE WAS ALSO
A MATHEMATICIAN AND ASTRONOMER IN ELEVENTH-CENTURY
PERSIA. DURING THIS TIME, PERSIA WAS UNDER THE RULE OF
THE SELJUK TURKS, THUS IT WAS BELIEVED THAT OMAR KHAYYAM
HAD TIES WITH SUFISM THAT LIKELY INFORMED HIS WORKS.

ISLAM, THE RELIGION OF THE BEDOUINS WHO INHABITED THE
SOUTHERN REGION OF THE ARABIAN PENINSULA, RAPIDLY EXPANDED
INTO PERSIA AFTER THE BEDOUINS OBLITERATED THE SASSANID EMPIRE
AND CONQUERED THE ROMAN TERRITORIES OF THE MIDDLE EAST AND
AFRICA. ORIGINALLY, THESE TERRITORIES LOOKED DOWN UPON THE STUDY
OF NATURAL PHILOSOPHY, WHICH INCLUDED ASTRONOMY, MATHEMATICS,
AND PHILOSOPHY, BUT THE ISLAMIC FAITH VIEWED THE STUDY OF NATURAL
PHILOSOPHY AS A WAY OF UNDERSTANDING GOD. THUS, GREEK PHILOSO-
PHY BEGAN TO FLOURISH IN THESE REGIONS, DESPITE THE OBVIOUS CON-
TRADICTION BETWEEN THE BELIEFS OF THE GREEKS AND THOSE OF ISLAM.

KHAYYAM WAS INFLUENCED BY THIS CULTURAL EXCHANGE, AND IT
WAS FROM THIS THAT HE CONCEIVED HIS MATHEMATICAL THEORY OF
CUBIC EQUATIONS AND INVENTED THE JALALI CALENDAR OF ASTRONOMY.
THIS CALENDAR NOT ONLY INFORMED THE IRANIAN CALENDAR, BUT
WAS EVEN MORE ACCURATE THAN THE GREGORIAN CALENDAR.

KHAYYAM'S INTEREST IN NATURAL PHILOSOPHY ALLOWED HIM TO
REALIZE THE DISCREPANCIES BETWEEN HIS RELIGIOUS BELIEFS AND
THE MORE EMPIRICALLY-DERIVED STUDY OF NATURAL SCIENCES.
BECAUSE OF THIS, HE ENGAGED IN BEHAVIORS SUCH AS DRINKING--
SOMETHING ORDINARILY PROHIBITED IN THE ISLAMIC FAITH.

IN HIS PERSONAL LIFE, KHAYYAM WAS KNOWN FOR BEING ANTAGONISTIC TOWARDS CLERGY,
AS WELL AS FOR HIS RELUCTANCE TO ENGAGE IN HUMAN INTERACTION--A RELUCTANCE SO STRONG
THAT HE OFTEN HESITATED TO TEACH. MANY OF HIS POEMS WERE PUBLISHED ANONYMOUSLY.
IN FACT, EVEN PARTS OF THE *RUBAIYAT* WERE NOT ADDED TO THE BOOK UNTIL MANY YEARS
LATER BECAUSE OF THEIR ANONYMOUS PUBLICATION.

THE *RUBAIYAT* CONTAINS MANY OF KHAYYAM'S ANECDOTES, AS WELL AS CONTENTS DETAILING
THE DISCOVERY OF HIS WORKS IN THE WEST. INTERESTINGLY, MEZHINSKY, THE HEAD OF THE
OGPU, THE SOVIET UNION'S SECRET POLICE, WAS SAID TO HAVE STUDIED A MEDIEVAL PERSIAN
EDITION OF THE *RUBAIYAT*.

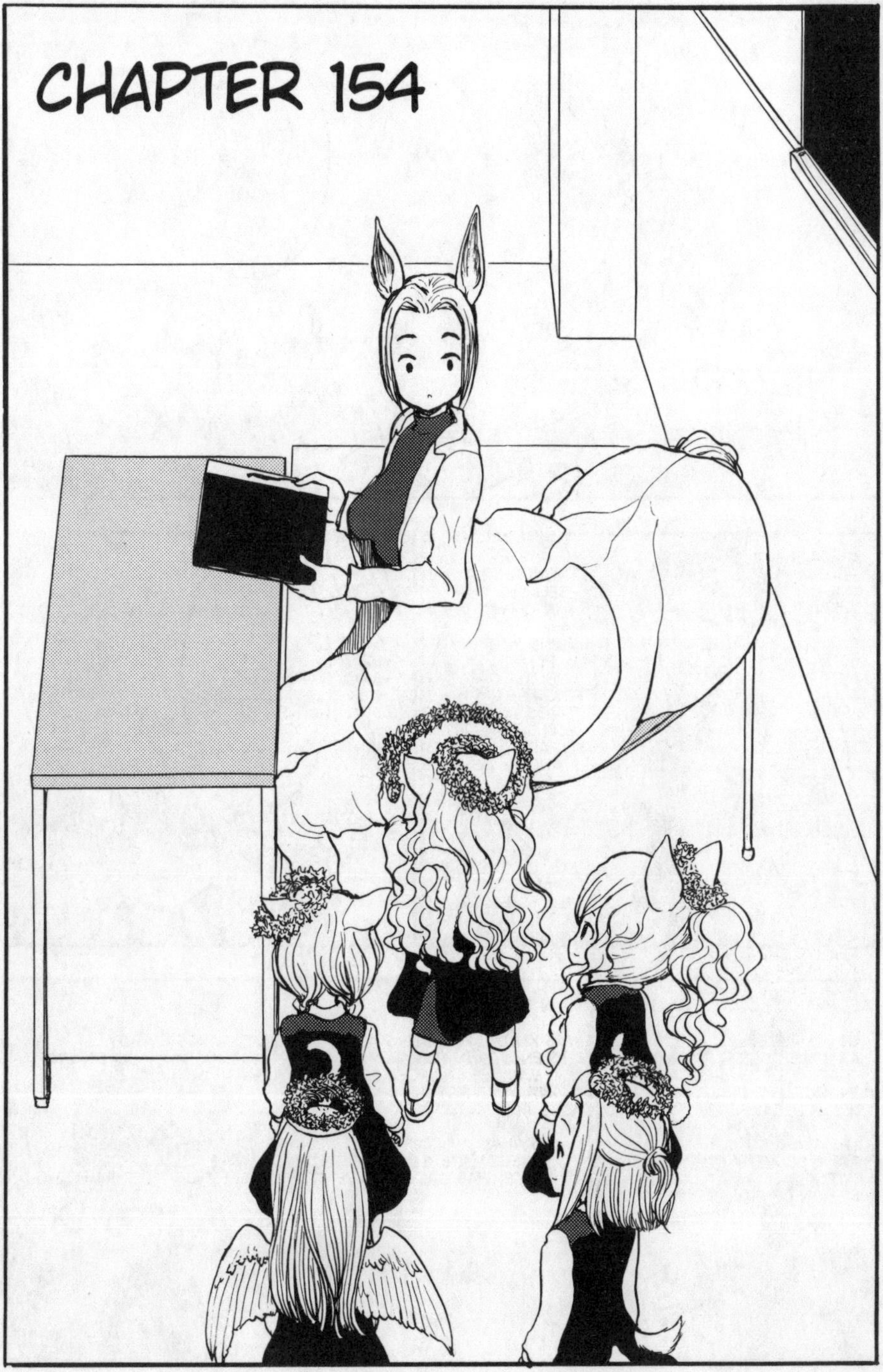
CHAPTER 154

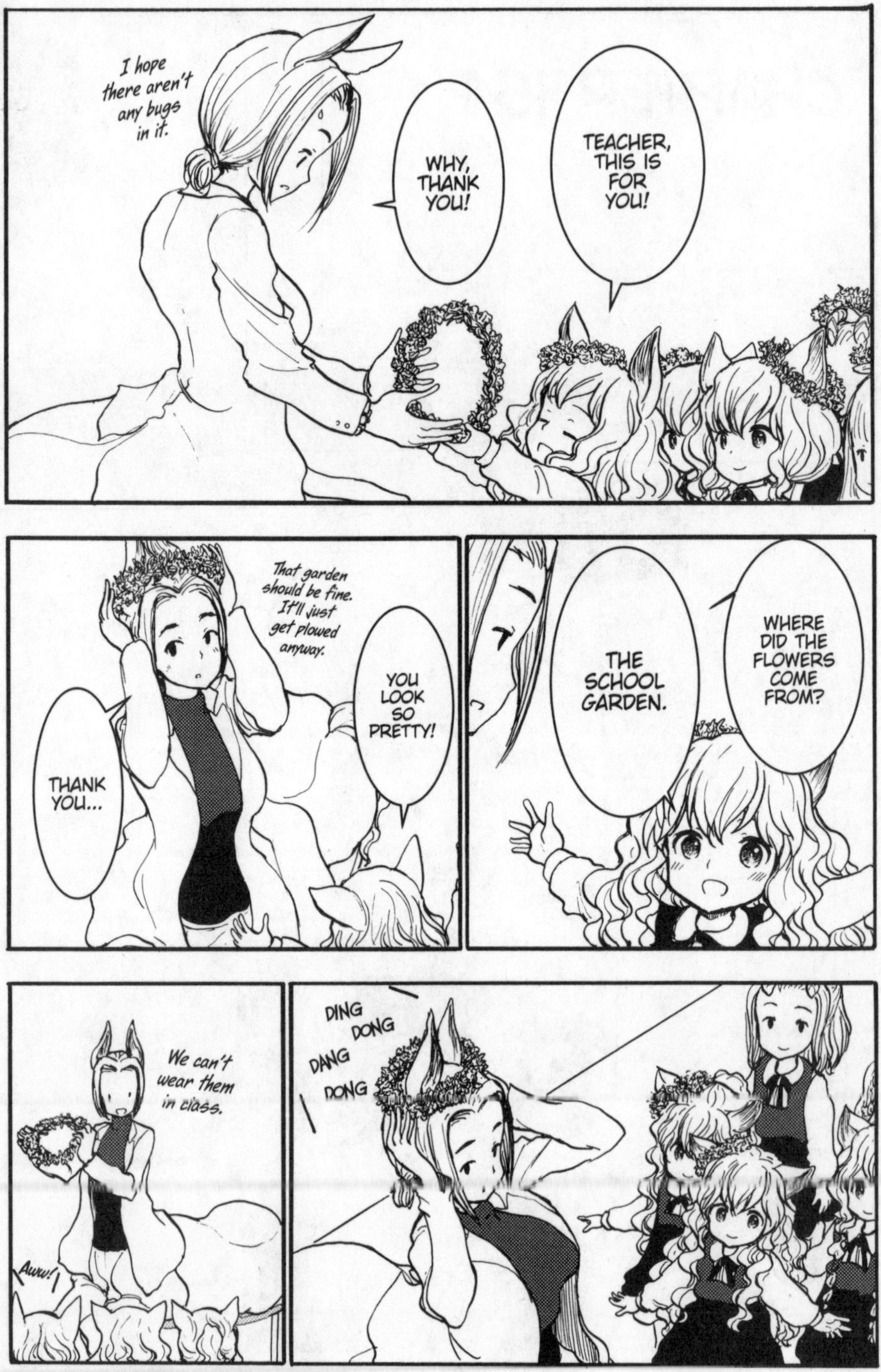
TEACHER, THIS IS FOR YOU!
WHY, THANK YOU!
I hope there aren't any bugs in it.
WHERE DID THE FLOWERS COME FROM?
THE SCHOOL GARDEN.
YOU LOOK SO PRETTY!
That garden should be fine. It'll just get plowed anyway.
THANK YOU...
DING DONG DANG DONG
We can't wear them in class.
Awww!

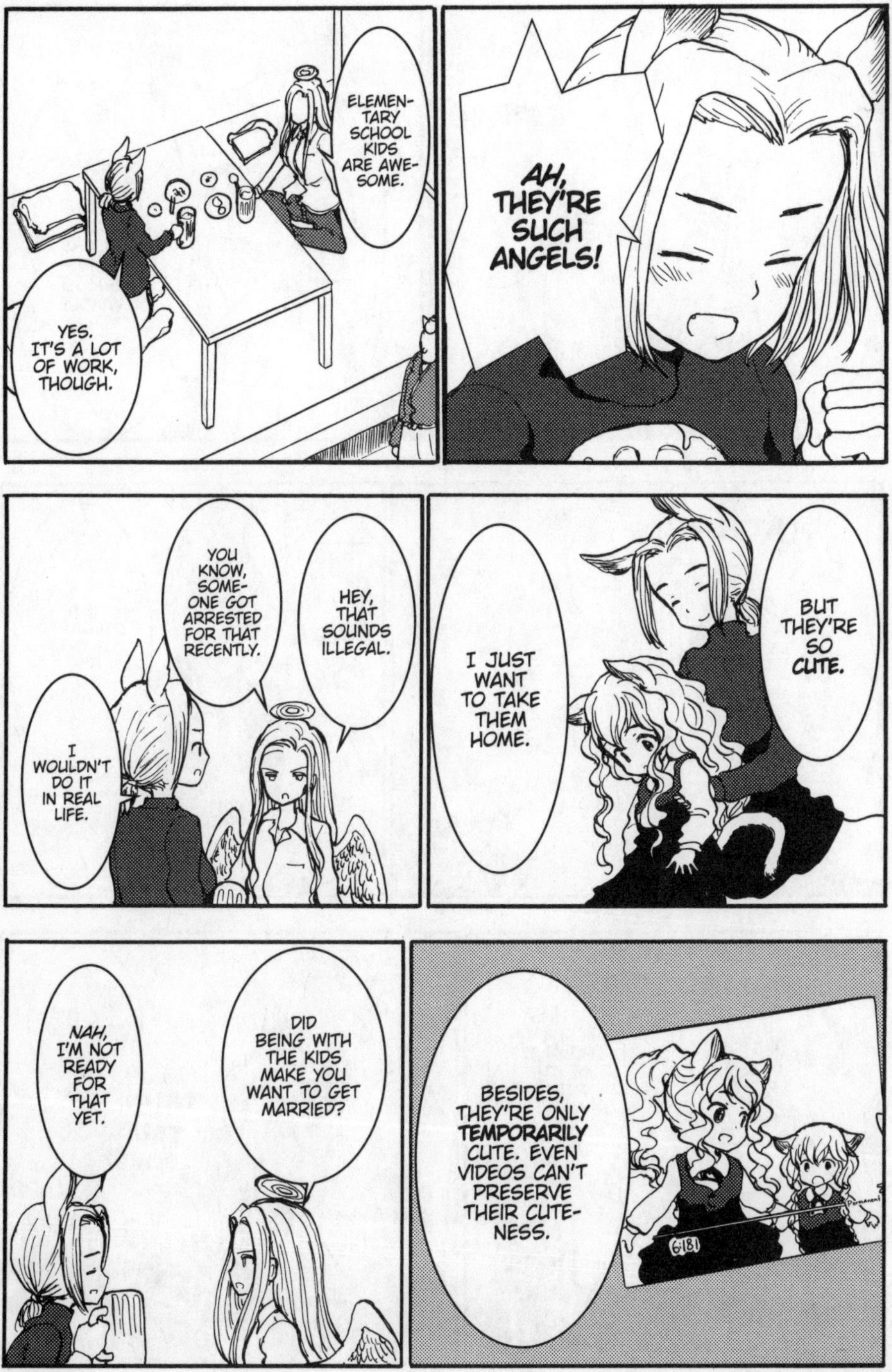
AH, THEY'RE SUCH ANGELS!
ELEMENTARY SCHOOL KIDS ARE AWESOME.
YES. IT'S A LOT OF WORK, THOUGH.
BUT THEY'RE SO CUTE.
I JUST WANT TO TAKE THEM HOME.
HEY, THAT SOUNDS ILLEGAL.
YOU KNOW, SOMEONE GOT ARRESTED FOR THAT RECENTLY.
I WOULDN'T DO IT IN REAL LIFE.
BESIDES, THEY'RE ONLY TEMPORARILY CUTE. EVEN VIDEOS CAN'T PRESERVE THEIR CUTENESS.
DID BEING WITH THE KIDS MAKE YOU WANT TO GET MARRIED?
NAH, I'M NOT READY FOR THAT YET.

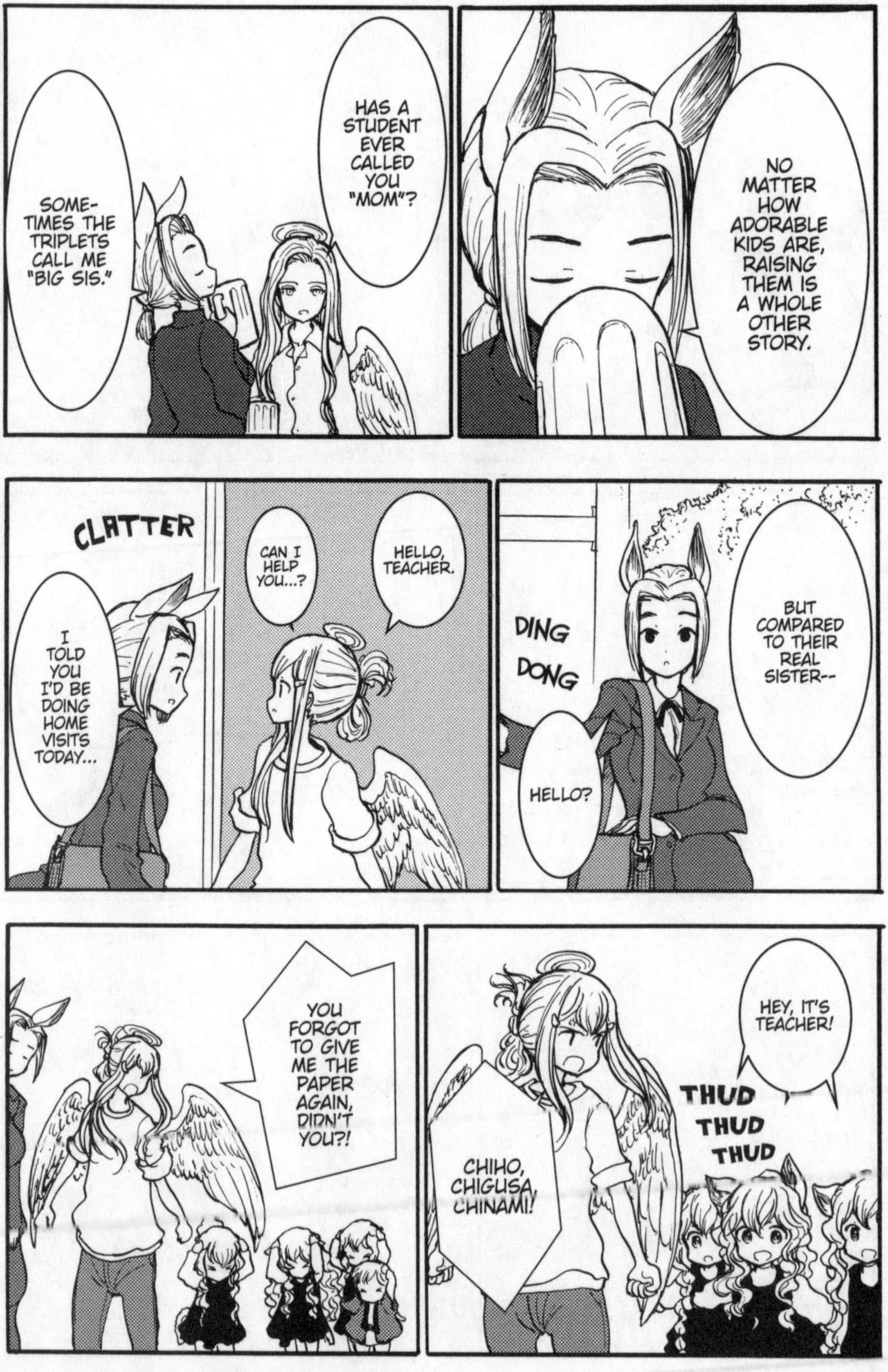
NO MATTER HOW ADORABLE KIDS ARE, RAISING THEM IS A WHOLE OTHER STORY.
HAS A STUDENT EVER CALLED YOU "MOM"?
SOME-TIMES THE TRIPLETS CALL ME "BIG SIS."
BUT COMPARED TO THEIR REAL SISTER--
DING DONG
HELLO?
HELLO, TEACHER.
CAN I HELP YOU...?
CLATTER
I TOLD YOU I'D BE DOING HOME VISITS TODAY...
HEY, IT'S TEACHER!
THUD THUD THUD
CHIHO, CHIGUSA, CHINAMI!
YOU FORGOT TO GIVE ME THE PAPER AGAIN, DIDN'T YOU?!

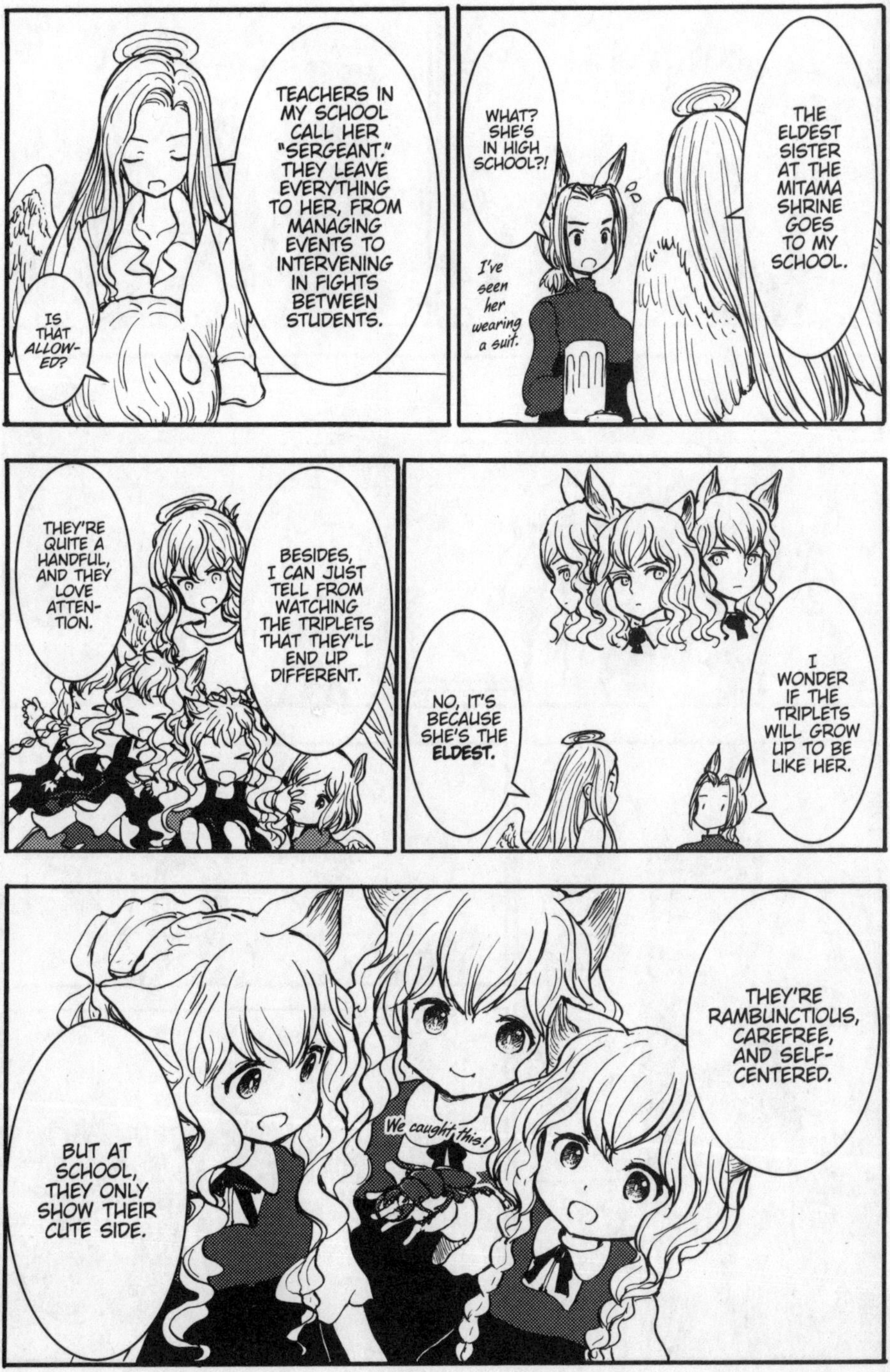
THE ELDEST SISTER AT THE MITAMA SHRINE GOES TO MY SCHOOL.
WHAT? SHE'S IN HIGH SCHOOL?!
I've seen her wearing a suit.
TEACHERS IN MY SCHOOL CALL HER "SERGEANT." THEY LEAVE EVERYTHING TO HER, FROM MANAGING EVENTS TO INTERVENING IN FIGHTS BETWEEN STUDENTS.
IS THAT ALLOWED?
I WONDER IF THE TRIPLETS WILL GROW UP TO BE LIKE HER.
NO, IT'S BECAUSE SHE'S THE **ELDEST.**
BESIDES, I CAN JUST TELL FROM WATCHING THE TRIPLETS THAT THEY'LL END UP DIFFERENT.
THEY'RE QUITE A HANDFUL, AND THEY LOVE ATTENTION.
THEY'RE RAMBUNCTIOUS, CAREFREE, AND SELF-CENTERED.
We caught this!
BUT AT SCHOOL, THEY ONLY SHOW THEIR CUTE SIDE.

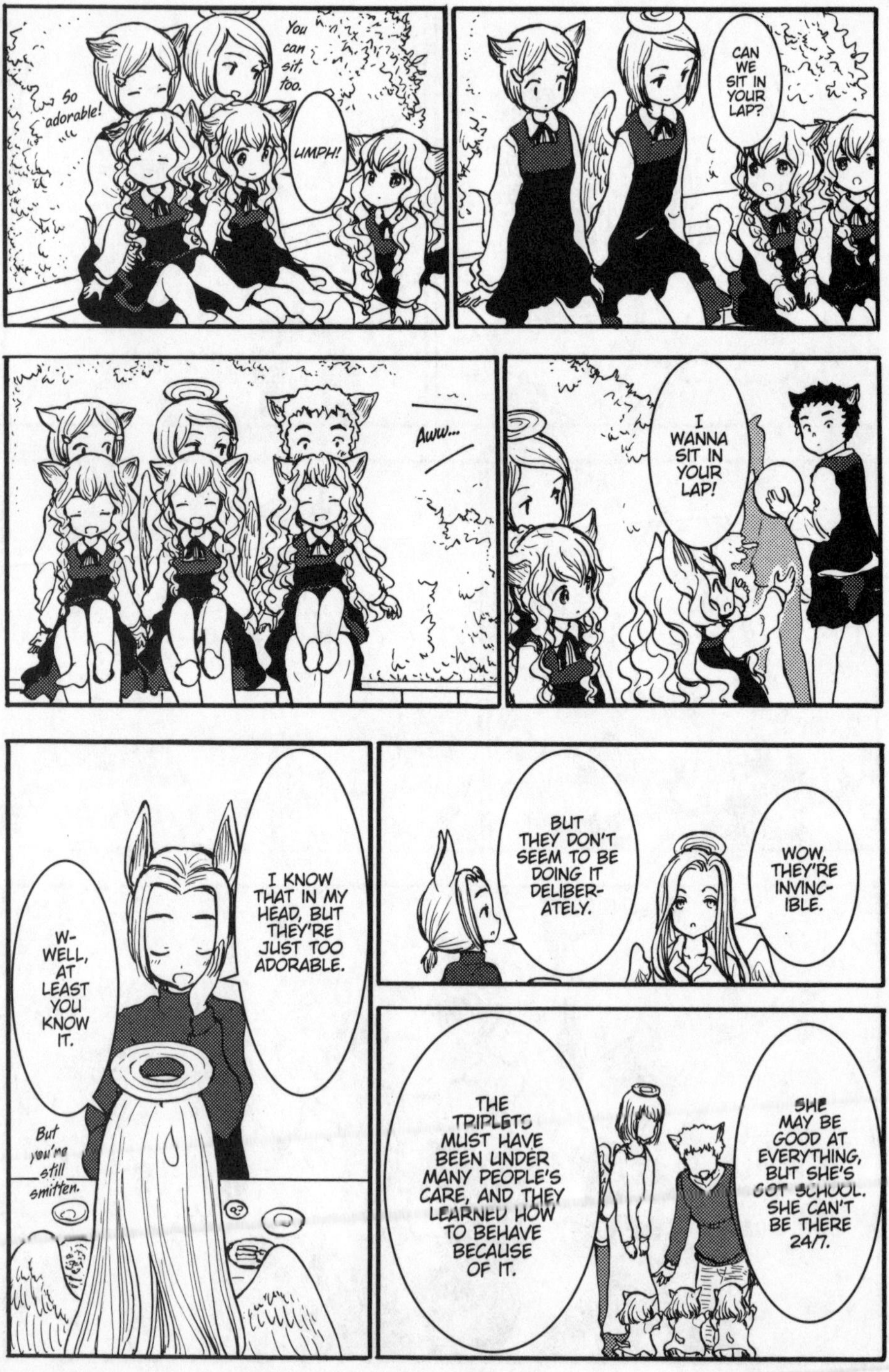
CAN WE SIT IN YOUR LAP?
You can sit, too.
UMPH!
So adorable!
I WANNA SIT IN YOUR LAP!
Aww...
WOW, THEY'RE INVINCIBLE.
BUT THEY DON'T SEEM TO BE DOING IT DELIBERATELY.
SHE MAY BE GOOD AT EVERYTHING, BUT SHE'S GOT SCHOOL. SHE CAN'T BE THERE 24/7.
THE TRIPLETS MUST HAVE BEEN UNDER MANY PEOPLE'S CARE, AND THEY LEARNED HOW TO BEHAVE BECAUSE OF IT.
I KNOW THAT IN MY HEAD, BUT THEY'RE JUST TOO ADORABLE.
W-WELL, AT LEAST YOU KNOW IT.
But you're still smitten.

A Centaur's Life

GREAT SCHOLARS OF THE WORLD:
<4> NICOLAUS COPERNICUS

NICOLAUS COPERNICUS IS KNOWN NOT ONLY FOR THE
COPERNICAN REVOLUTION, BUT ALSO FOR CREATING A PARADIGM
SHIFT IN HUMANITY'S VIEW OF THE UNIVERSE WITH HIS HELIOCENTRIC
THEORY. GUIDED BY THEN-MODERN TECHNOLOGY AND ACADEMIA, HE
BROUGHT A LIFE-CHANGING THEORY OF THE COSMOS TO THE WORLD.

NICOLAUS COPERNICUS WAS BORN IN 1473 IN TORUN--A PART OF THE
KINGDOM OF PRUSSIA IN MODERN-DAY POLAND. AT THIS TIME, THE FIRST
LETTERPRESS PRINTING BUSINESS HAD OPENED IN KRAKOW, THE CAPITAL
OF POLAND. THIS INVENTION WOULD LATER MAKE A HUGE IMPACT ON
COPERNICUS, WHO WENT ON TO STUDY AT KRAKOW UNIVERSITY.

AT THIS TIME, EUROPE WAS UNDER RELIGIOUS DOMINATION. BECAUSE
THE BIBLE MADE NO MENTION OF NATURAL SCIENCE, AN ECUMENICAL
COUNCIL SOUGHT TO ENDORSE ARISTOTLE'S THEORIES. ARISTOTLE'S
COSMOLOGY, A GEOCENTRIC MODEL, WAS DEVELOPED FROM PLATO'S
THEORY OF FORMS. ARISTOTLE BELIEVED THAT THE SUN, THE MOON,
AND EVERY OTHER CELESTIAL BODY ORBITED THE EARTH IN PERFECT
CONCENTRIC CIRCLES AND THAT THE EARTH WAS THE CENTER OF THE
UNIVERSE. THIS MODEL'S FLAW, HOWEVER, WAS THAT IT WAS
IDEALISTIC AND NOT BASED ON OBSERVATION.

A MORE COMPLEX MODEL OF THE UNIVERSE AROSE TO REPLACE IT--ONE WITH A GREATER BASE IN
EMPIRICISM. IT DEPICTED AN EPICYCLE (OR CIRCLE WITHIN A CIRCLE) WHICH CARRIED THE PLANETS
AROUND A VIRTUAL POINT CALLED THE EQUANT RATHER THAN AROUND THE EARTH. THIS MODEL
WAS DISTRIBUTED THROUGH MASS PUBLICATIONS WITH THE HELP OF THE PRINTING BUSINESS.

IN THE LATE 1400S, THE PRINTING BUSINESS WAS OFTEN RUN BY SCHOLARS AND ASTRONOMERS.
THUS, COPERNICUS ACQUIRED THE MEANS TO STUDY THIS MODEL AND EVENTUALLY PROVE IT WRONG.
HE DEVELOPED A HELIOCENTRIC THEORY--THE IDEA THAT THE EARTH REVOLVES AROUND THE SUN--
AND CONCLUDED THAT THE EPICYCLE AND THE EQUANT WERE UNNECESSARY CONCEPTS IF HIS
THEORY WERE TRUE.

ORIGINALLY, COPERNICUS KEPT THIS REVELATION TO HIMSELF. HOWEVER, AFTER HIS DEATH, HIS
DISCIPLE PRINTED HIS FINDINGS. UNFORTUNATELY, THIS MEANT THAT COPERNICUS NEVER SAW THE
PUBLICATION OF HIS OWN THEORY, BUT NEVERTHELESS, THAT THEORY WOULD FUNDAMENTALLY
CHANGE OUR VIEW OF THE UNIVERSE.

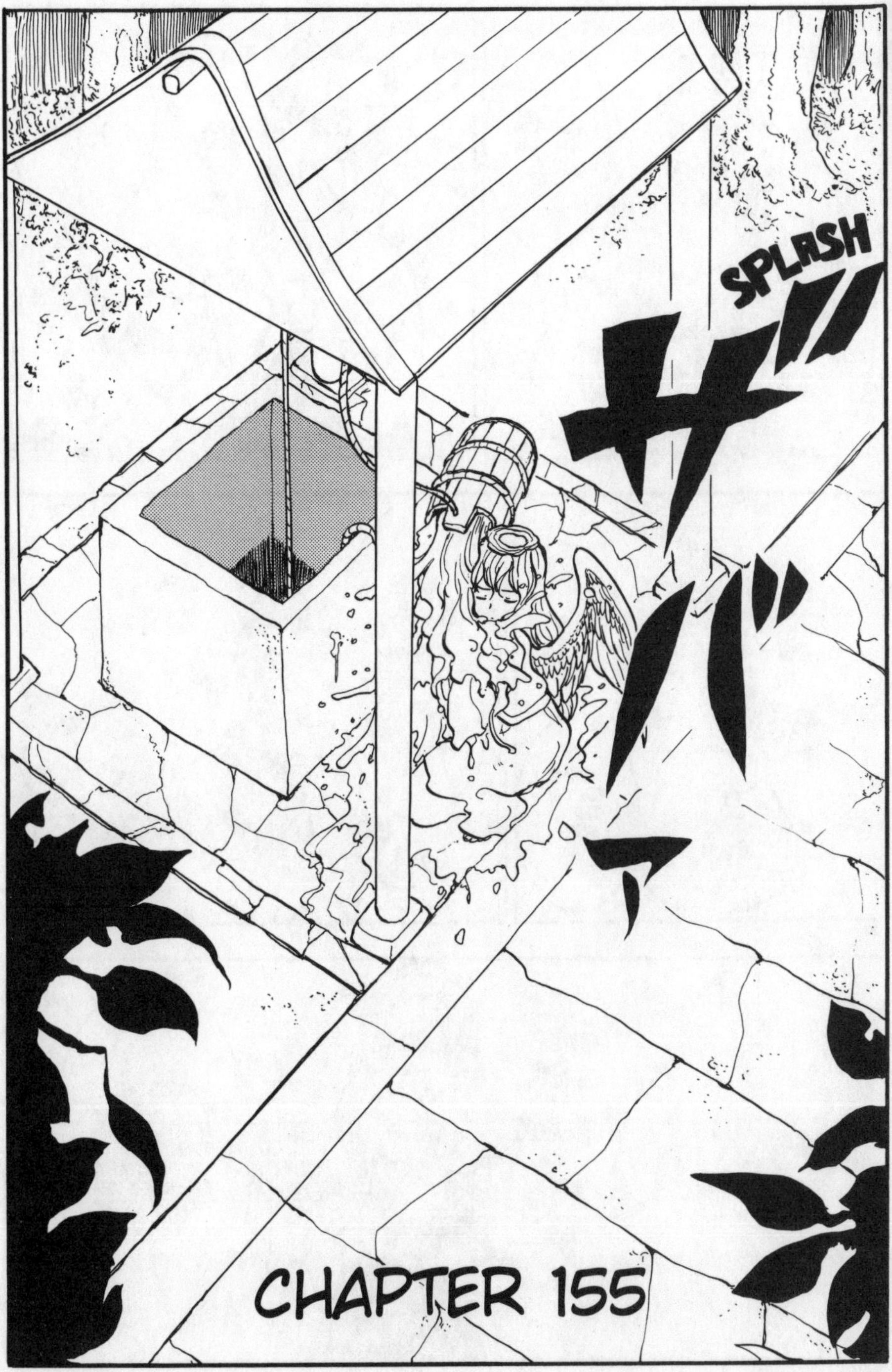
SPLASH
ザバァ
CHAPTER 155

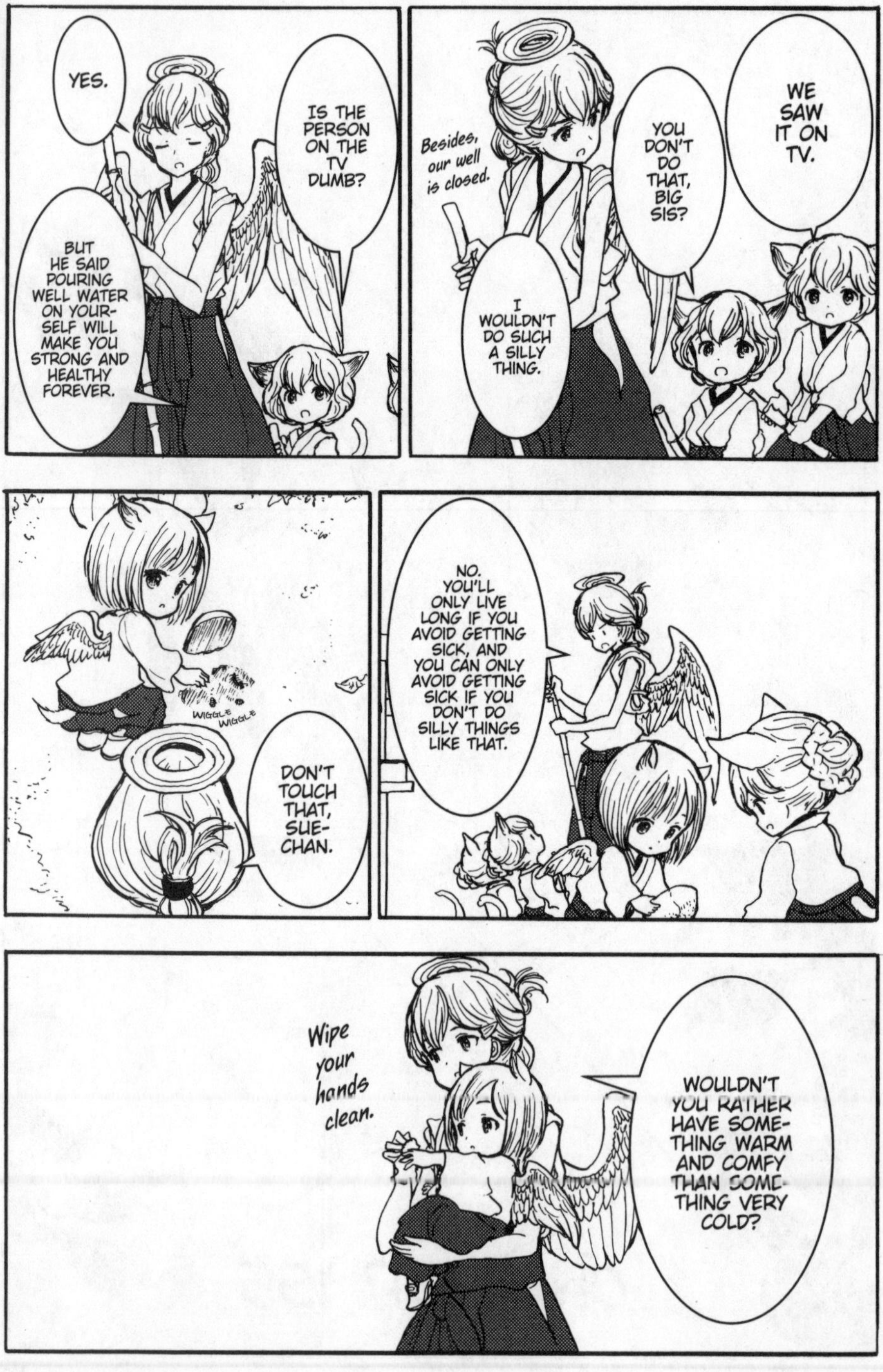

WE SAW IT ON TV.
YOU DON'T DO THAT, BIG SIS?
I WOULDN'T DO SUCH A SILLY THING.
Besides, our well is closed.
BUT HE SAID POURING WELL WATER ON YOURSELF WILL MAKE YOU STRONG AND HEALTHY FOREVER.
IS THE PERSON ON THE TV DUMB?
YES.
NO. YOU'LL ONLY LIVE LONG IF YOU AVOID GETTING SICK, AND YOU CAN ONLY AVOID GETTING SICK IF YOU DON'T DO SILLY THINGS LIKE THAT.
DON'T TOUCH THAT, SUE-CHAN.
WIGGLE WIGGLE
WOULDN'T YOU RATHER HAVE SOMETHING WARM AND COMFY THAN SOMETHING VERY COLD?
Wipe your hands clean.

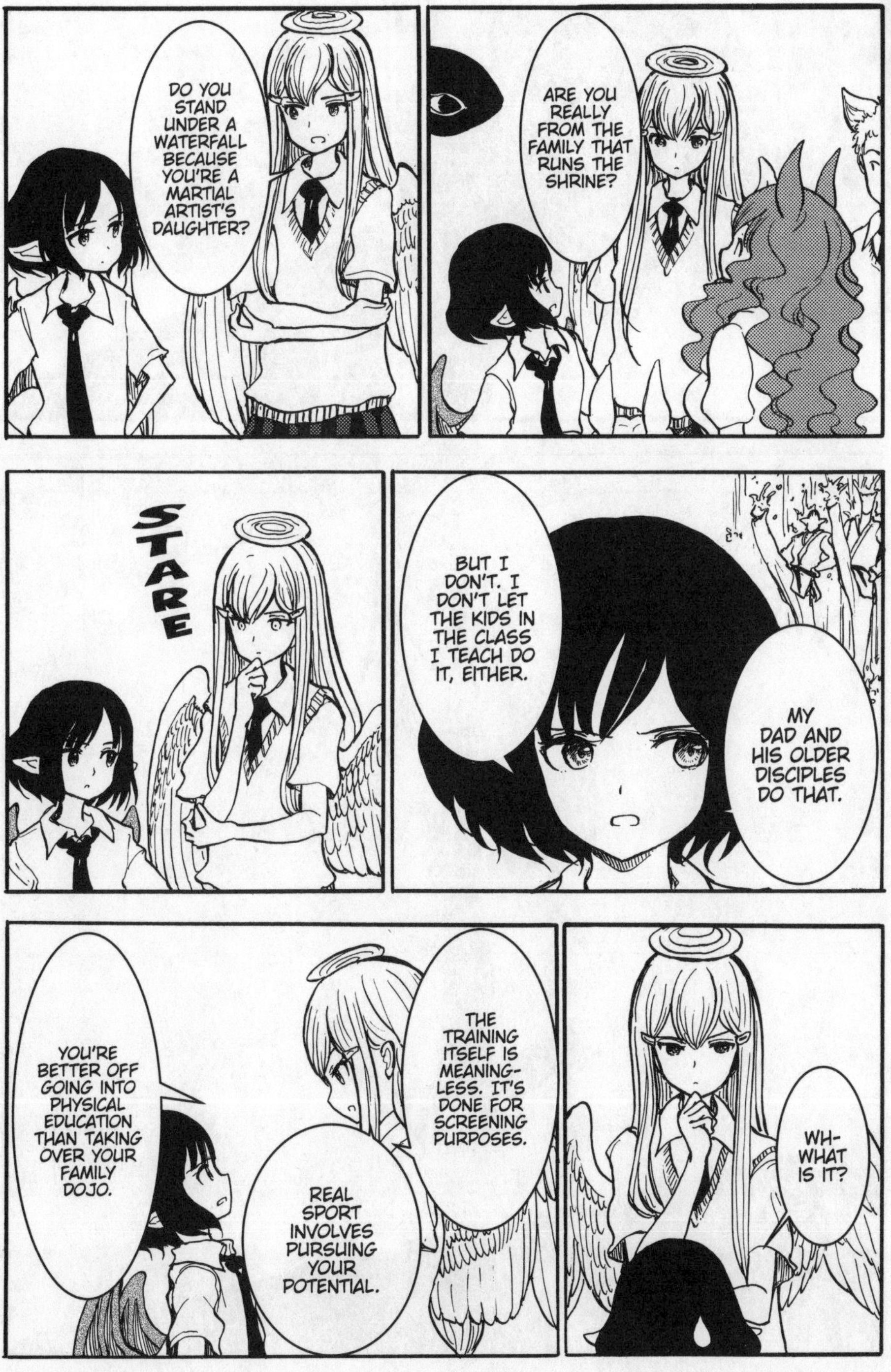
ARE YOU REALLY FROM THE FAMILY THAT RUNS THE SHRINE?
DO YOU STAND UNDER A WATERFALL BECAUSE YOU'RE A MARTIAL ARTIST'S DAUGHTER?
MY DAD AND HIS OLDER DISCIPLES DO THAT.
BUT I DON'T. I DON'T LET THE KIDS IN THE CLASS I TEACH DO IT, EITHER.
STARE
WH-WHAT IS IT?
THE TRAINING ITSELF IS MEANING-LESS. IT'S DONE FOR SCREENING PURPOSES.
REAL SPORT INVOLVES PURSUING YOUR POTENTIAL.
YOU'RE BETTER OFF GOING INTO PHYSICAL EDUCATION THAN TAKING OVER YOUR FAMILY DOJO.

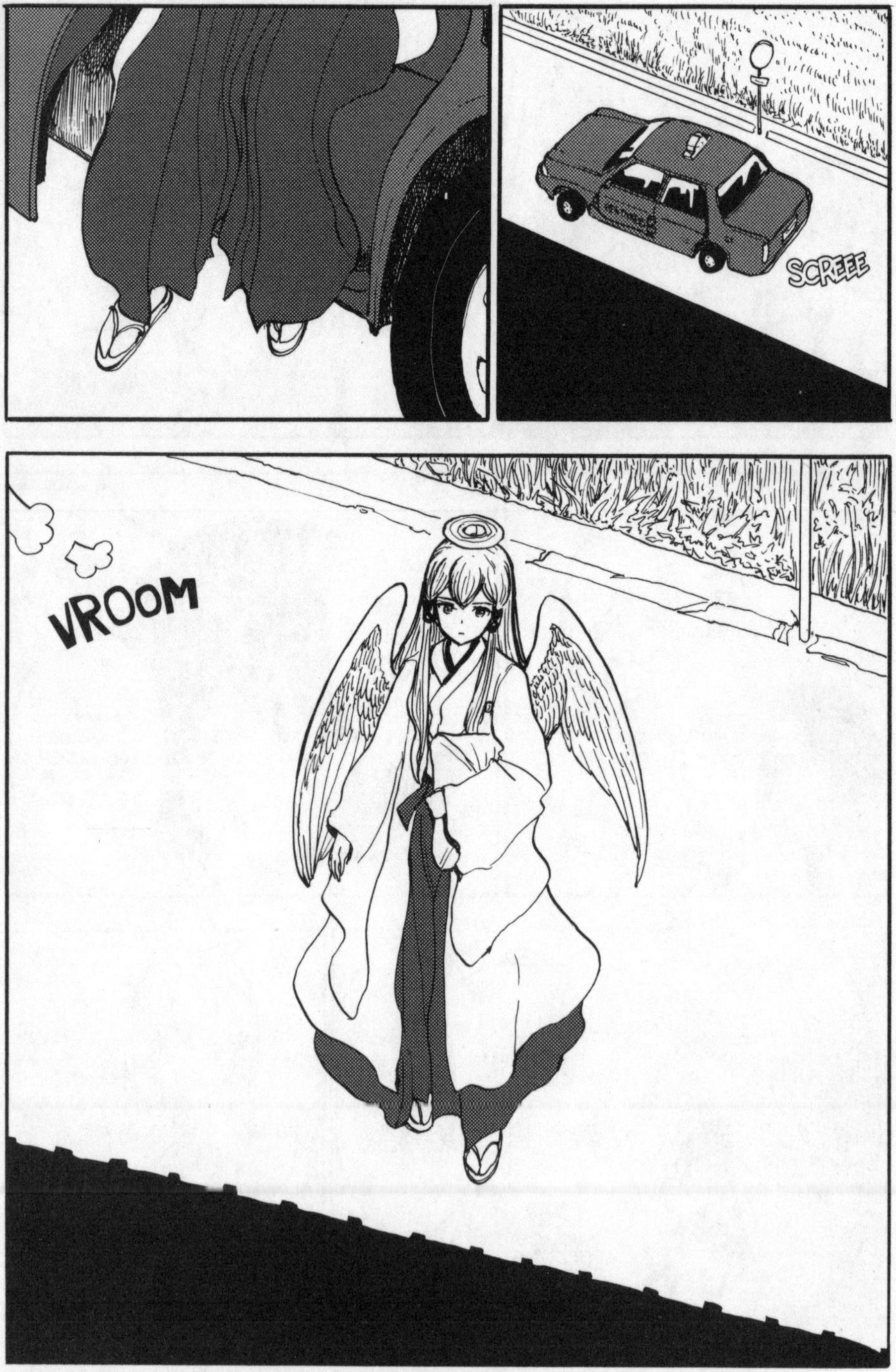
SCREEE
VROOM

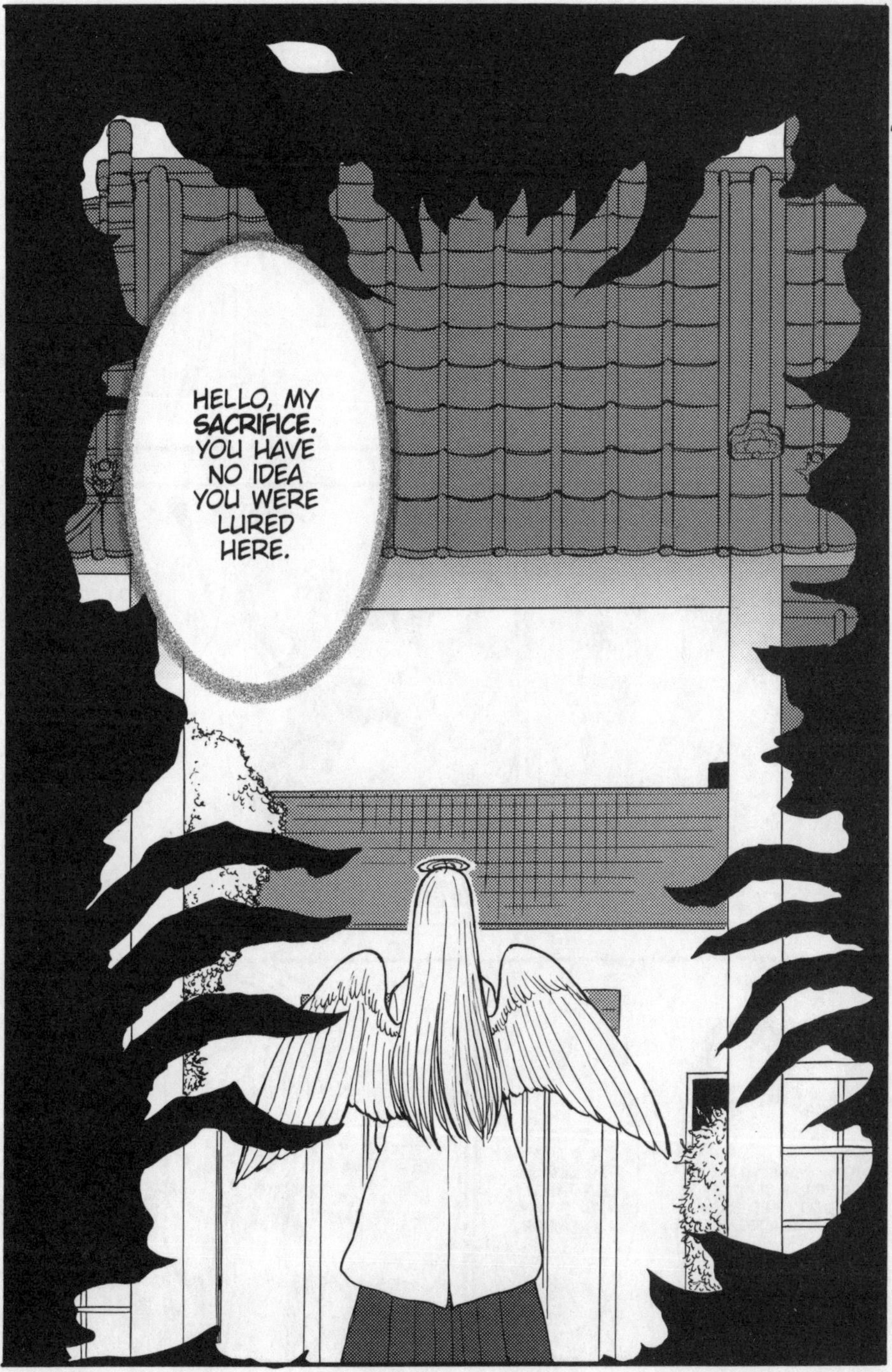
HELLO, MY SACRIFICE. YOU HAVE NO IDEA YOU WERE LURED HERE.

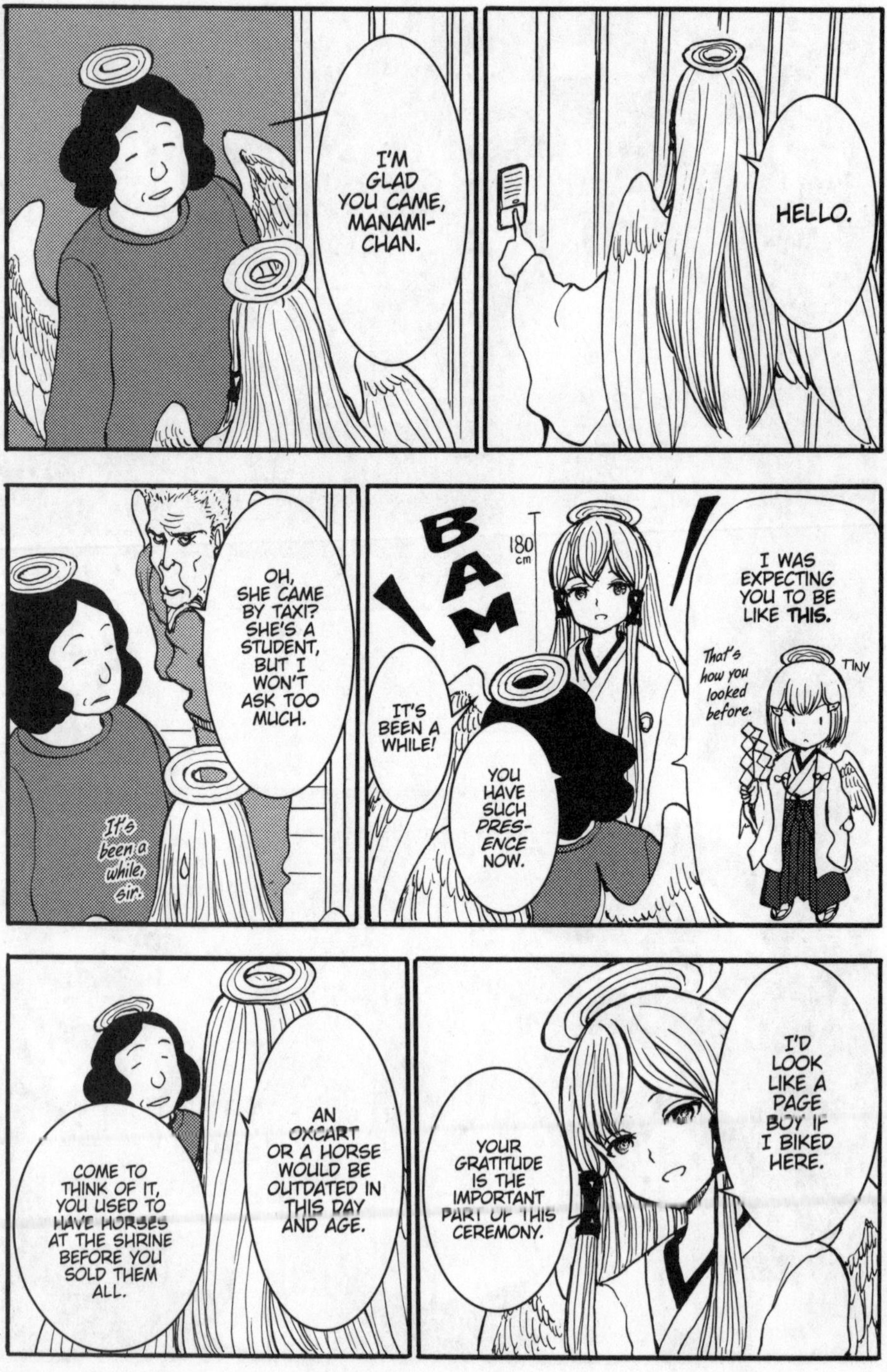
HELLO.
I'M GLAD YOU CAME, MANAMI-CHAN.
I WAS EXPECTING YOU TO BE LIKE THIS.
TINY
That's how you looked before.
180 cm
BAM
IT'S BEEN A WHILE!
YOU HAVE SUCH PRESENCE NOW.
OH, SHE CAME BY TAXI? SHE'S A STUDENT, BUT I WON'T ASK TOO MUCH.
It's been a while, sir.
I'D LOOK LIKE A PAGE BOY IF I BIKED HERE.
YOUR GRATITUDE IS THE IMPORTANT PART OF THIS CEREMONY.
AN OXCART OR A HORSE WOULD BE OUTDATED IN THIS DAY AND AGE.
COME TO THINK OF IT, YOU USED TO HAVE HORSES AT THE SHRINE BEFORE YOU SOLD THEM ALL.

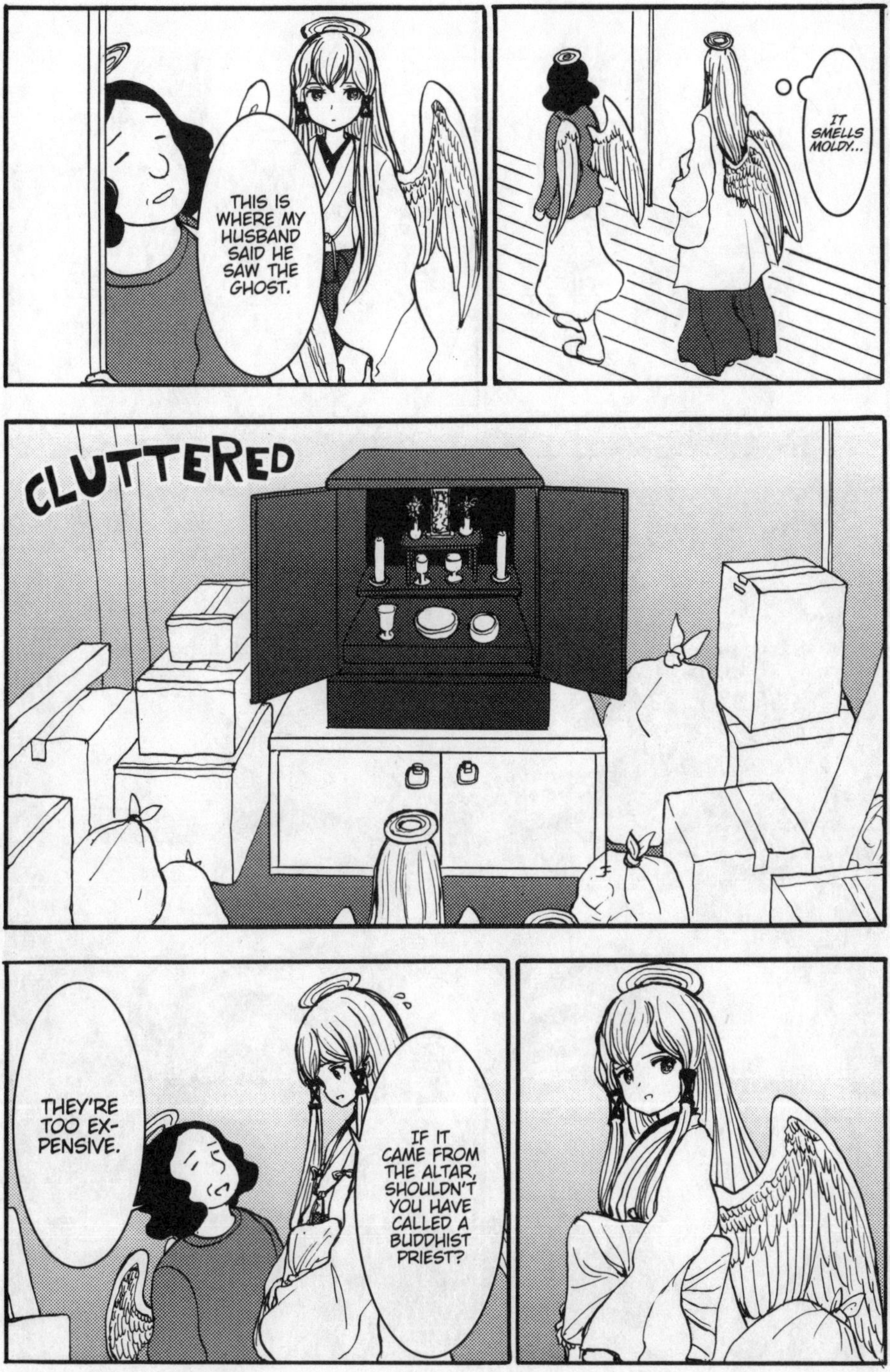
IT SMELLS MOLDY...
THIS IS WHERE MY HUSBAND SAID HE SAW THE GHOST.
CLUTTERED
IF IT CAME FROM THE ALTAR, SHOULDN'T YOU HAVE CALLED A BUDDHIST PRIEST?
THEY'RE TOO EX-PENSIVE.

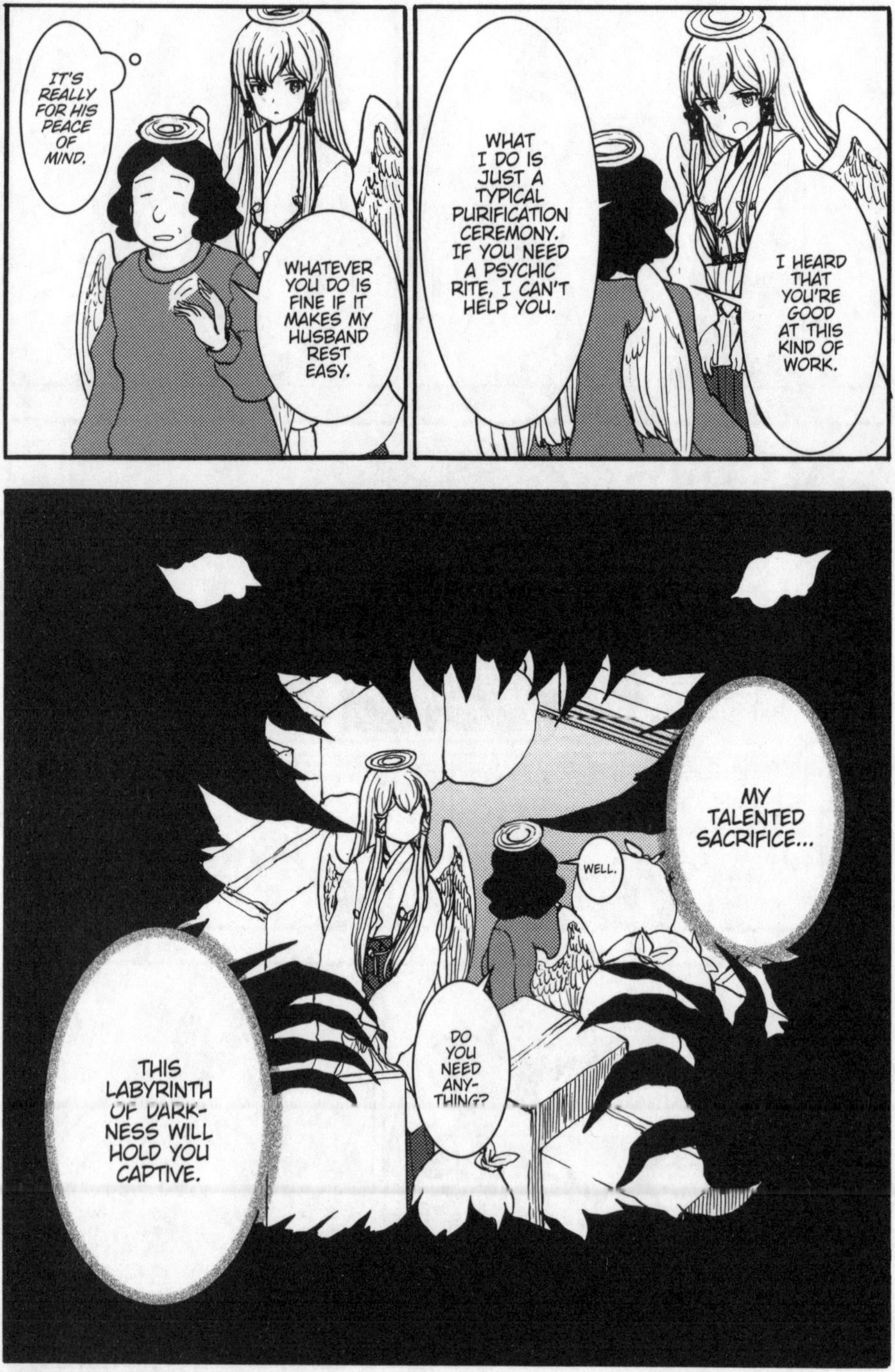
I HEARD THAT YOU'RE GOOD AT THIS KIND OF WORK.
WHAT I DO IS JUST A TYPICAL PURIFICATION CEREMONY. IF YOU NEED A PSYCHIC RITE, I CAN'T HELP YOU.
IT'S REALLY FOR HIS PEACE OF MIND.
WHATEVER YOU DO IS FINE IF IT MAKES MY HUSBAND REST EASY.
MY TALENTED SACRIFICE...
WELL.
DO YOU NEED ANY-THING?
THIS LABYRINTH OF DARK-NESS WILL HOLD YOU CAPTIVE.

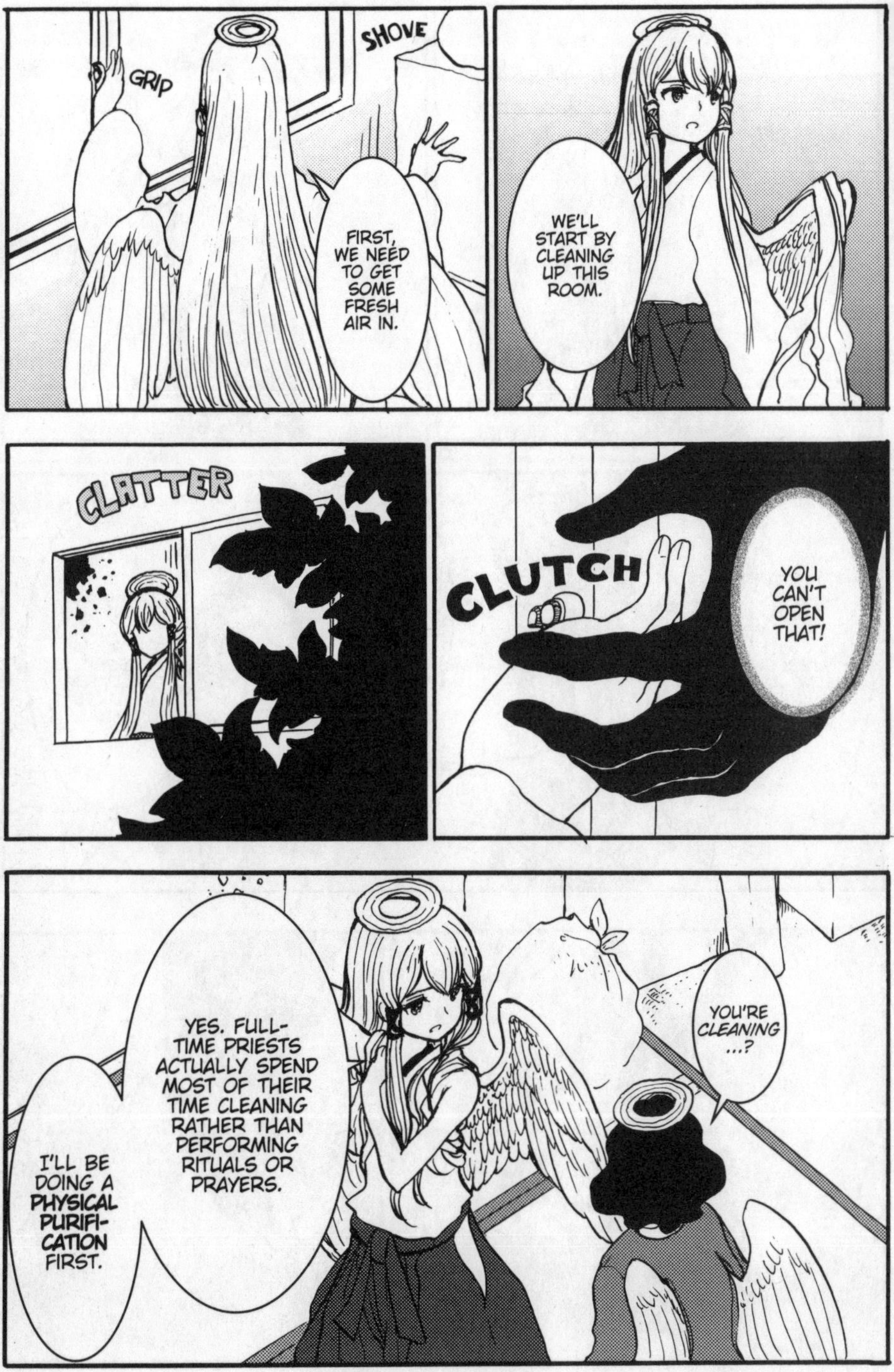
WE'LL START BY CLEANING UP THIS ROOM.
SHOVE
GRIP
FIRST, WE NEED TO GET SOME FRESH AIR IN.
YOU CAN'T OPEN THAT!
CLUTCH
CLATTER
YOU'RE CLEANING ...?
YES. FULL-TIME PRIESTS ACTUALLY SPEND MOST OF THEIR TIME CLEANING RATHER THAN PERFORMING RITUALS OR PRAYERS.
I'LL BE DOING A PHYSICAL PURIFICATION FIRST.

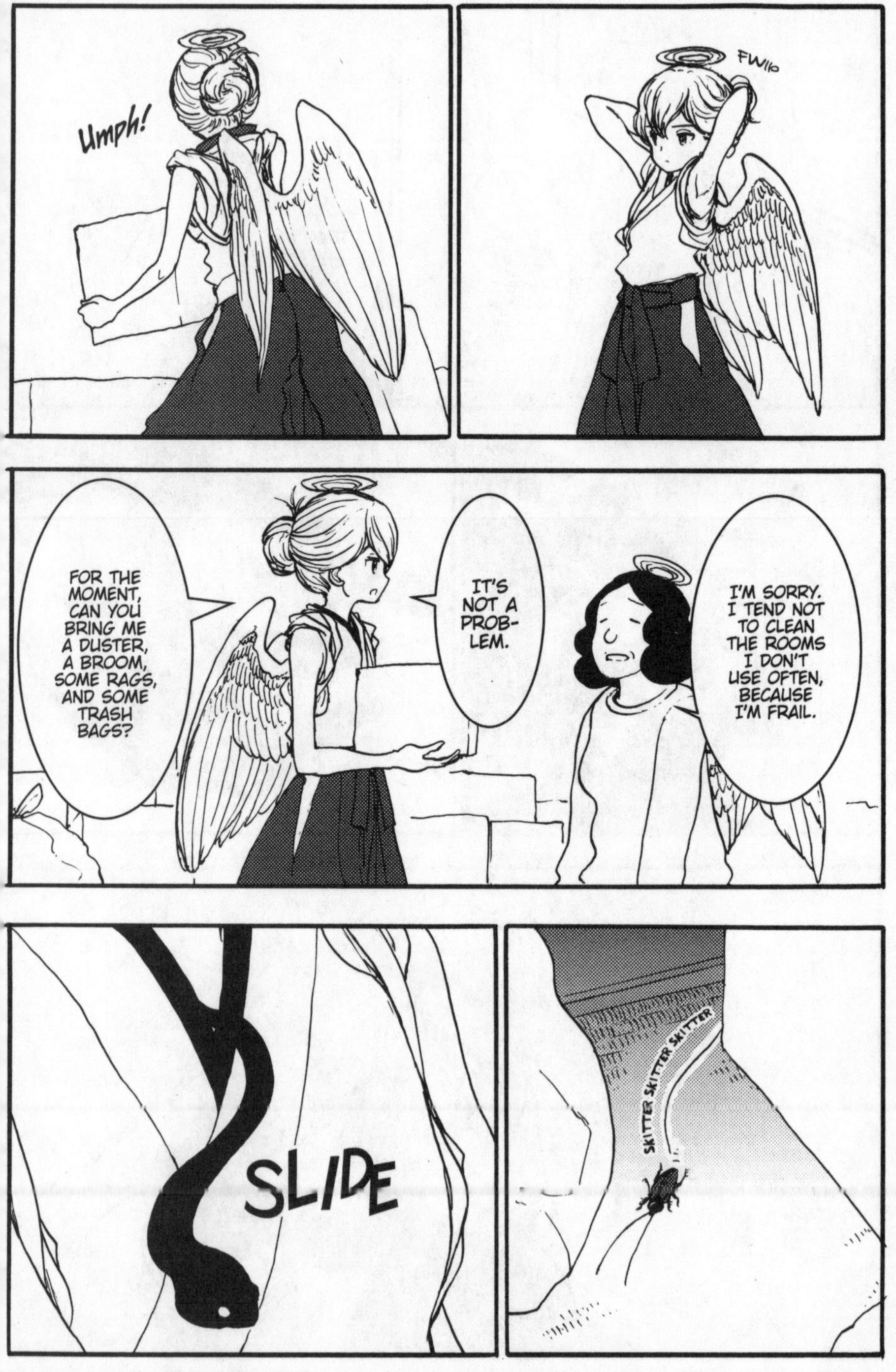
FWIP
Umph!
I'M SORRY. I TEND NOT TO CLEAN THE ROOMS I DON'T USE OFTEN, BECAUSE I'M FRAIL.
IT'S NOT A PROB-LEM.
FOR THE MOMENT, CAN YOU BRING ME A DUSTER, A BROOM, SOME RAGS, AND SOME TRASH BAGS?
SKITTER SKITTER SKITTER
SLIDE

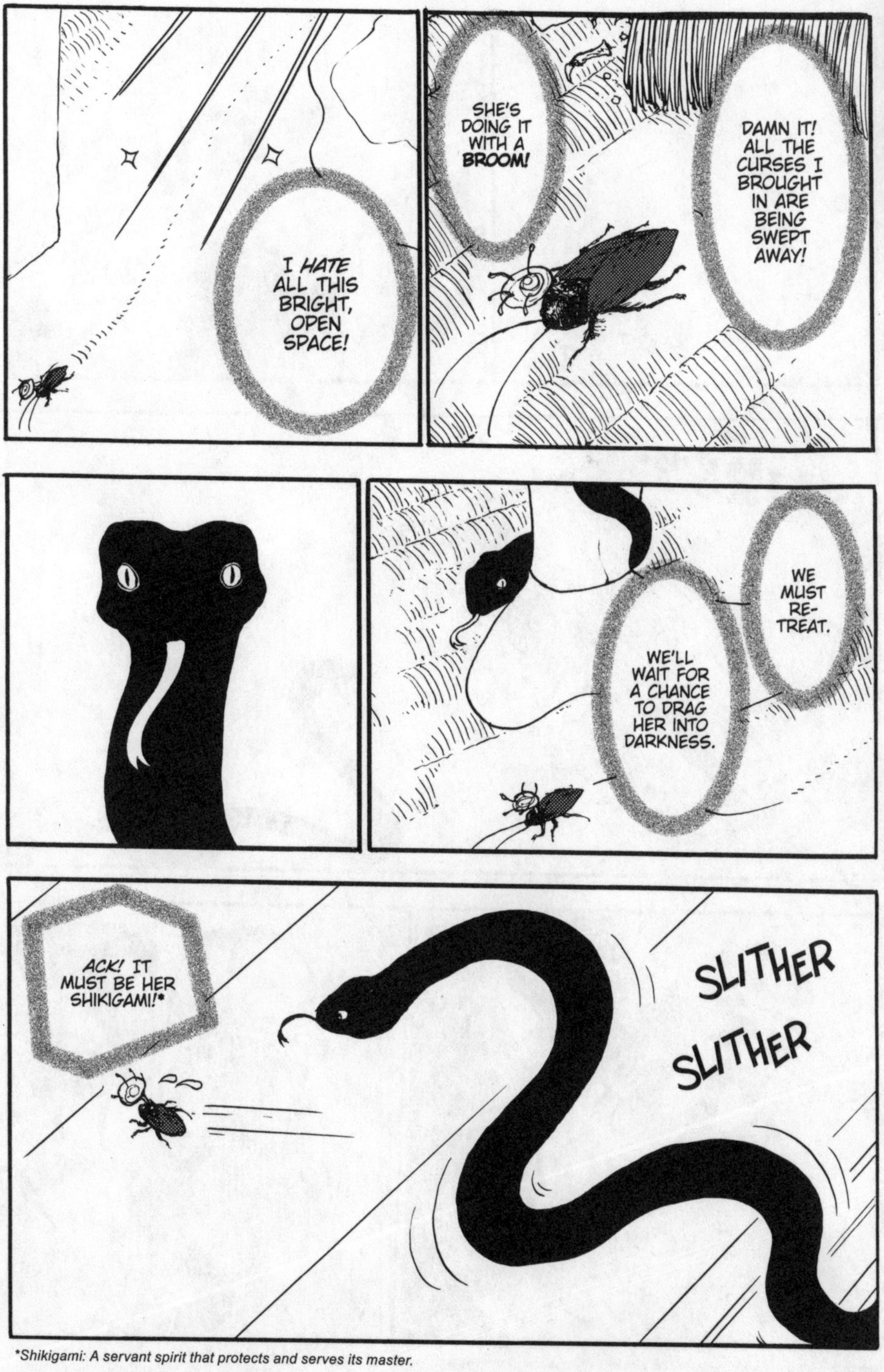
DAMN IT! ALL THE CURSES I BROUGHT IN ARE BEING SWEPT AWAY!
SHE'S DOING IT WITH A **BROOM!**
I *HATE* ALL THIS BRIGHT, OPEN SPACE!
WE MUST RE-TREAT.
WE'LL WAIT FOR A CHANCE TO DRAG HER INTO DARKNESS.
SLITHER
SLITHER
ACK! IT MUST BE HER SHIKIGAMI!*

*Shikigami: A servant spirit that protects and serves its master.

WRIGGLE
BYOING
ぴょん
I DON'T WANT TO GO OUT-SIDE, BUT I HAVE NO CHOICE!
SKITTER SKITTER SKITTER
BURST
ROAR
AN INU-GAMI!*
URAH
YOU RIVICU-LOUS FAKE GOD!

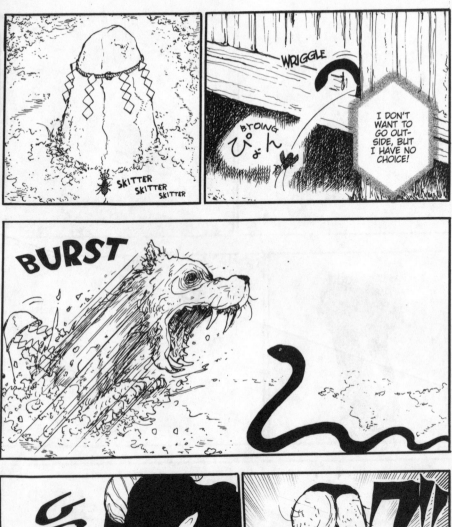

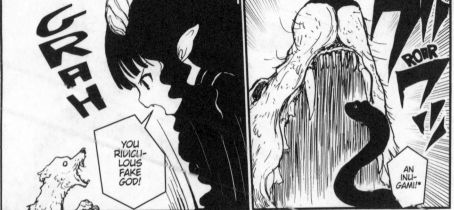

*Inugami: A type of shikigami that carries out vengeance or acts as a guardian to its master.

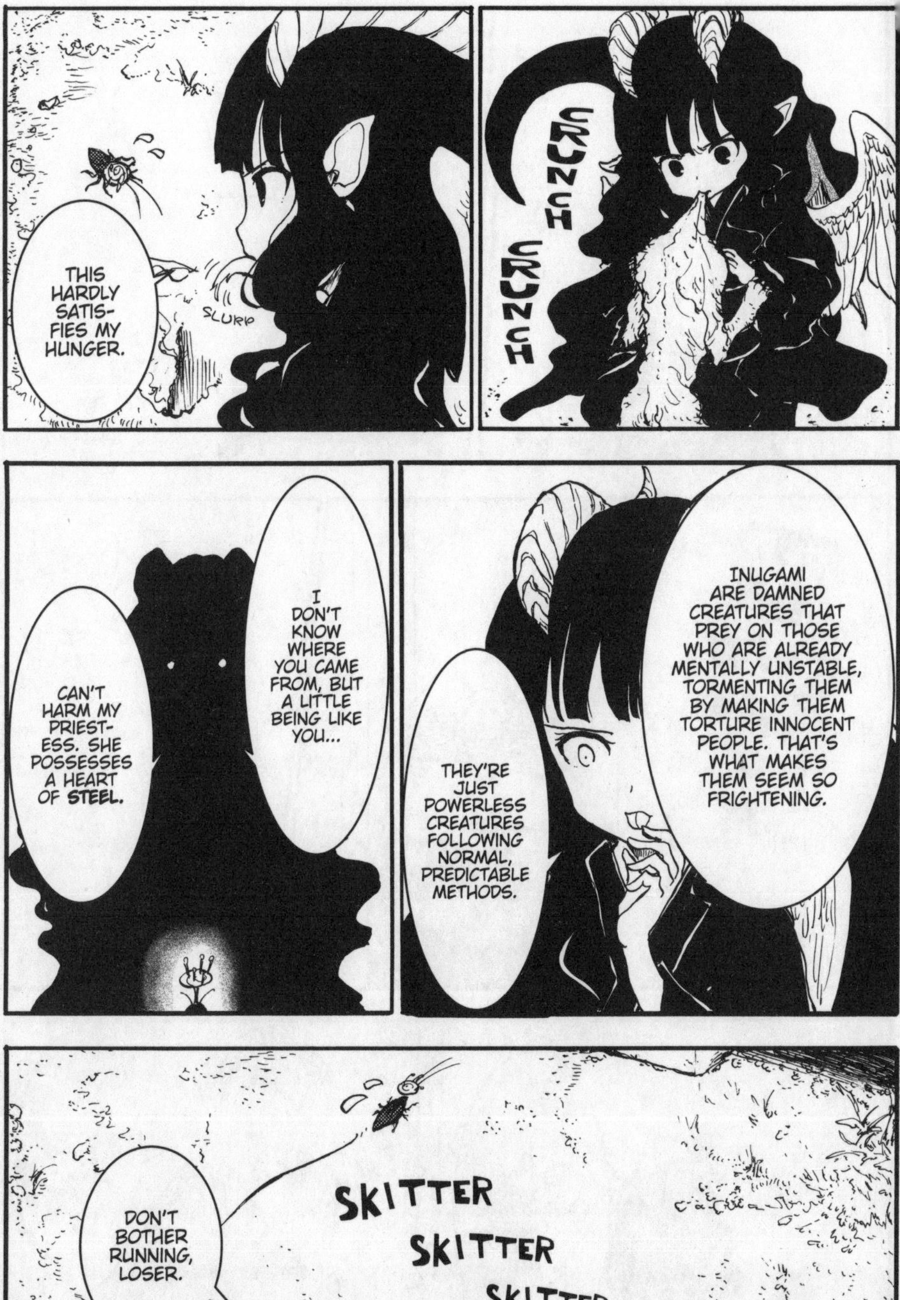
CRUNCH
CRUNCH
THIS HARDLY SATIS-FIES MY HUNGER.
SLURP
INUGAMI ARE DAMNED CREATURES THAT PREY ON THOSE WHO ARE ALREADY MENTALLY UNSTABLE, TORMENTING THEM BY MAKING THEM TORTURE INNOCENT PEOPLE. THAT'S WHAT MAKES THEM SEEM SO FRIGHTENING.
THEY'RE JUST POWERLESS CREATURES FOLLOWING NORMAL, PREDICTABLE METHODS.
I DON'T KNOW WHERE YOU CAME FROM, BUT A LITTLE BEING LIKE YOU...
CAN'T HARM MY PRIEST-ESS. SHE POSSESSES A HEART OF **STEEL.**
SKITTER
SKITTER
SKITTER
DON'T BOTHER RUNNING, LOSER.

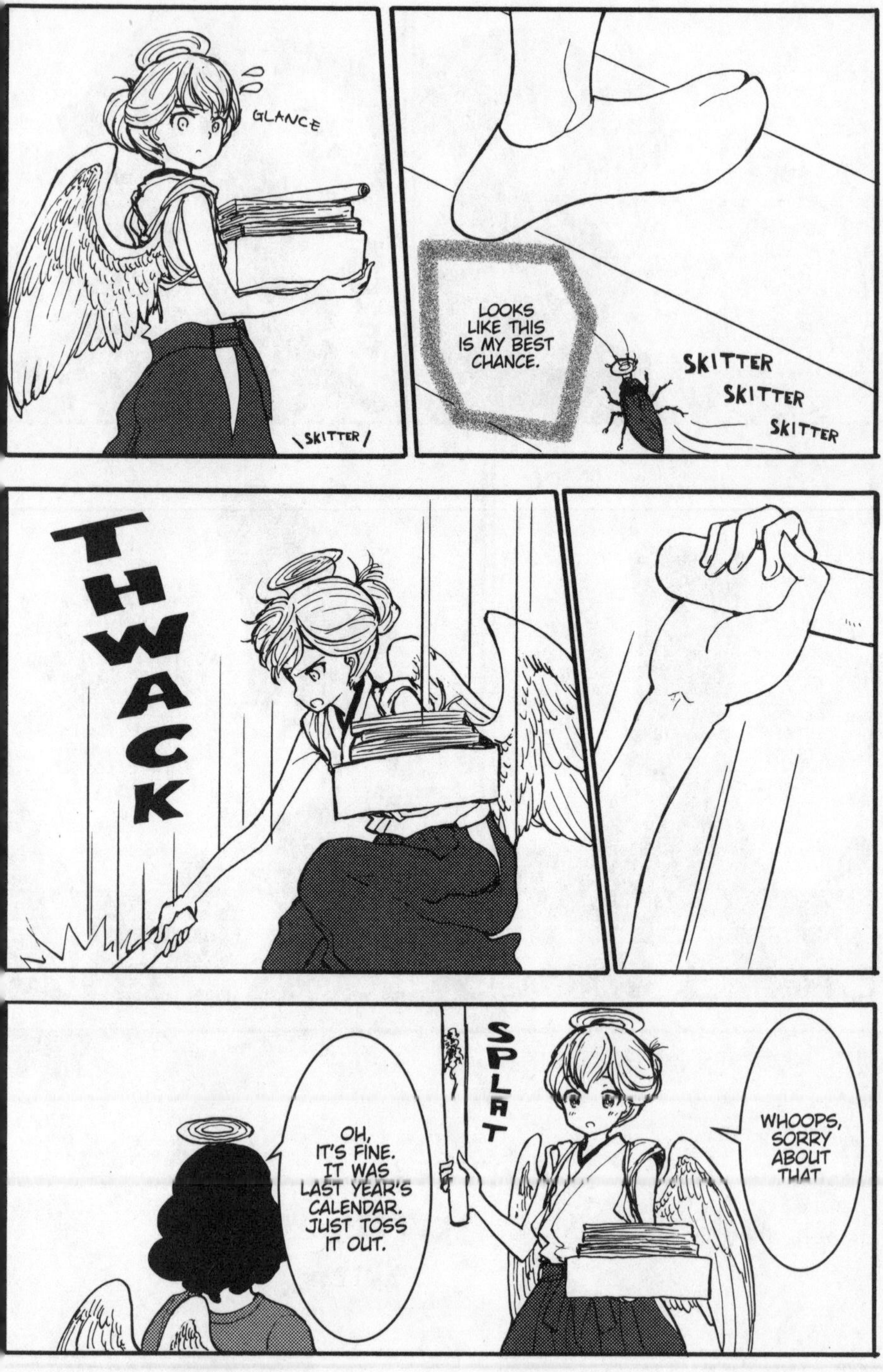
LOOKS LIKE THIS IS MY BEST CHANCE.
SKITTER
SKITTER
SKITTER
GLANCE
SKITTER
THWACK
WHOOPS, SORRY ABOUT THAT
SPLAT
OH, IT'S FINE. IT WAS LAST YEAR'S CALENDAR. JUST TOSS IT OUT.

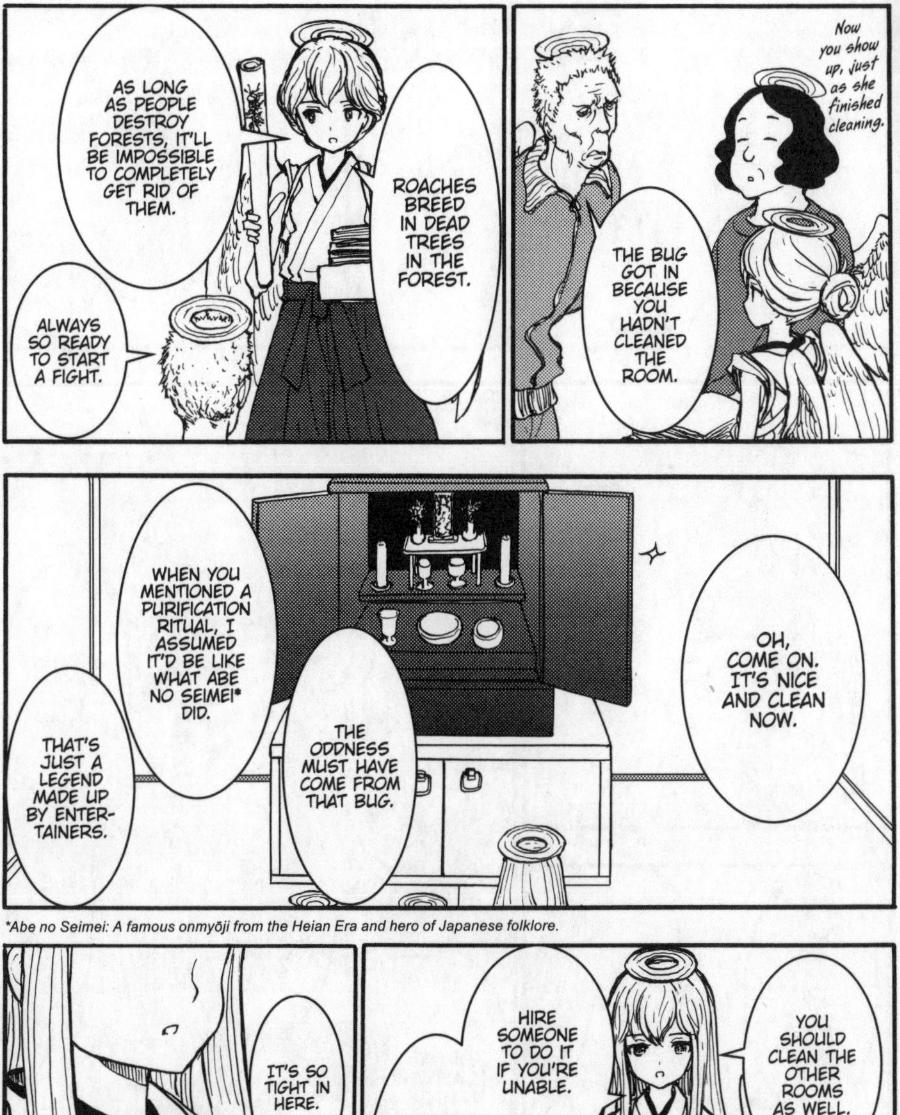
Now you show up, just as she finished cleaning.
THE BUG GOT IN BECAUSE YOU HADN'T CLEANED THE ROOM.
ROACHES BREED IN DEAD TREES IN THE FOREST.
AS LONG AS PEOPLE DESTROY FORESTS, IT'LL BE IMPOSSIBLE TO COMPLETELY GET RID OF THEM.
ALWAYS SO READY TO START A FIGHT.
OH, COME ON. IT'S NICE AND CLEAN NOW.
THE ODDNESS MUST HAVE COME FROM THAT BUG.
WHEN YOU MENTIONED A PURIFICATION RITUAL, I ASSUMED IT'D BE LIKE WHAT ABE NO SEIMEI* DID.
THAT'S JUST A LEGEND MADE UP BY ENTERTAINERS.

*Abe no Seimei: A famous onmyōji from the Heian Era and hero of Japanese folklore.

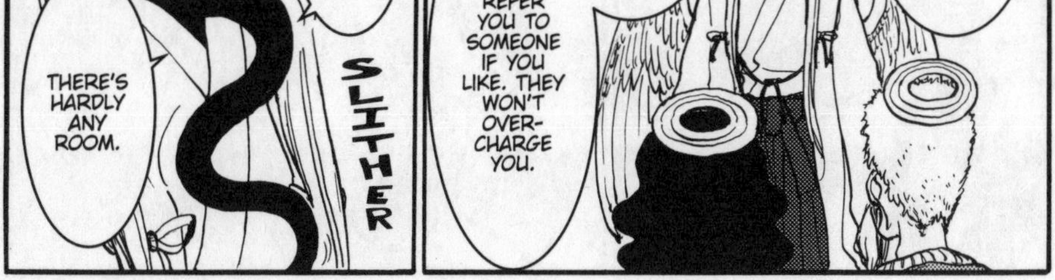
YOU SHOULD CLEAN THE OTHER ROOMS AS WELL.
HIRE SOMEONE TO DO IT IF YOU'RE UNABLE.
I CAN REFER YOU TO SOMEONE IF YOU LIKE. THEY WON'T OVER-CHARGE YOU.
IT'S SO TIGHT IN HERE.
SLITHER
THERE'S HARDLY ANY ROOM.

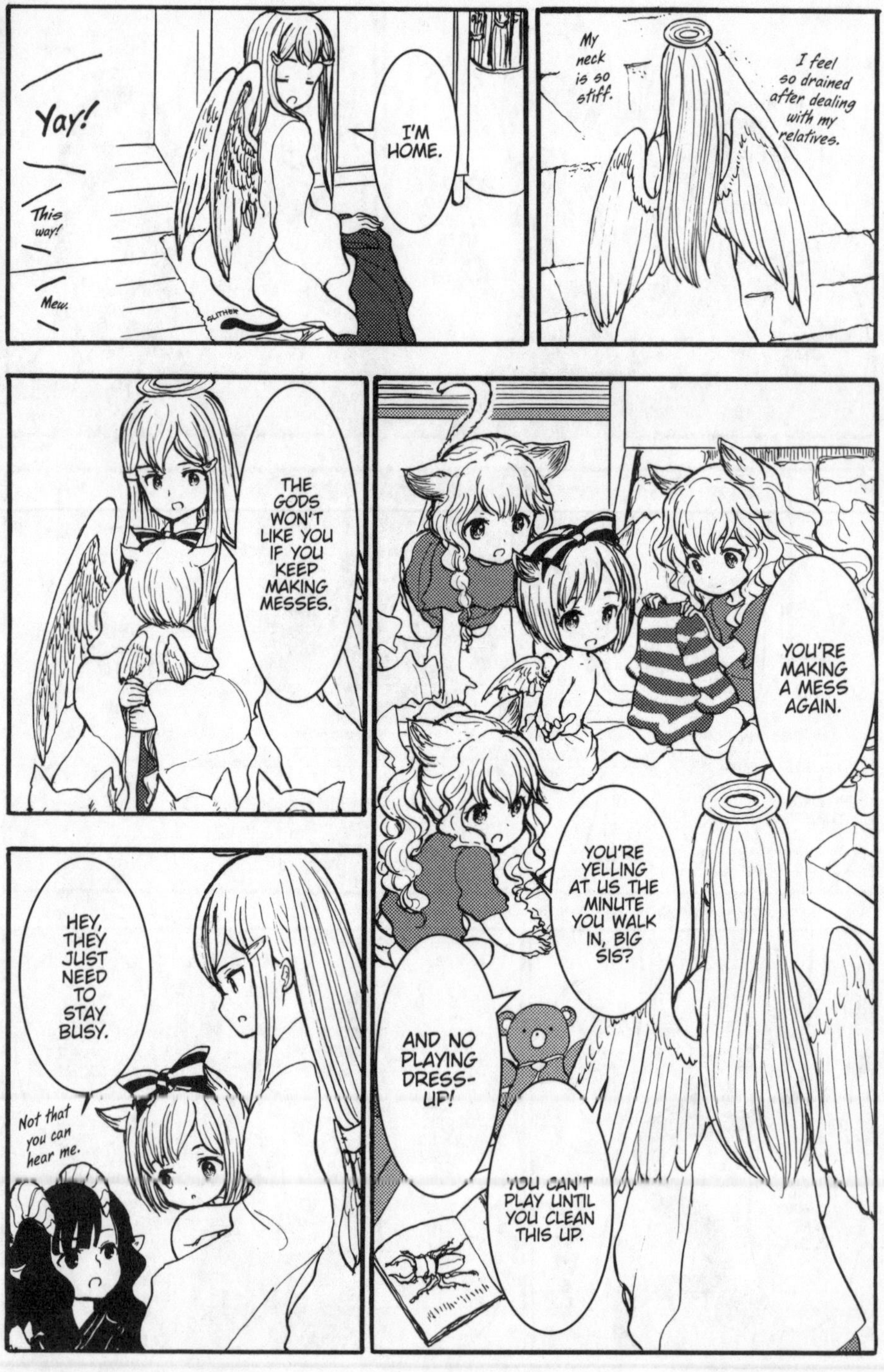
My neck is so stiff.
I feel so drained after dealing with my relatives.
I'M HOME.
Yay!
This way!
Mew.
SLITHER
YOU'RE MAKING A MESS AGAIN.
YOU'RE YELLING AT US THE MINUTE YOU WALK IN, BIG SIS?
AND NO PLAYING DRESS-UP!
YOU CAN'T PLAY UNTIL YOU CLEAN THIS UP.
THE GODS WON'T LIKE YOU IF YOU KEEP MAKING MESSES.
HEY, THEY JUST NEED TO STAY BUSY.
Not that you can hear me.

A Centaur's Life

GREAT SCHOLARS OF THE WORLD:
<5> CHARLES ROBERT DARWIN

CHARLES DARWIN WAS BEST KNOWN FOR HIS FAMOUS THEORY OF
EVOLUTION. AS A YOUNG MAN, HE VISITED THE GALÁPAGOS ISLANDS,
WHERE HE STUDIED VARIOUS SPECIES AND REALIZED THAT, ALTHOUGH
SIMILAR, THESE SPECIES VARIED FROM ISLAND TO ISLAND. FROM THIS,
HE BEGAN TO UNDERSTAND THE CONCEPT OF EVOLUTION.

THE FIELD OF EVOLUTIONARY SCIENCE VIEWS DARWIN AS A MAN WHO
SINGLE-HANDEDLY CAME TO UNDERSTAND THE EVOLUTION OF LIFE-
FORMS--BEINGS WHICH WERE COMMONLY BELIEVED TO HAVE BEEN
CREATED BY GOD. DARWIN IS BELIEVED TO HAVE DEDUCED THAT
EVOLUTION WAS A MECHANICAL PROCESS--NOT ONLY A MONUMENTAL
FEAT, BUT ONE CLEARLY AT ODDS WITH THE DOMINANT TEACHINGS OF
RELIGION. HOWEVER, CONTRARY TO POPULAR BELIEF, EVOLUTIONARY
THEORY WAS NOT DERIVED FROM DARWIN'S INSIGHTS ALONE.

TODAY, THE THEORY OF EVOLUTION HAS EXPANDED. IT IS COMMONLY EMPLOYED IN BUSINESS
AND USED TO PROMOTE ORGANIZATIONAL GROWTH THROUGH THE IDEA OF "SURVIVAL OF THE
FITTEST." THIS APPLICATION, HOWEVER, IS A FAR CRY FROM DARWIN'S ORIGINAL THEORY. "THE
SURVIVAL OF THE FITTEST," ACCORDING TO DARWIN, IS MEANT TO DESCRIBE A SITUATION IN WHICH
SURVIVORS IN A GIVEN ENVIRONMENT GO ON TO PRODUCE OFFSPRING, WHICH THEN GO ON TO
SURVIVE AND REPRODUCE AS WELL. IN OTHER WORDS, THESE INDIVIDUALS ARE CONSIDERED
THE "FITTEST" BECAUSE THEY HAVE SURVIVED TO PASS ON THEIR GENES.

THE EVOLUTIONARY THEORY THAT IS EMPLOYED IN THE FIELD OF BUSINESS, HOWEVER, IS CLOSER
TO A FORM OF SOCIAL EVOLUTIONISM. THE THEORY OF SOCIAL EVOLUTION DEPICTS THE EVOLUTION
OF A SOCIAL SYSTEM SUCH AS THE EVOLUTION FROM MONARCHY TO DEMOCRACY. IT IS COMMONLY
USED AS AN EXCUSE FOR THE COLONIZATION OF UNDERDEVELOPED REGIONS OF THE WORLD OR
FOR WAR BETWEEN NATIONS. THIS FORM OF EVOLUTIONARY THEORY, HOWEVER, IS UNRELATED TO
DARWIN'S ORIGINAL THEORY AND WAS NOT AT ALL WHAT DARWIN INTENDED.

HOWEVER, DARWIN'S ASSOCIATION WITH THE THEORY OF EVOLUTION IN ANY FORM IS SO DEEPLY
EMBEDDED IN EVERYONE'S MINDS THAT ANTI-EVOLUTIONISTS OFTEN ASSOCIATE THE FALLACIES OF
SOCIAL EVOLUTIONISM WITH DARWINISM. IT IS TRUE THAT DARWIN ISN'T COMPLETELY INFALLIBLE.
AFTER ALL, WHILE HE CORRECTLY RECOGNIZED THAT ALL HORSE BREEDS BELONG TO A SINGLE
SPECIES, HE WAS VERY WRONG IN ASSUMING THAT THE EARTHWORM WAS ABLE TO FORM SOIL
IN ONLY A FEW DAYS. HOWEVER, METHODS OF SPECIATION WERE NOT FULLY UNDERSTOOD DURING
DARWIN'S TIME. AFTER ALL, GENES HAD YET TO BE DISCOVERED, AND DARWIN BASED HIS THEORY OF
EVOLUTION ON OBSERVATION AND PRIOR EXISTING THEORIES, RATHER THAN ON GENETIC EVIDENCE.

WHAT WE CAN LEARN FROM THIS IS THAT EVEN WIDELY-ACCEPTED THEORIES ARE NEVER STATIC.
ANY THEORY, NO MATTER HOW BRILLIANT, IS EVENTUALLY REPLACED WITH ONE THAT IS MORE
REFINED ONCE A CONTRADICTORY OBSERVATION IS DISCOVERED. IN SOME CASES, A THEORY MAY
BE COMPLETELY REJECTED IF ENOUGH CONTRADICTORY EVIDENCE IS FOUND. WITH CONTINUAL
REFINEMENT, THE THEORY OF EVOLUTION ITSELF HAS EVOLVED. BUT THANKS TO DARWIN'S DIS-
COVERIES, WE UNDERSTAND THAT THE EVOLUTION OF A SPECIES RESULTS IN DIVERSITY, AND THAT
SPECIES WERE CREATED BY THE PROCESS OF EVOLUTION RATHER THAN A SUPERNATURAL BEING.

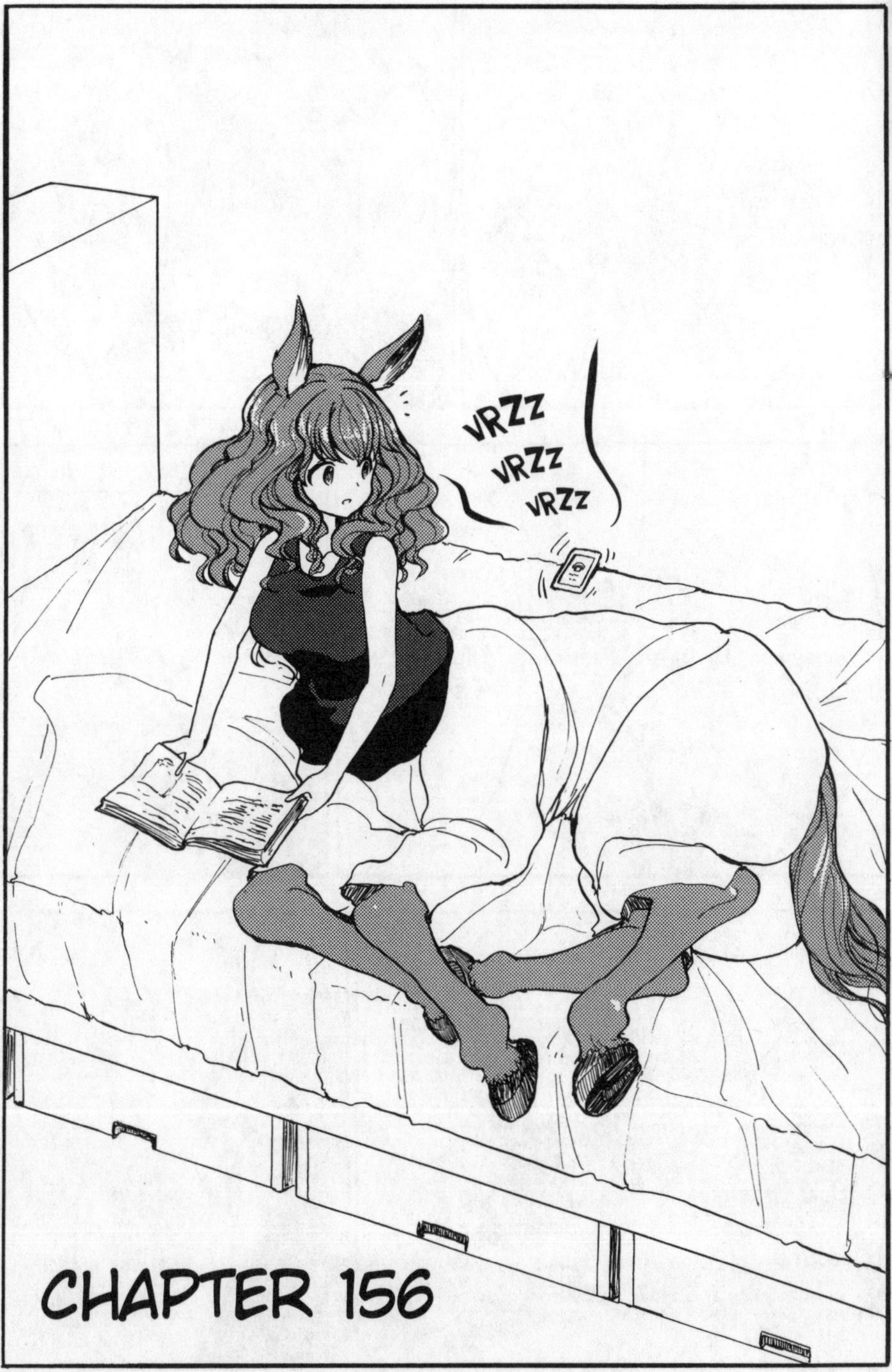
VRZZ
VRZZ
VRZZ
CHAPTER 156

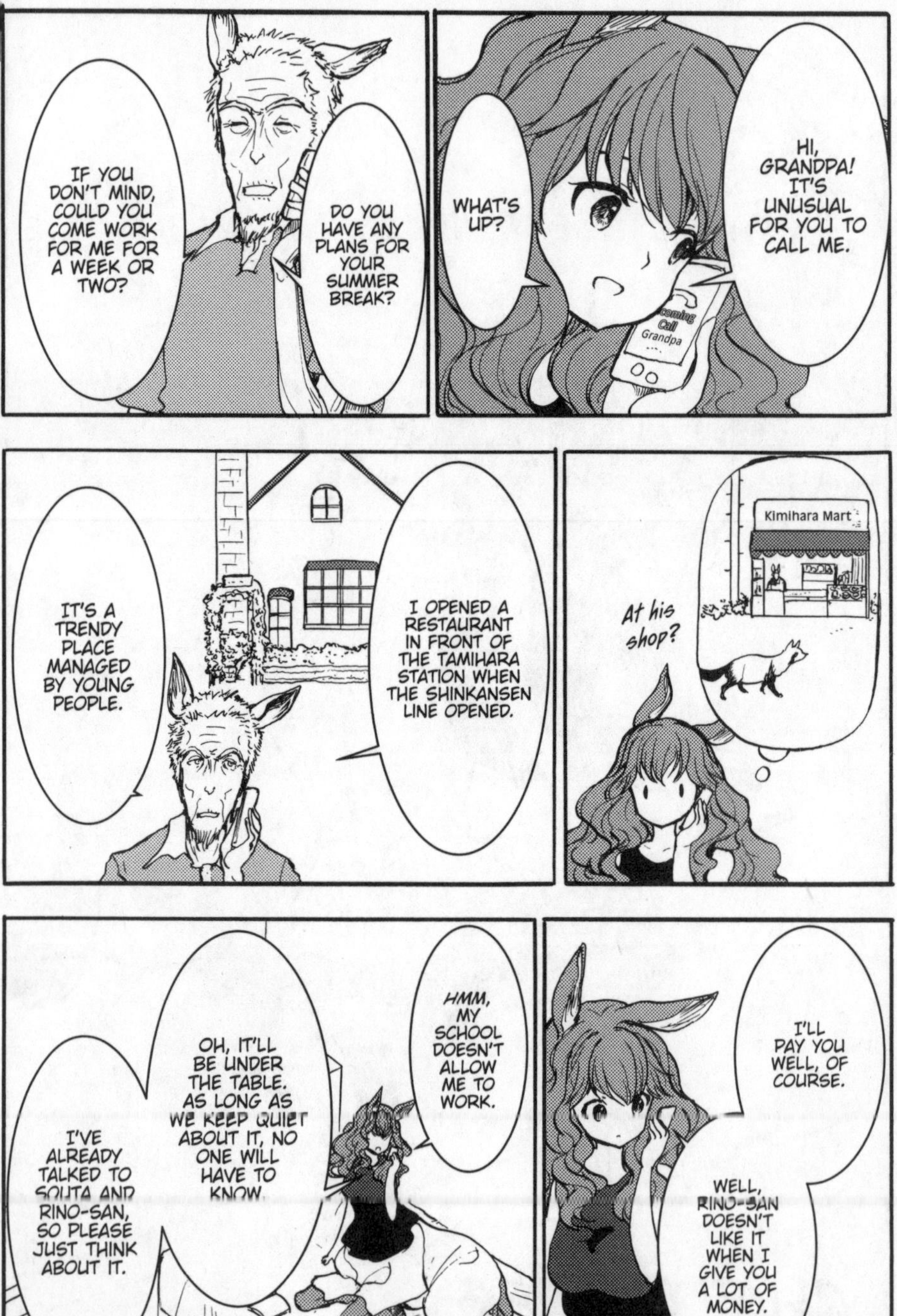
HI, GRANDPA! IT'S UNUSUAL FOR YOU TO CALL ME.
WHAT'S UP?
Call
Grandpa
DO YOU HAVE ANY PLANS FOR YOUR SUMMER BREAK?
IF YOU DON'T MIND, COULD YOU COME WORK FOR ME FOR A WEEK OR TWO?
Kimihara Mart
At his shop?
I OPENED A RESTAURANT IN FRONT OF THE TAMIHARA STATION WHEN THE SHINKANSEN LINE OPENED.
IT'S A TRENDY PLACE MANAGED BY YOUNG PEOPLE.
I'LL PAY YOU WELL, OF COURSE.
WELL, RINO-SAN DOESN'T LIKE IT WHEN I GIVE YOU A LOT OF MONEY.
HMM, MY SCHOOL DOESN'T ALLOW ME TO WORK.
OH, IT'LL BE UNDER THE TABLE. AS LONG AS WE KEEP QUIET ABOUT IT, NO ONE WILL HAVE TO KNOW.
I'VE ALREADY TALKED TO SOUTA AND RINO-SAN, SO PLEASE JUST THINK ABOUT IT.

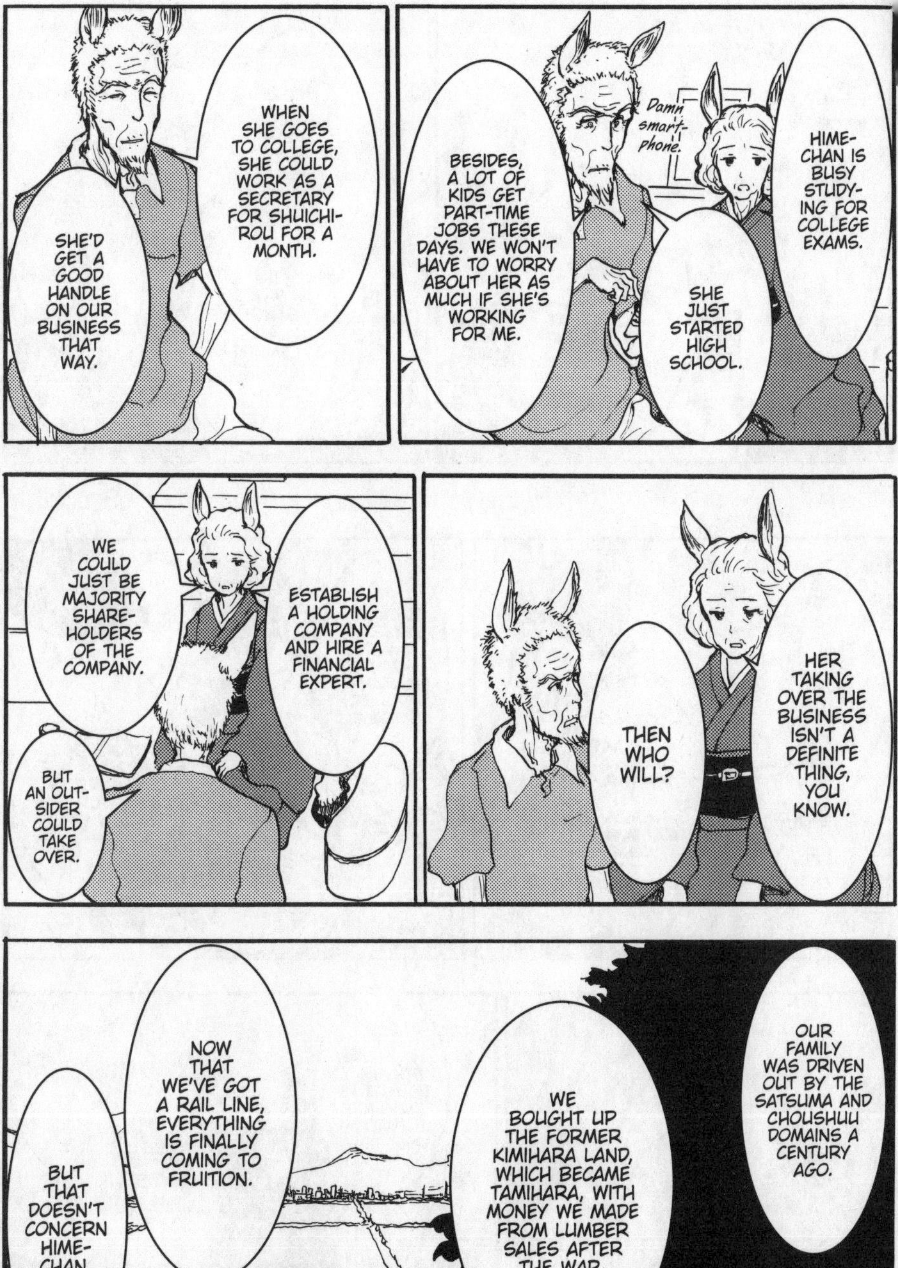
HIME-CHAN IS BUSY STUDYING FOR COLLEGE EXAMS.
SHE JUST STARTED HIGH SCHOOL.
Damn smart-phone.
BESIDES, A LOT OF KIDS GET PART-TIME JOBS THESE DAYS. WE WON'T HAVE TO WORRY ABOUT HER AS MUCH IF SHE'S WORKING FOR ME.
WHEN SHE GOES TO COLLEGE, SHE COULD WORK AS A SECRETARY FOR SHUICHIROU FOR A MONTH.
SHE'D GET A GOOD HANDLE ON OUR BUSINESS THAT WAY.
HER TAKING OVER THE BUSINESS ISN'T A DEFINITE THING, YOU KNOW.
THEN WHO WILL?
ESTABLISH A HOLDING COMPANY AND HIRE A FINANCIAL EXPERT.
WE COULD JUST BE MAJORITY SHARE-HOLDERS OF THE COMPANY.
BUT AN OUT-SIDER COULD TAKE OVER.
OUR FAMILY WAS DRIVEN OUT BY THE SATSUMA AND CHOUSHUU DOMAINS A CENTURY AGO.
WE BOUGHT UP THE FORMER KIMIHARA LAND, WHICH BECAME TAMIHARA, WITH MONEY WE MADE FROM LUMBER SALES AFTER THE WAR.
NOW THAT WE'VE GOT A RAIL LINE, EVERYTHING IS FINALLY COMING TO FRUITION.
BUT THAT DOESN'T CONCERN HIME-CHAN.

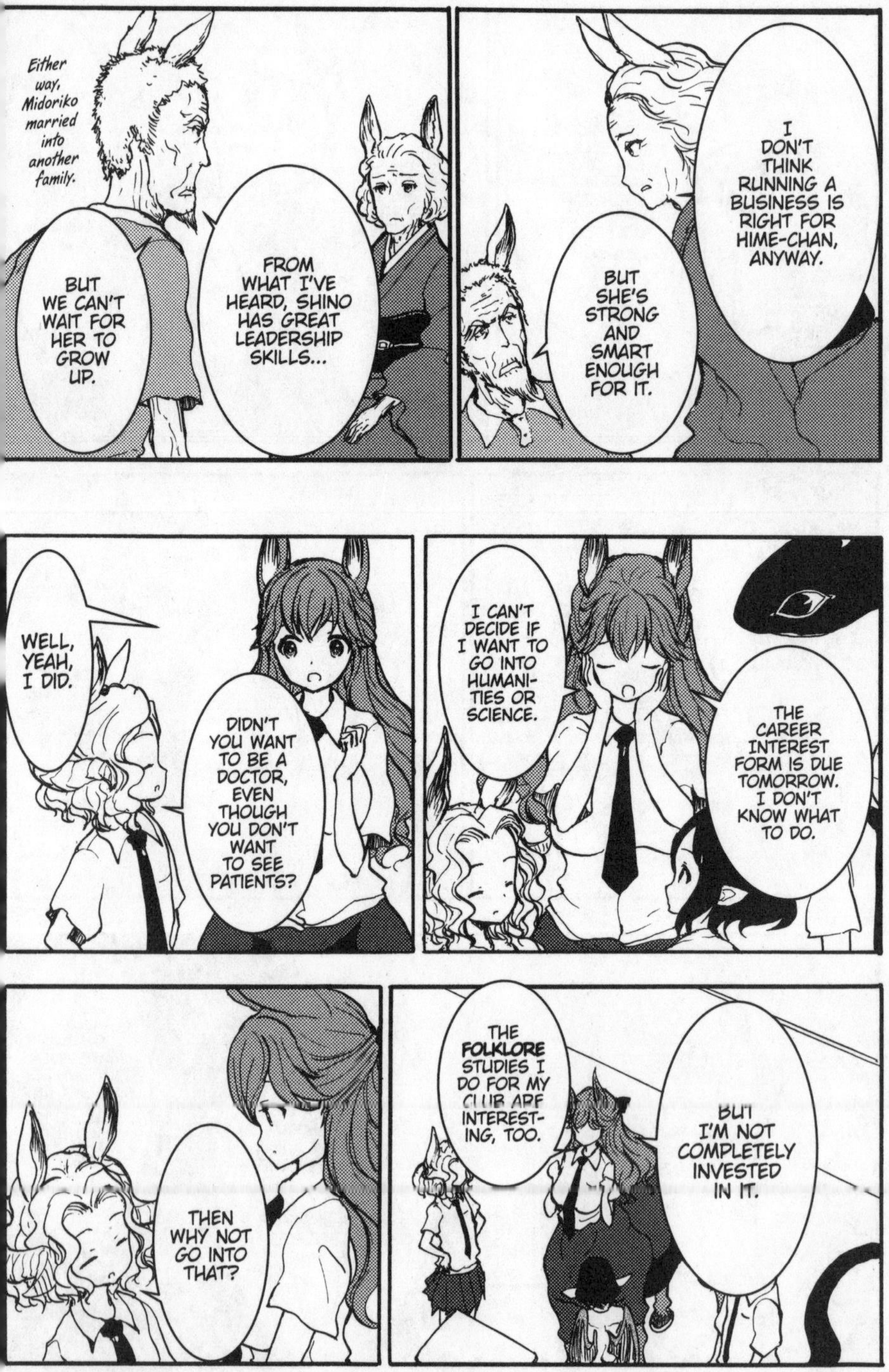
I DON'T THINK RUNNING A BUSINESS IS RIGHT FOR HIME-CHAN, ANYWAY.
BUT SHE'S STRONG AND SMART ENOUGH FOR IT.
FROM WHAT I'VE HEARD, SHINO HAS GREAT LEADERSHIP SKILLS...
BUT WE CAN'T WAIT FOR HER TO GROW UP.
Either way, Midoriko married into another family.
THE CAREER INTEREST FORM IS DUE TOMORROW. I DON'T KNOW WHAT TO DO.
I CAN'T DECIDE IF I WANT TO GO INTO HUMANITIES OR SCIENCE.
DIDN'T YOU WANT TO BE A DOCTOR, EVEN THOUGH YOU DON'T WANT TO SEE PATIENTS?
WELL, YEAH, I DID.
BUT I'M NOT COMPLETELY INVESTED IN IT.
THE **FOLKLORE** STUDIES I DO FOR MY CLUB ARE INTERESTING, TOO.
THEN WHY NOT GO INTO THAT?

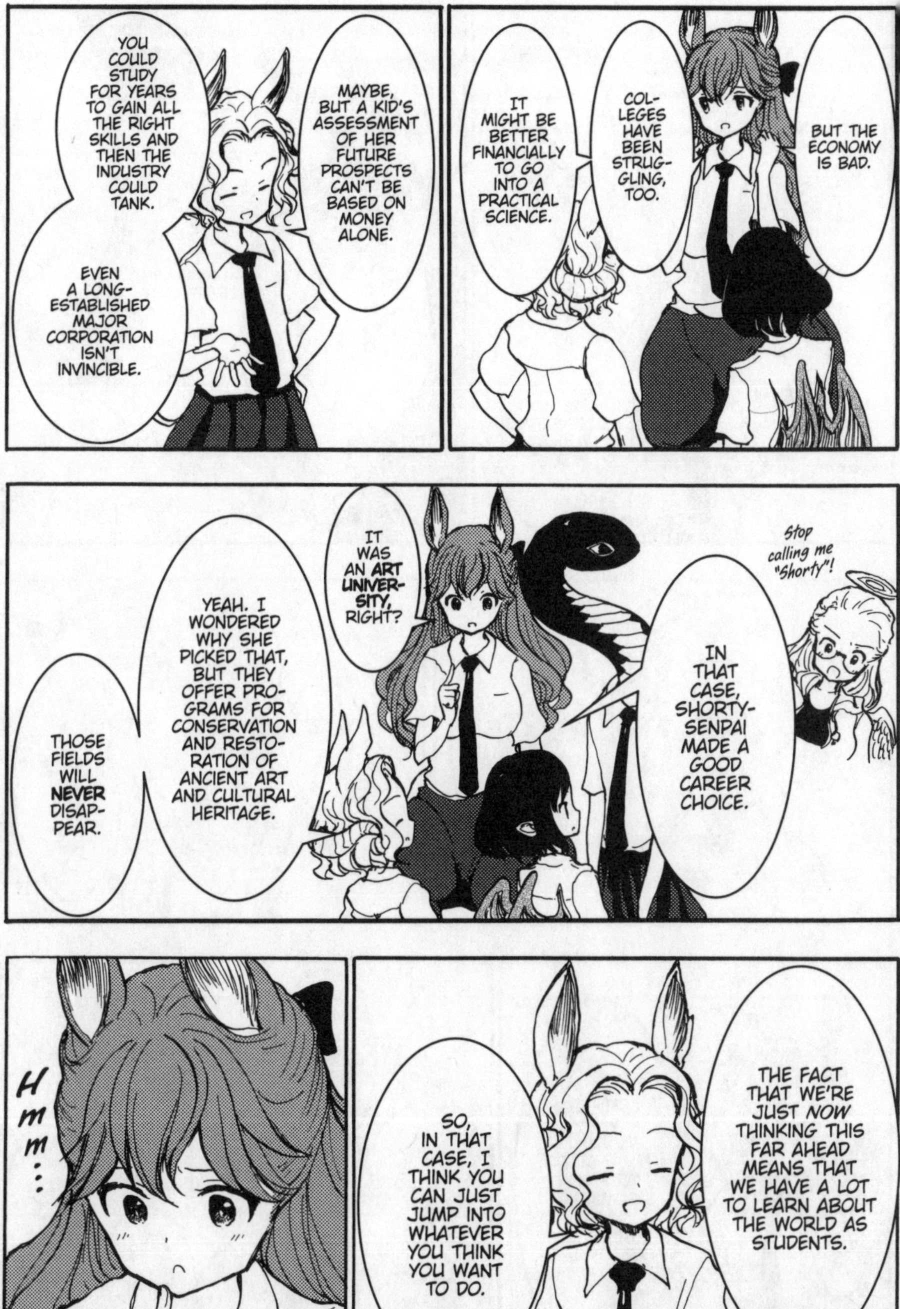
BUT THE ECONOMY IS BAD.
COLLEGES HAVE BEEN STRUGGLING, TOO.
IT MIGHT BE BETTER FINANCIALLY TO GO INTO A PRACTICAL SCIENCE.
MAYBE, BUT A KID'S ASSESSMENT OF HER FUTURE PROSPECTS CAN'T BE BASED ON MONEY ALONE.
YOU COULD STUDY FOR YEARS TO GAIN ALL THE RIGHT SKILLS AND THEN THE INDUSTRY COULD TANK.
EVEN A LONG-ESTABLISHED MAJOR CORPORATION ISN'T INVINCIBLE.
Stop calling me "Shorty"!
IN THAT CASE, SHORTY-SENPAI MADE A GOOD CAREER CHOICE.
IT WAS AN **ART UNIVERSITY**, RIGHT?
YEAH. I WONDERED WHY SHE PICKED THAT, BUT THEY OFFER PROGRAMS FOR CONSERVATION AND RESTORATION OF ANCIENT ART AND CULTURAL HERITAGE.
THOSE FIELDS WILL **NEVER** DISAPPEAR.
THE FACT THAT WE'RE JUST *NOW* THINKING THIS FAR AHEAD MEANS THAT WE HAVE A LOT TO LEARN ABOUT THE WORLD AS STUDENTS.
SO, IN THAT CASE, I THINK YOU CAN JUST JUMP INTO WHATEVER YOU THINK YOU WANT TO DO.
Hmm...

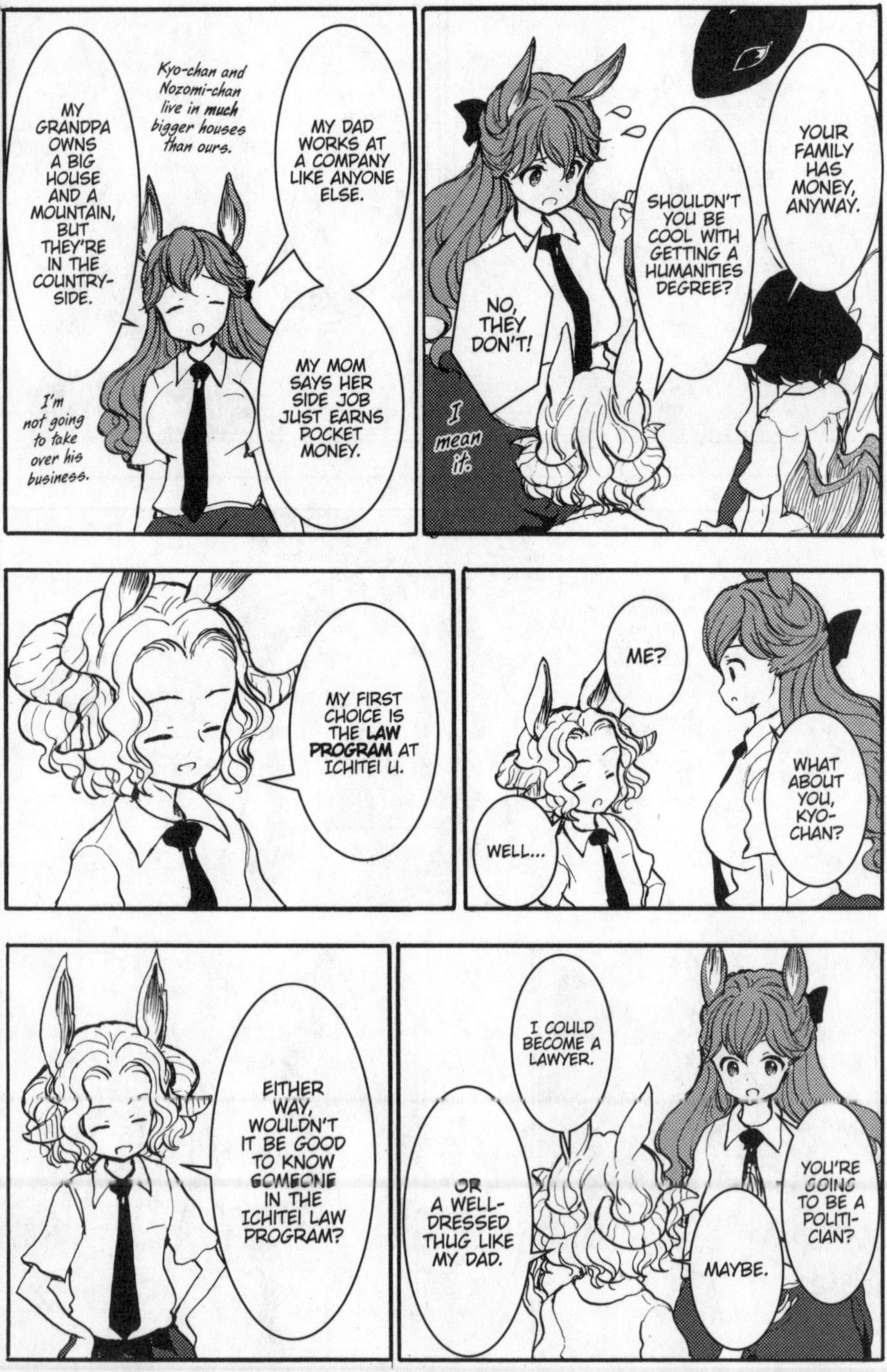
YOUR FAMILY HAS MONEY, ANYWAY.
SHOULDN'T YOU BE COOL WITH GETTING A HUMANITIES DEGREE?
NO, THEY DON'T!
I mean it.
MY DAD WORKS AT A COMPANY LIKE ANYONE ELSE.
Kyo-chan and Nozomi-chan live in much bigger houses than ours.
MY MOM SAYS HER SIDE JOB JUST EARNS POCKET MONEY.
MY GRANDPA OWNS A BIG HOUSE AND A MOUNTAIN, BUT THEY'RE IN THE COUNTRYSIDE.
I'm not going to take over his business.
WHAT ABOUT YOU, KYO-CHAN?
ME?
WELL...
MY FIRST CHOICE IS THE LAW PROGRAM AT ICHITEI U.
YOU'RE GOING TO BE A POLITICIAN?
MAYBE.
I COULD BECOME A LAWYER.
OR A WELL-DRESSED THUG LIKE MY DAD.
EITHER WAY, WOULDN'T IT BE GOOD TO KNOW SOMEONE IN THE ICHITEI LAW PROGRAM?

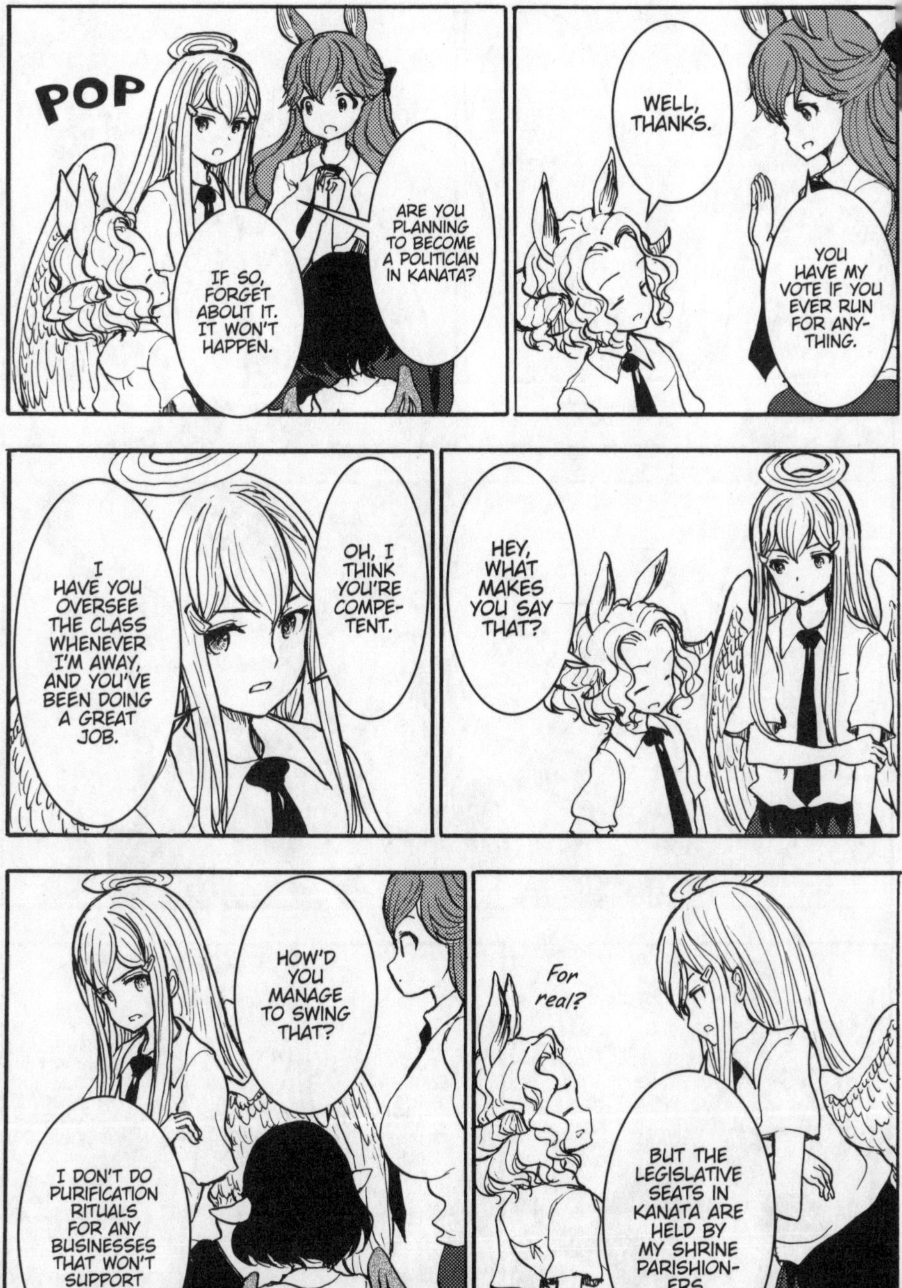
YOU HAVE MY VOTE IF YOU EVER RUN FOR ANY-THING.
WELL, THANKS.
POP
ARE YOU PLANNING TO BECOME A POLITICIAN IN KANATA?
IF SO, FORGET ABOUT IT. IT WON'T HAPPEN.
HEY, WHAT MAKES YOU SAY THAT?
OH, I THINK YOU'RE COMPE-TENT.
I HAVE YOU OVERSEE THE CLASS WHENEVER I'M AWAY, AND YOU'VE BEEN DOING A GREAT JOB.
For real?
BUT THE LEGISLATIVE SEATS IN KANATA ARE HELD BY MY SHRINE PARISHION-ERS.
HOW'D YOU MANAGE TO SWING THAT?
I DON'T DO PURIFICATION RITUALS FOR ANY BUSINESSES THAT WON'T SUPPORT THEM.

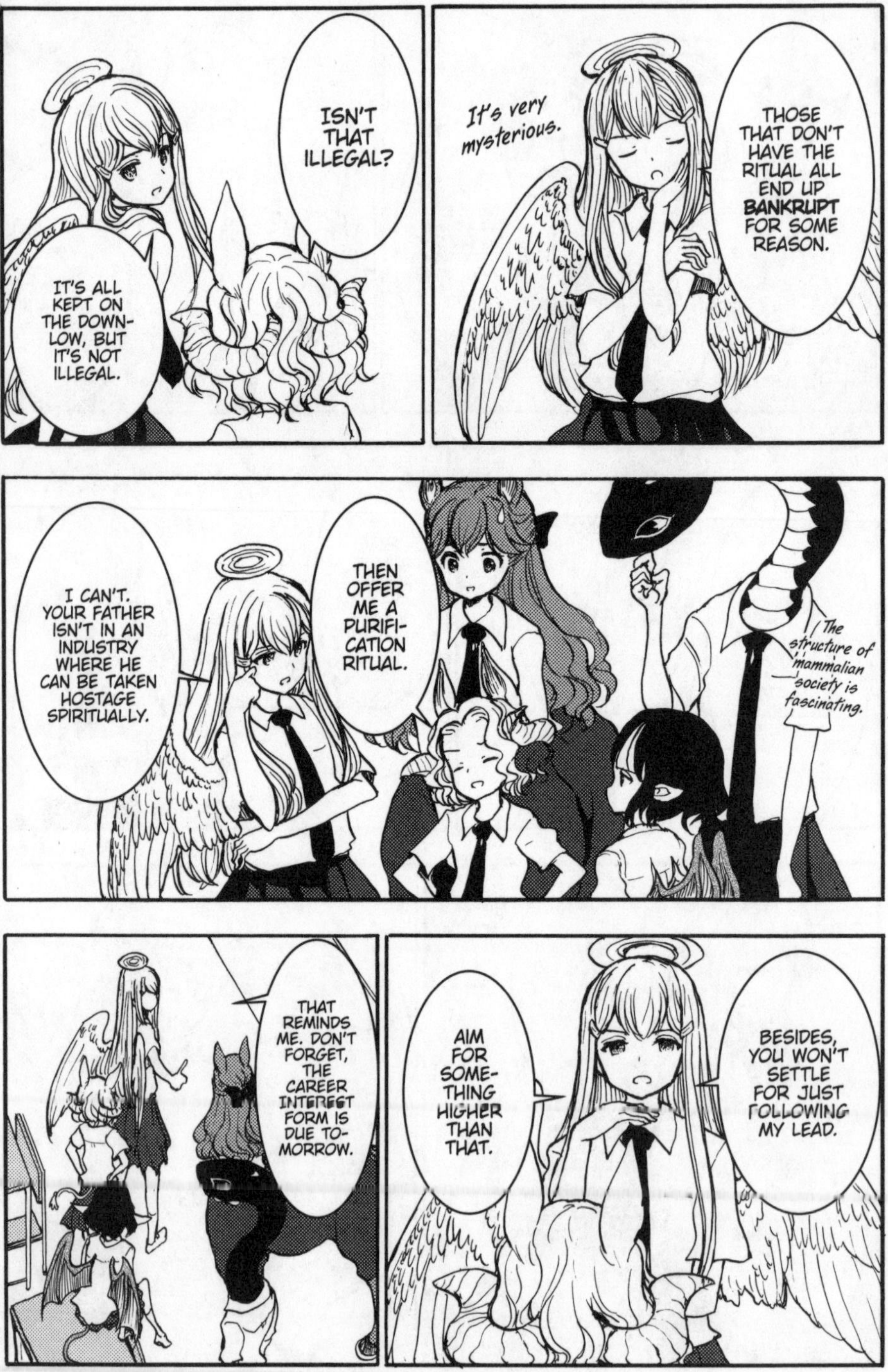
THOSE THAT DON'T HAVE THE RITUAL ALL END UP **BANKRUPT** FOR SOME REASON.
It's very mysterious.
ISN'T THAT ILLEGAL?
IT'S ALL KEPT ON THE DOWN-LOW, BUT IT'S NOT ILLEGAL.
The structure of mammalian society is fascinating.
THEN OFFER ME A PURIFICATION RITUAL.
I CAN'T. YOUR FATHER ISN'T IN AN INDUSTRY WHERE HE CAN BE TAKEN HOSTAGE SPIRITUALLY.
BESIDES, YOU WON'T SETTLE FOR JUST FOLLOWING MY LEAD.
AIM FOR SOMETHING HIGHER THAN THAT.
THAT REMINDS ME. DON'T FORGET, THE CAREER INTEREST FORM IS DUE TOMORROW.

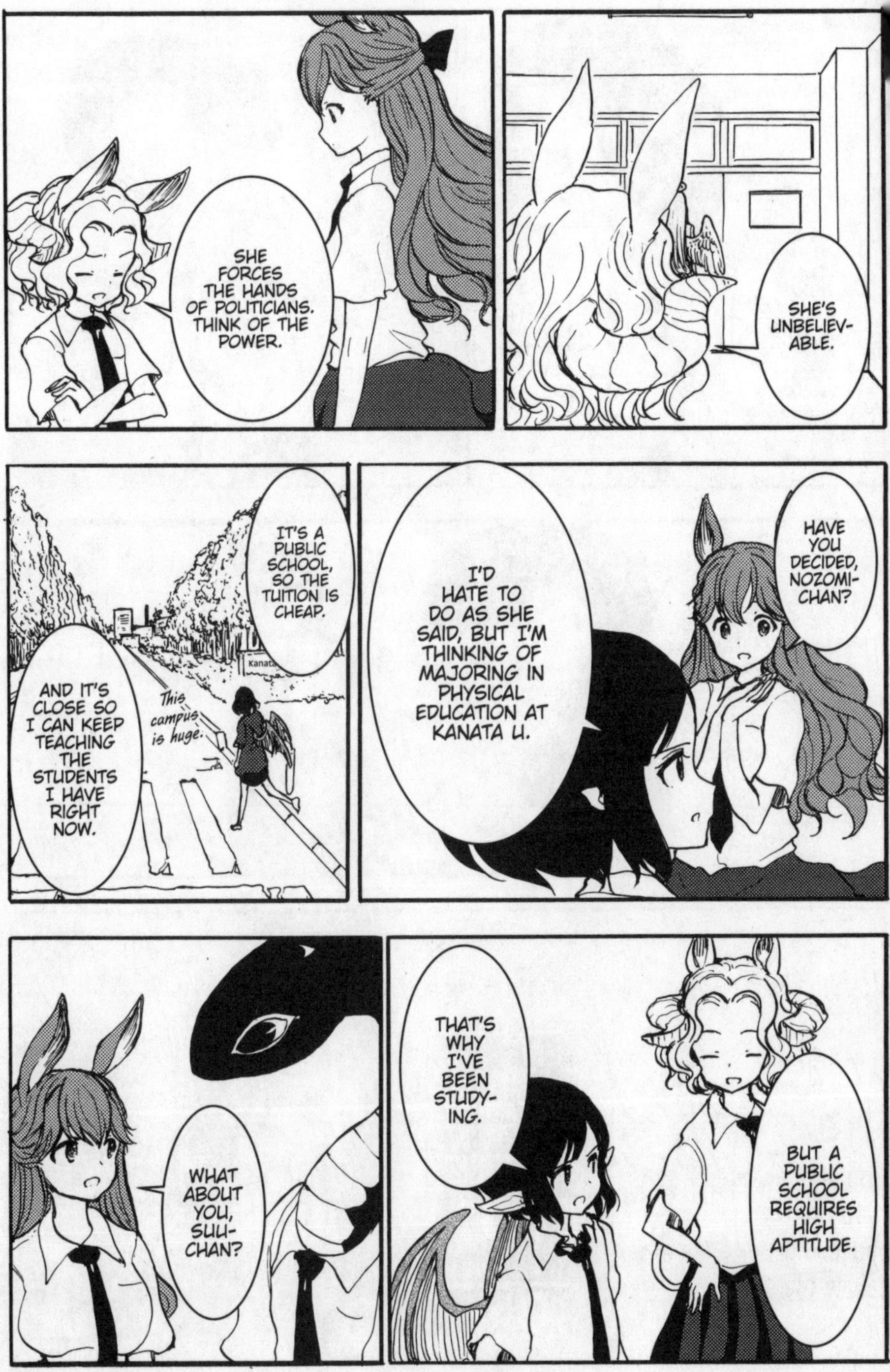
SHE'S UNBELIEVABLE.
SHE FORCES THE HANDS OF POLITICIANS. THINK OF THE POWER.
HAVE YOU DECIDED, NOZOMI-CHAN?
I'D HATE TO DO AS SHE SAID, BUT I'M THINKING OF MAJORING IN PHYSICAL EDUCATION AT KANATA U.
IT'S A PUBLIC SCHOOL, SO THE TUITION IS CHEAP.
Kanata
This campus is huge.
AND IT'S CLOSE SO I CAN KEEP TEACHING THE STUDENTS I HAVE RIGHT NOW.
BUT A PUBLIC SCHOOL REQUIRES HIGH APTITUDE.
THAT'S WHY I'VE BEEN STUDYING.
WHAT ABOUT YOU, SUU-CHAN?

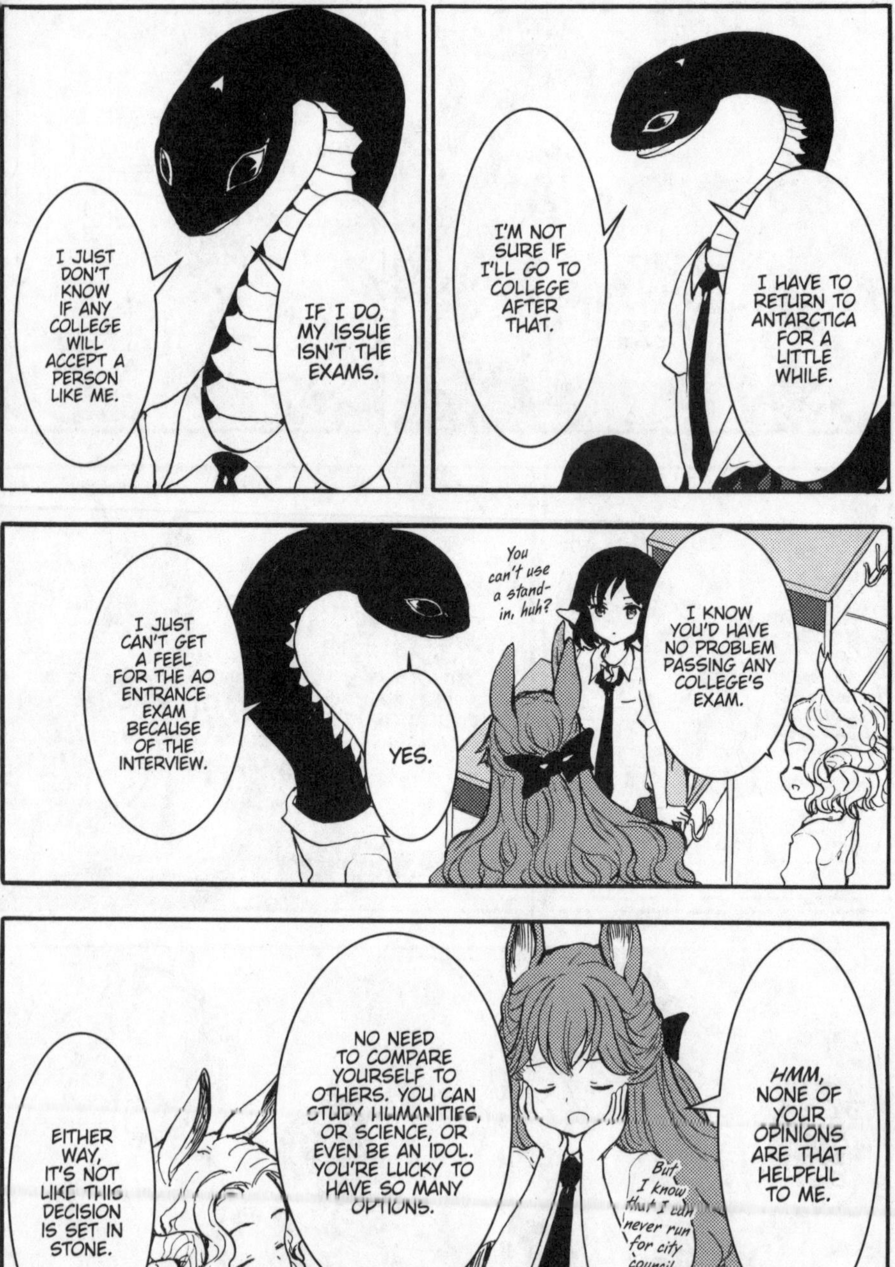
I HAVE TO RETURN TO ANTARCTICA FOR A LITTLE WHILE.
I'M NOT SURE IF I'LL GO TO COLLEGE AFTER THAT.
IF I DO, MY ISSUE ISN'T THE EXAMS.
I JUST DON'T KNOW IF ANY COLLEGE WILL ACCEPT A PERSON LIKE ME.
I KNOW YOU'D HAVE NO PROBLEM PASSING ANY COLLEGE'S EXAM.
You can't use a stand-in, huh?
YES.
I JUST CAN'T GET A FEEL FOR THE AO ENTRANCE EXAM BECAUSE OF THE INTERVIEW.
HMM, NONE OF YOUR OPINIONS ARE THAT HELPFUL TO ME.
But I know that I can never run for city council.
NO NEED TO COMPARE YOURSELF TO OTHERS. YOU CAN STUDY HUMANITIES, OR SCIENCE, OR EVEN BE AN IDOL. YOU'RE LUCKY TO HAVE SO MANY OPTIONS.
EITHER WAY, IT'S NOT LIKE THIS DECISION IS SET IN STONE.

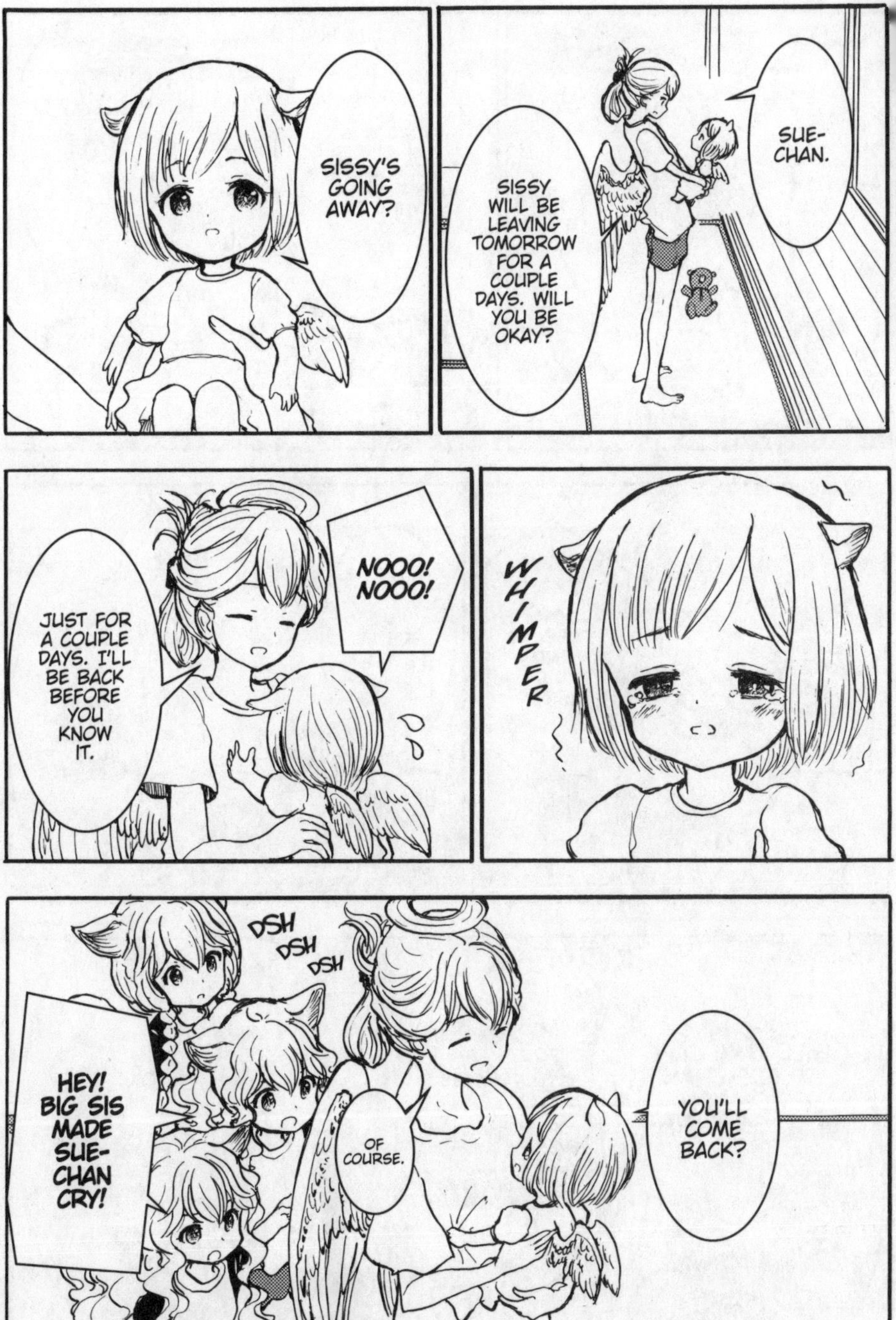
SUE-CHAN.
SISSY WILL BE LEAVING TOMORROW FOR A COUPLE DAYS. WILL YOU BE OKAY?
SISSY'S GOING AWAY?
WHIMPER
NOOO! NOOO!
JUST FOR A COUPLE DAYS. I'LL BE BACK BEFORE YOU KNOW IT.
YOU'LL COME BACK?
OF COURSE.
DSH DSH DSH
HEY! BIG SIS MADE SUE-CHAN CRY!

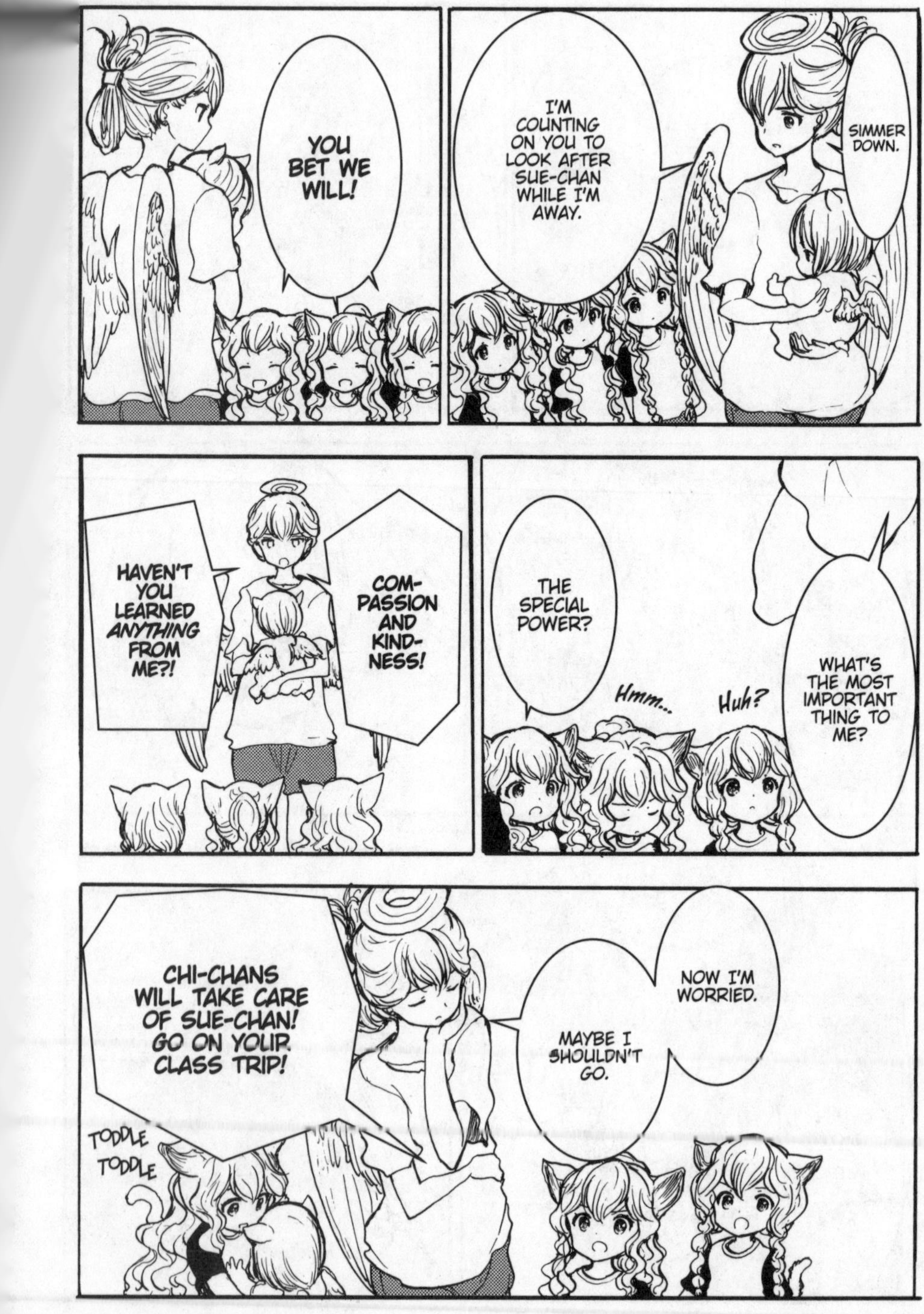
SIMMER DOWN.
I'M COUNTING ON YOU TO LOOK AFTER SUE-CHAN WHILE I'M AWAY.
YOU BET WE WILL!
WHAT'S THE MOST IMPORTANT THING TO ME?
Huh?
Hmm...
THE SPECIAL POWER?
COM-PASSION AND KIND-NESS!
HAVEN'T YOU LEARNED *ANYTHING* FROM ME?!
NOW I'M WORRIED.
MAYBE I SHOULDN'T GO.
CHI-CHANS WILL TAKE CARE OF SUE-CHAN! GO ON YOUR CLASS TRIP!
TODDLE TODDLE

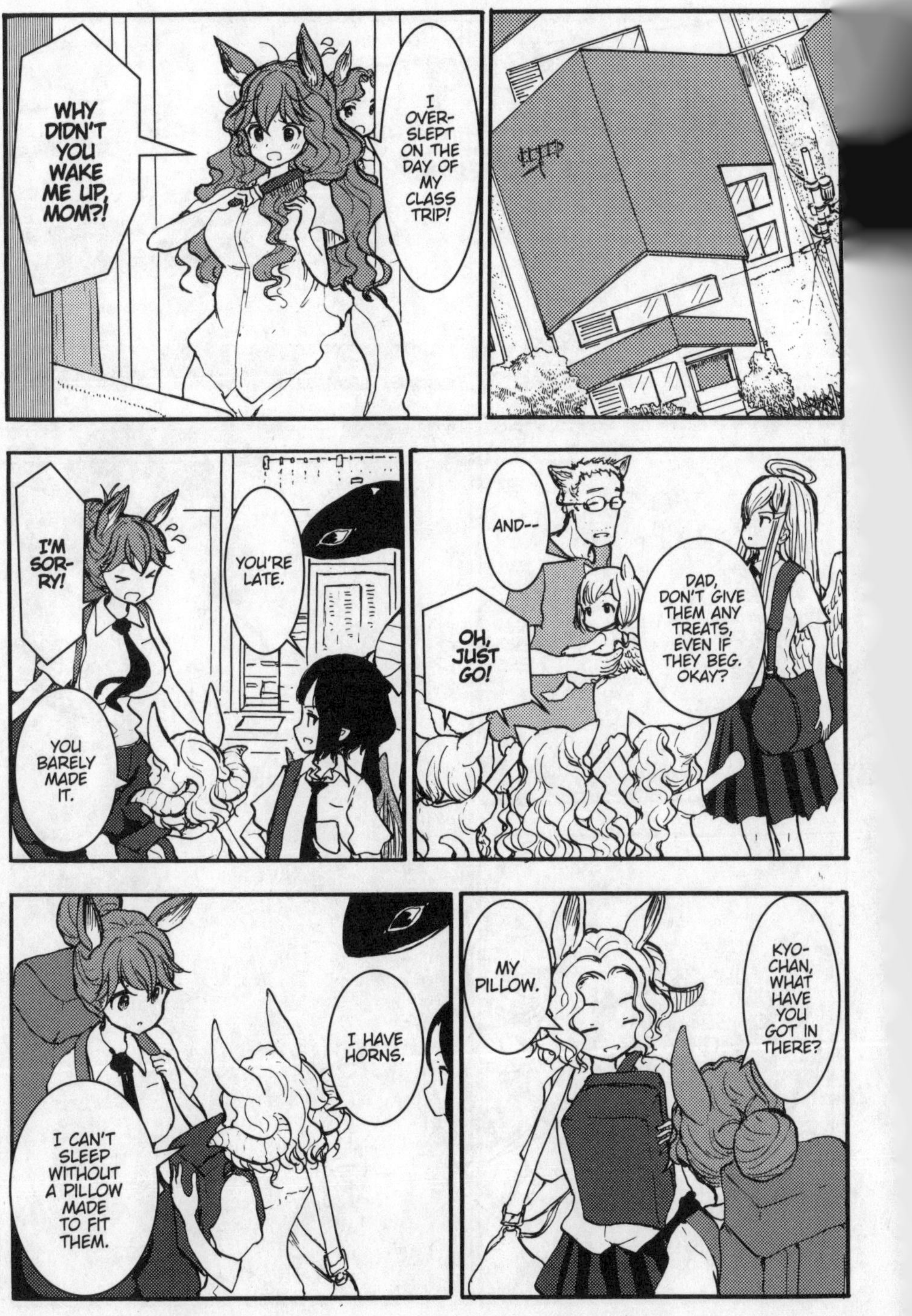
I OVER-SLEPT ON THE DAY OF MY CLASS TRIP!
WHY DIDN'T YOU WAKE ME UP, MOM?!
DAD, DON'T GIVE THEM ANY TREATS, EVEN IF THEY BEG. OKAY?
AND--
OH, JUST GO!
YOU'RE LATE.
I'M SOR-RY!
YOU BARELY MADE IT.
KYO-CHAN, WHAT HAVE YOU GOT IN THERE?
MY PILLOW.
I HAVE HORNS.
I CAN'T SLEEP WITHOUT A PILLOW MADE TO FIT THEM.

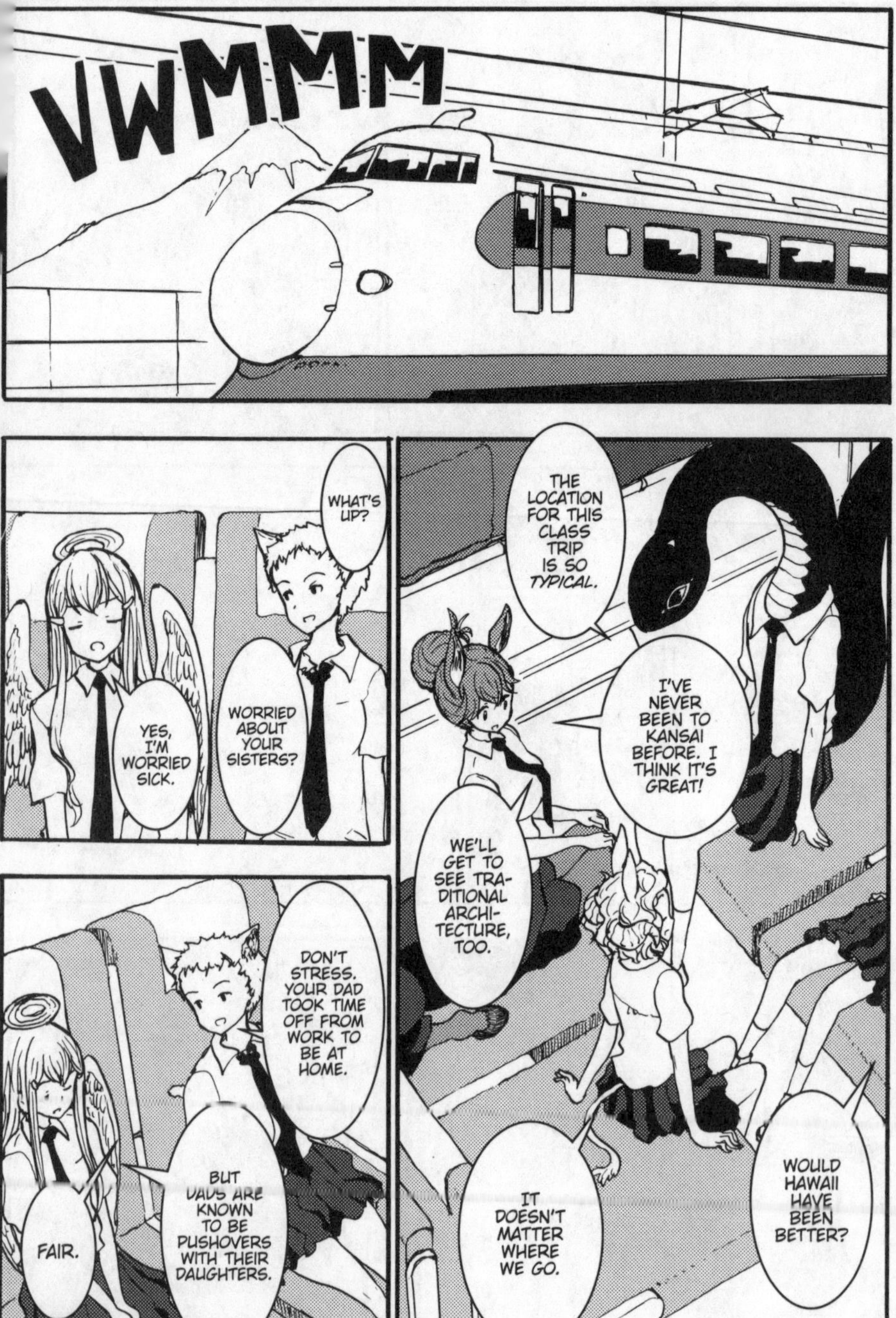
VWMMMM
THE LOCATION FOR THIS CLASS TRIP IS SO *TYPICAL*.
I'VE NEVER BEEN TO KANSAI BEFORE. I THINK IT'S GREAT!
WE'LL GET TO SEE TRA-DITIONAL ARCHI-TECTURE, TOO.
WOULD HAWAII HAVE BEEN BETTER?
IT DOESN'T MATTER WHERE WE GO.
WHAT'S UP?
WORRIED ABOUT YOUR SISTERS?
YES, I'M WORRIED SICK.
DON'T STRESS. YOUR DAD TOOK TIME OFF FROM WORK TO BE AT HOME.
BUT DADS ARE KNOWN TO BE PUSHOVERS WITH THEIR DAUGHTERS.
FAIR.

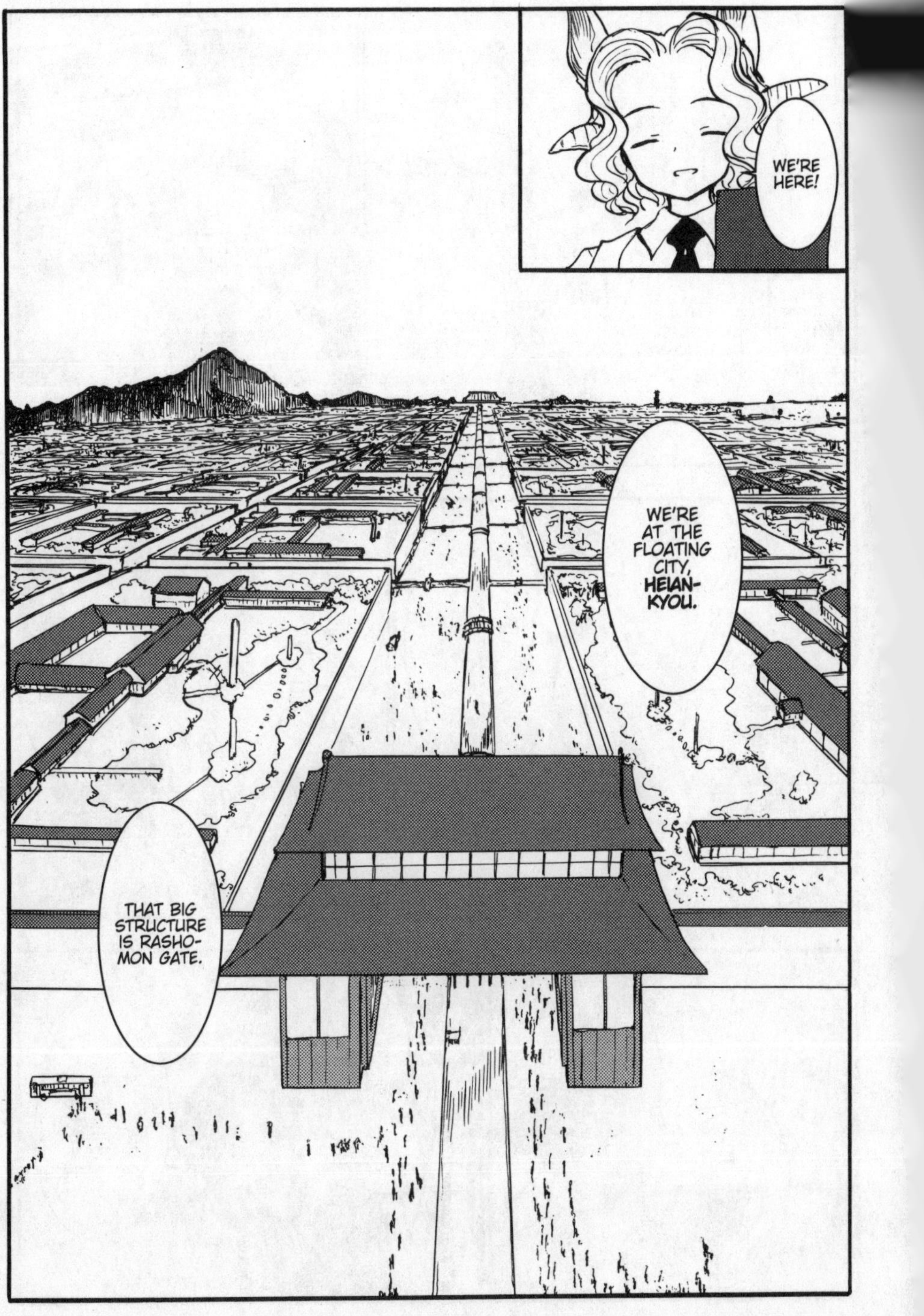
WE'RE HERE!
WE'RE AT THE FLOATING CITY, HEIAN-KYOU.
THAT BIG STRUCTURE IS RASHO-MON GATE.

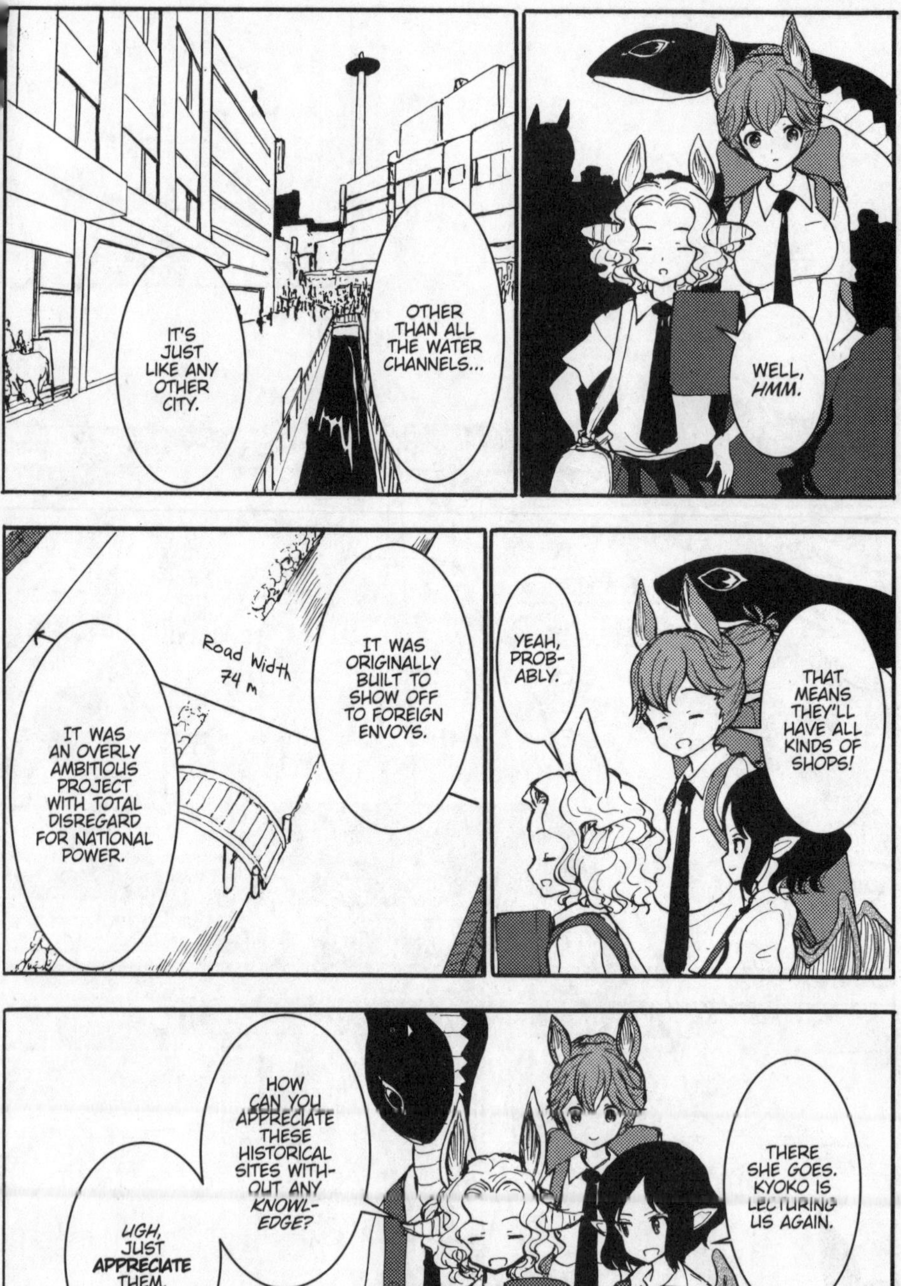
WELL, HMM.
OTHER THAN ALL THE WATER CHANNELS...
IT'S JUST LIKE ANY OTHER CITY.
THAT MEANS THEY'LL HAVE ALL KINDS OF SHOPS!
YEAH, PROBABLY.
IT WAS ORIGINALLY BUILT TO SHOW OFF TO FOREIGN ENVOYS.
Road Width 74 m
IT WAS AN OVERLY AMBITIOUS PROJECT WITH TOTAL DISREGARD FOR NATIONAL POWER.
THERE SHE GOES. KYOKO IS LECTURING US AGAIN.
HOW CAN YOU APPRECIATE THESE HISTORICAL SITES WITHOUT ANY KNOWLEDGE?
UGH, JUST APPRECIATE THEM.

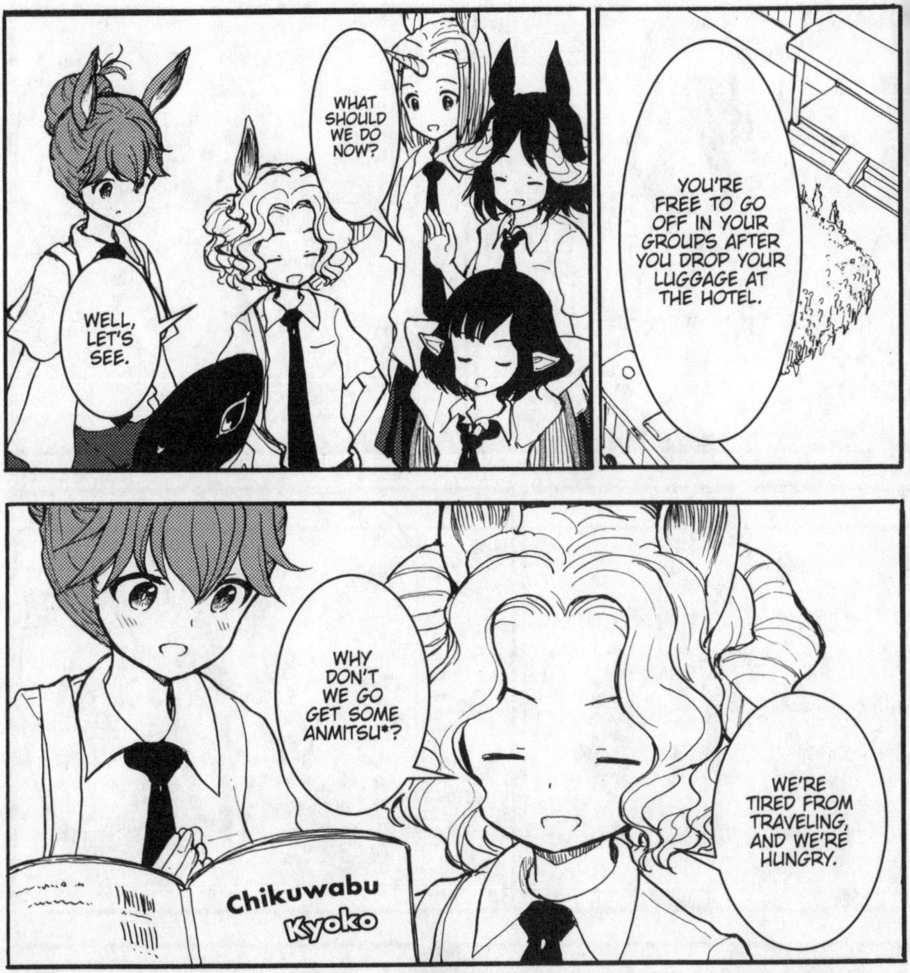
YOU'RE FREE TO GO OFF IN YOUR GROUPS AFTER YOU DROP YOUR LUGGAGE AT THE HOTEL.
WHAT SHOULD WE DO NOW?
WELL, LET'S SEE.
WE'RE TIRED FROM TRAVELING, AND WE'RE HUNGRY.
WHY DON'T WE GO GET SOME ANMITSU*?
Chikuwabu
Kyoko

*Anmitsu: A cold Japanese dessert.

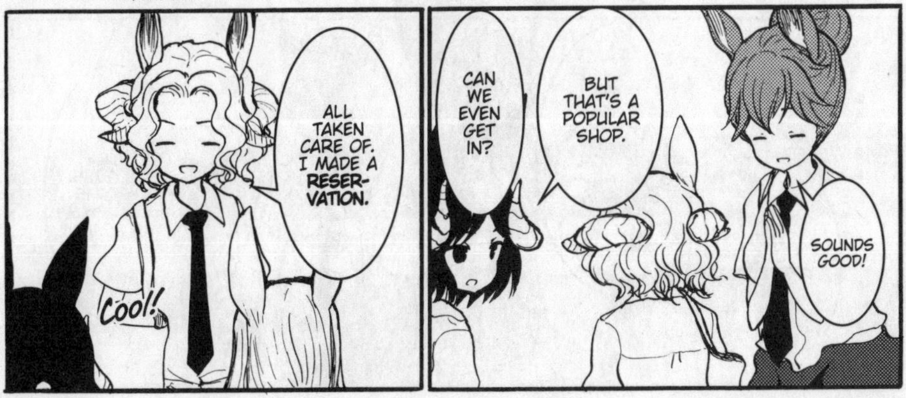
SOUNDS GOOD!
BUT THAT'S A POPULAR SHOP.
CAN WE EVEN GET IN?
ALL TAKEN CARE OF. I MADE A RESER-VATION.
COOL!

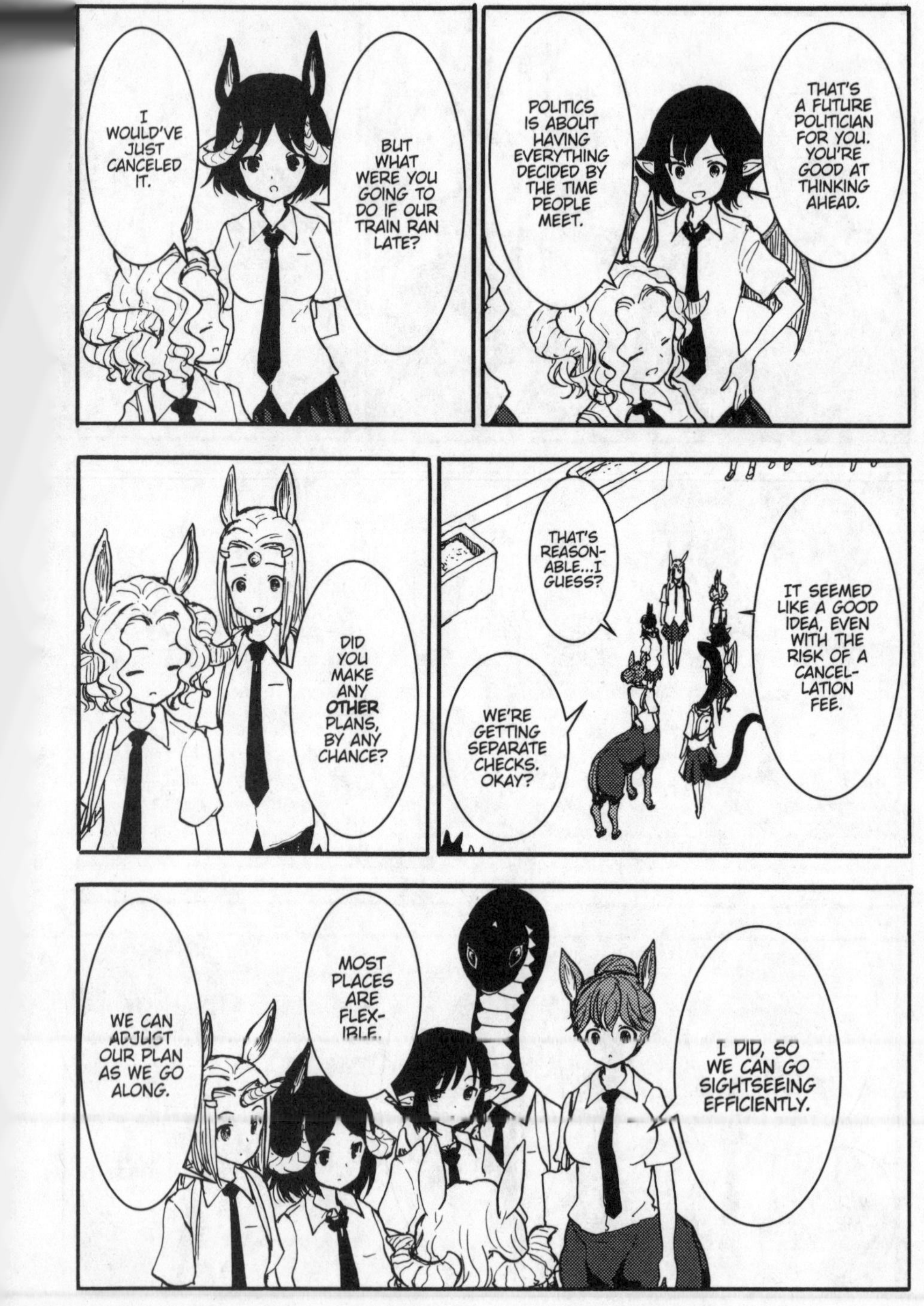
THAT'S A FUTURE POLITICIAN FOR YOU. YOU'RE GOOD AT THINKING AHEAD.
POLITICS IS ABOUT HAVING EVERYTHING DECIDED BY THE TIME PEOPLE MEET.
BUT WHAT WERE YOU GOING TO DO IF OUR TRAIN RAN LATE?
I WOULD'VE JUST CANCELED IT.
IT SEEMED LIKE A GOOD IDEA, EVEN WITH THE RISK OF A CANCELLATION FEE.
THAT'S REASONABLE...I GUESS?
WE'RE GETTING SEPARATE CHECKS. OKAY?
DID YOU MAKE ANY **OTHER** PLANS, BY ANY CHANCE?
I DID, SO WE CAN GO SIGHTSEEING EFFICIENTLY.
MOST PLACES ARE FLEXIBLE.
WE CAN ADJUST OUR PLAN AS WE GO ALONG.

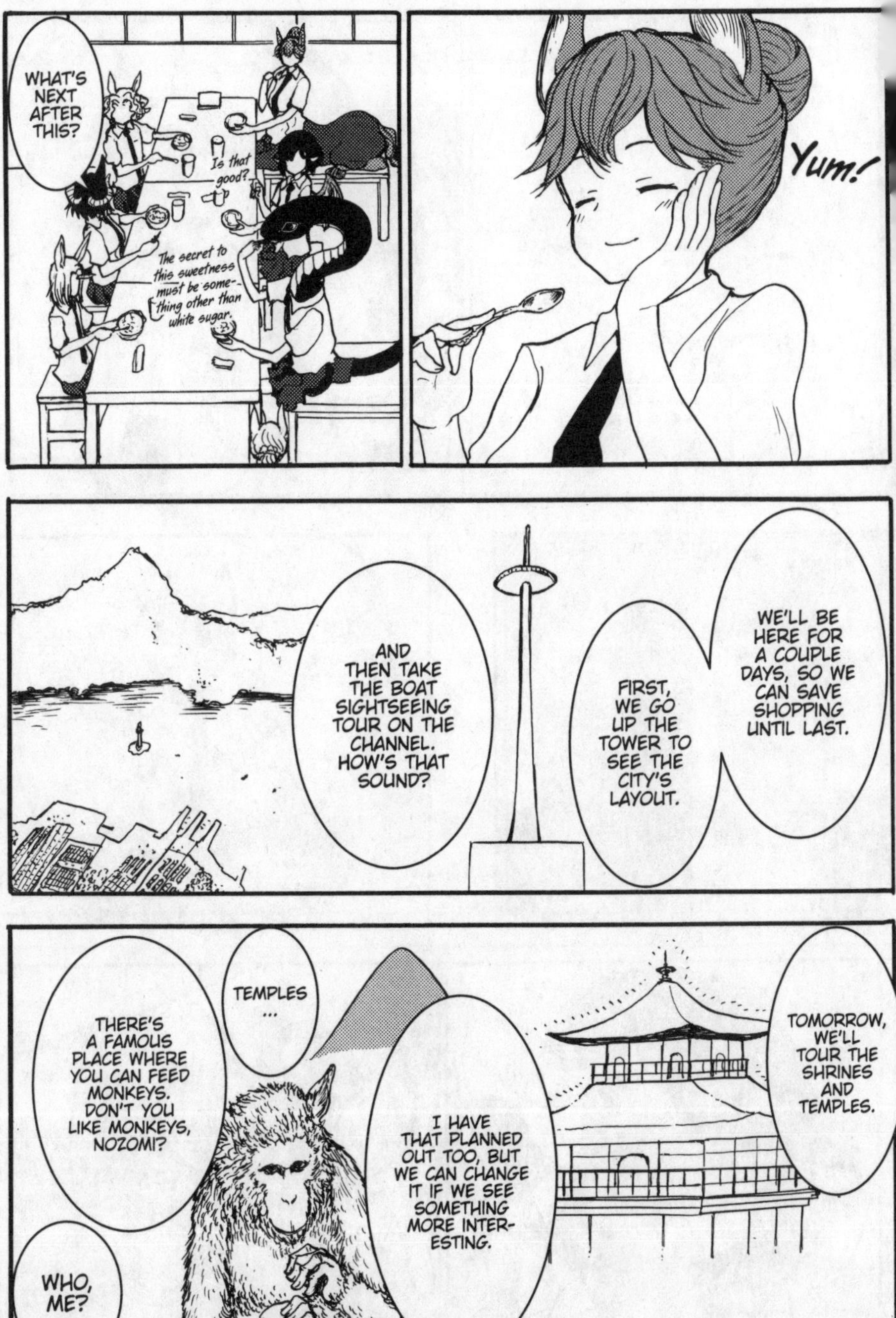
Yum!
WHAT'S NEXT AFTER THIS?
Is that good?
The secret to this sweetness must be some-thing other than white sugar.
WE'LL BE HERE FOR A COUPLE DAYS, SO WE CAN SAVE SHOPPING UNTIL LAST.
FIRST, WE GO UP THE TOWER TO SEE THE CITY'S LAYOUT.
AND THEN TAKE THE BOAT SIGHTSEEING TOUR ON THE CHANNEL. HOW'S THAT SOUND?
TOMORROW, WE'LL TOUR THE SHRINES AND TEMPLES.
I HAVE THAT PLANNED OUT TOO, BUT WE CAN CHANGE IT IF WE SEE SOMETHING MORE INTER-ESTING.
TEMPLES ...
THERE'S A FAMOUS PLACE WHERE YOU CAN FEED MONKEYS. DON'T YOU LIKE MONKEYS, NOZOMI?
WHO, ME?

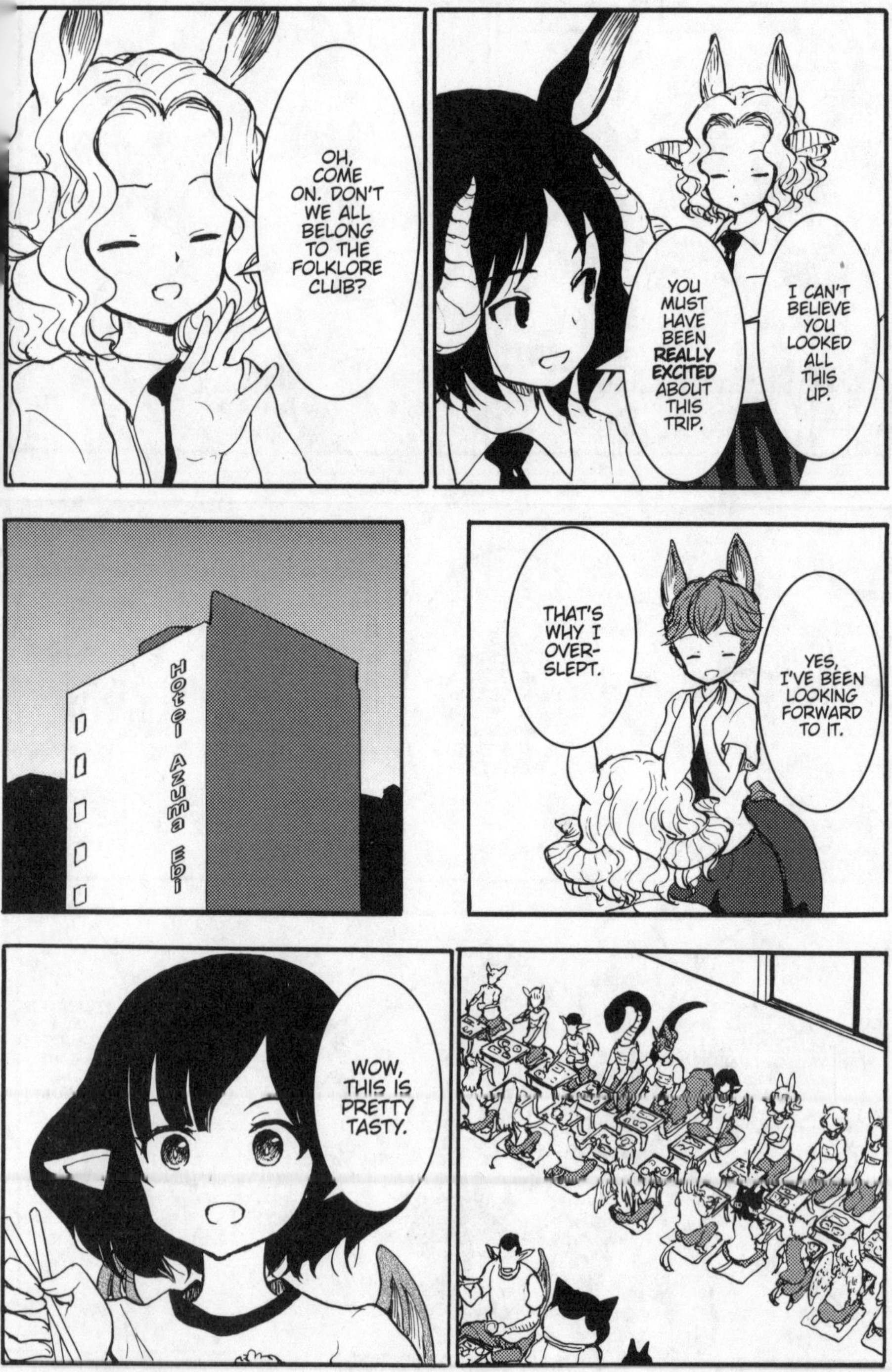
I CAN'T BELIEVE YOU LOOKED ALL THIS UP.
YOU MUST HAVE BEEN **REALLY EXCITED** ABOUT THIS TRIP.
OH, COME ON. DON'T WE ALL BELONG TO THE FOLKLORE CLUB?
YES, I'VE BEEN LOOKING FORWARD TO IT.
THAT'S WHY I OVER-SLEPT.
Hotel Azuma Ebi
WOW, THIS IS PRETTY TASTY.

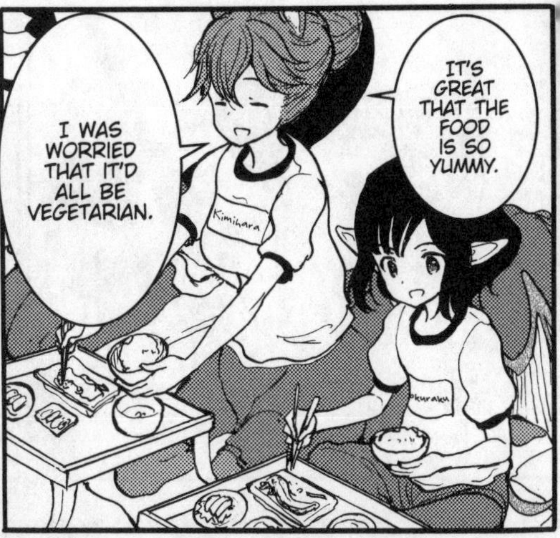
IT'S GREAT THAT THE FOOD IS SO YUMMY.
I WAS WORRIED THAT IT'D ALL BE VEGETARIAN.
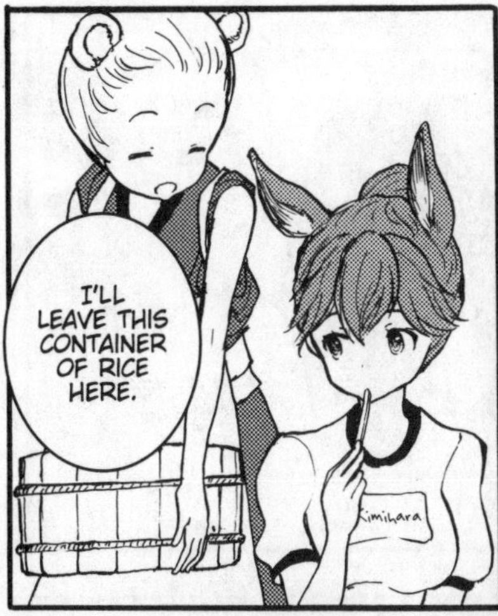
I'LL LEAVE THIS CONTAINER OF RICE HERE.
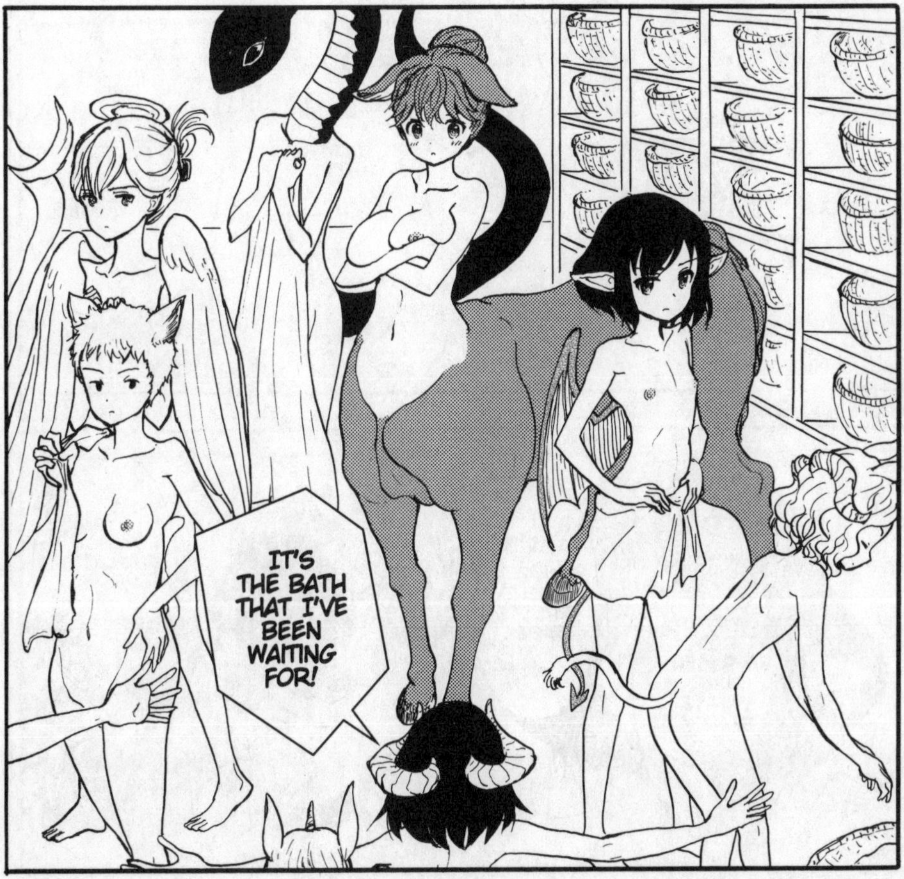
IT'S THE BATH THAT I'VE BEEN WAITING FOR!

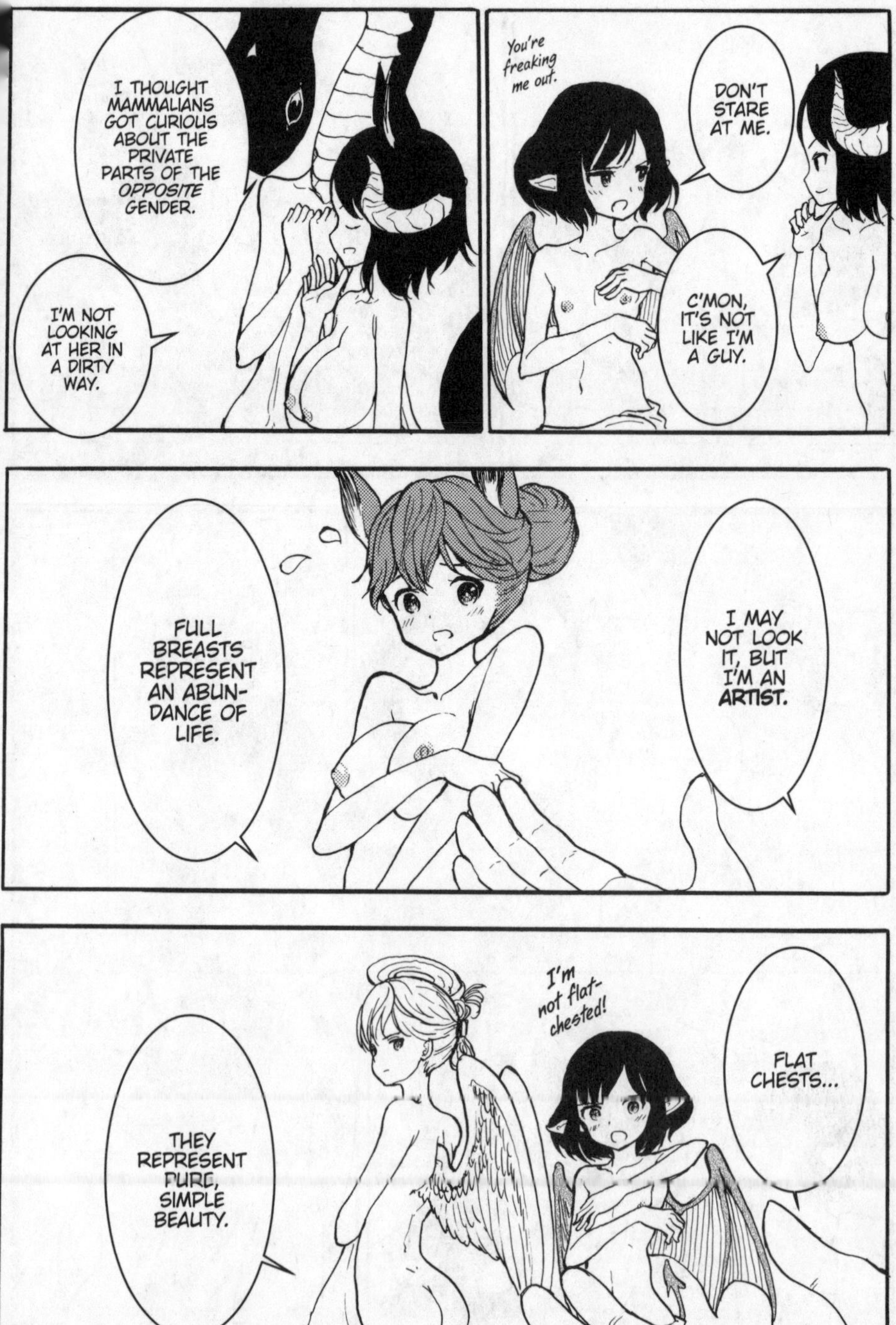
DON'T STARE AT ME.
You're freaking me out.
C'MON, IT'S NOT LIKE I'M A GUY.
I THOUGHT MAMMALIANS GOT CURIOUS ABOUT THE PRIVATE PARTS OF THE *OPPOSITE* GENDER.
I'M NOT LOOKING AT HER IN A DIRTY WAY.
I MAY NOT LOOK IT, BUT I'M AN **ARTIST.**
FULL BREASTS REPRESENT AN ABUN-DANCE OF LIFE.
FLAT CHESTS...
I'm not flat-chested!
THEY REPRESENT PURE, SIMPLE BEAUTY.

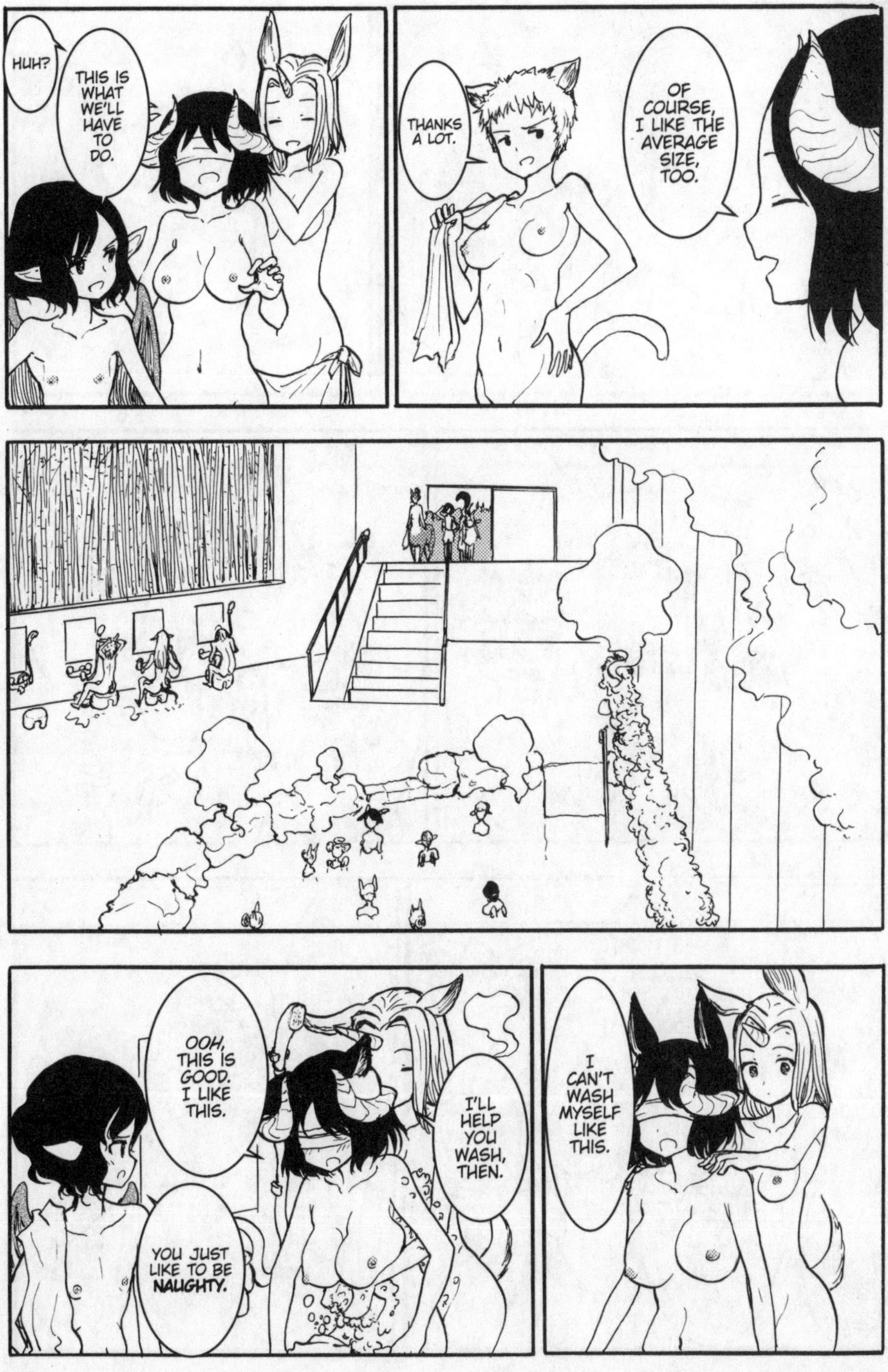
OF COURSE, I LIKE THE AVERAGE SIZE, TOO.
THANKS A LOT.
THIS IS WHAT WE'LL HAVE TO DO.
HUH?
I CAN'T WASH MYSELF LIKE THIS.
I'LL HELP YOU WASH, THEN.
OOH, THIS IS GOOD. I LIKE THIS.
YOU JUST LIKE TO BE **NAUGHTY.**

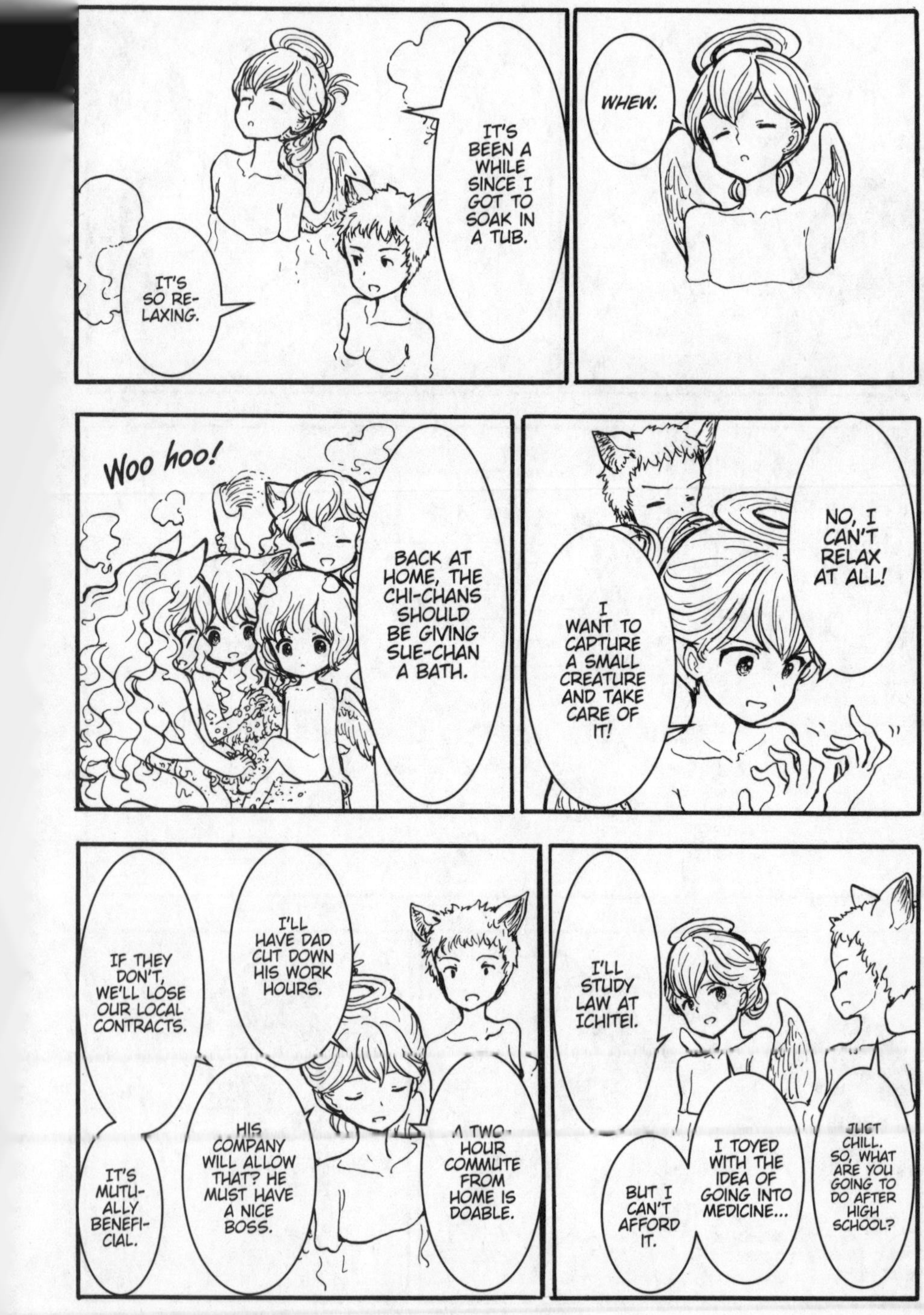
WHEW.
IT'S BEEN A WHILE SINCE I GOT TO SOAK IN A TUB.
IT'S SO RE-LAXING.
NO, I CAN'T RELAX AT ALL!
I WANT TO CAPTURE A SMALL CREATURE AND TAKE CARE OF IT!
BACK AT HOME, THE CHI-CHANS SHOULD BE GIVING SUE-CHAN A BATH.
Woo hoo!
JUST CHILL. SO, WHAT ARE YOU GOING TO DO AFTER HIGH SCHOOL?
I TOYED WITH THE IDEA OF GOING INTO MEDICINE...
BUT I CAN'T AFFORD IT.
I'LL STUDY LAW AT ICHITEI.
A TWO-HOUR COMMUTE FROM HOME IS DOABLE.
I'LL HAVE DAD CUT DOWN HIS WORK HOURS.
HIS COMPANY WILL ALLOW THAT? HE MUST HAVE A NICE BOSS.
IF THEY DON'T, WE'LL LOSE OUR LOCAL CONTRACTS.
IT'S MUTU-ALLY BENEFI-CIAL.

A CentaUr's Life

GREAT SCHOLARS OF THE WORLD:
<6> FRITZ HABER

FRITZ HABER IS COMMONLY KNOWN AS "DR. POISON" BECAUSE OF
HIS ROLE IN SUPERVISING A CHEMICAL WARFARE PROGRAM FOR
GERMANY DURING WORLD WAR I, BUT HE IS ALSO THE CREATOR OF
THE HABER-BOSCH PROCESS, WHICH INVOLVES THE FIXATION OF
NITROGEN. NITROGEN, A NECESSARY ELEMENT FOR PLANT GROWTH,
IS PRESENT IN THE ATMOSPHERE IN LARGE AMOUNTS. HOWEVER,
ATMOSPHERIC NITROGEN IS UNUSABLE BY PLANTS, AND IT IS
DIFFICULT TO CONVERT IT INTO A USABLE FORM. AT THE TIME, IT
TOOK A TREMENDOUS AMOUNT OF ENERGY TO PRODUCE A USABLE
NITROGEN COMPOUND. HOWEVER, HABER FOUND A MORE ENERGY-
EFFICIENT METHOD BY USING A CATALYST TO LOWER THE ACTIVATION
ENERGY. HE WON A NOBEL PRIZE FOR THIS INNOVATION.

IN ADDITION TO HIS CONTRIBUTIONS TO SCIENCE, HABER WAS WELL-
VERSED IN LITERATURE AND POLITICS. HE WAS HIGHLY INTELLIGENT AND
A GREAT SPEAKER, AND HIS WIDE BREADTH OF KNOWLEDGE INFORMED
HIS DEDICATION TO MULTIDISCIPLINARY RESEARCH. AS SUCH, HE WAS
A GREAT SCIENTIST OF BOTH KNOWLEDGE AND CHARACTER.

AS MENTIONED BEFORE, HABER PLAYED AN IMPORTANT ROLE DURING WORLD WAR I. ORIGINALLY,
THE WAR WAS EXPECTED TO END BY CHRISTMAS OF 1915; HOWEVER, IT DRAGGED ON FOR YEARS.
TRENCH WARFARE LED TO STALEMATES, SO GERMANY SHIFTED ITS FOCUS TO A NEW STRATEGY--
CHEMICAL WARFARE. ALTHOUGH HE WASN'T THE FIRST TO USE GAS ON THE BATTLEFIELD, HABER
WAS INSTRUMENTAL IN DEVELOPING GERMANY'S CHEMICAL WARFARE PROGRAM. AFTER HIS WIFE'S
SUICIDE, HE SUPERVISED THE PROGRAM IN HOPES OF BRINGING THE WAR TO AN END AND SAVING
THE LIVES OF HIS PEOPLE. HE WAS A BRILLIANT CHEMIST AND DEVELOPED SEVERAL POISONOUS
GASES, INCLUDING THE INFAMOUS DICHLORODIETHYL SULFIDE, ALSO KNOWN AS MUSTARD GAS.
AFTER GERMANY'S DEFEAT, HE TOOK PART IN HIS COUNTRY'S RECONSTRUCTION BY
DEVELOPING THE ZYKLON B PESTICIDE.

ALTHOUGH HABER WAS DEDICATED TO HIS WORK FOR GERMANY, HE WAS EXPELLED
FROM THE COUNTRY AFTER HITLER'S RISE TO POWER DUE TO HIS JEWISH HERITAGE.

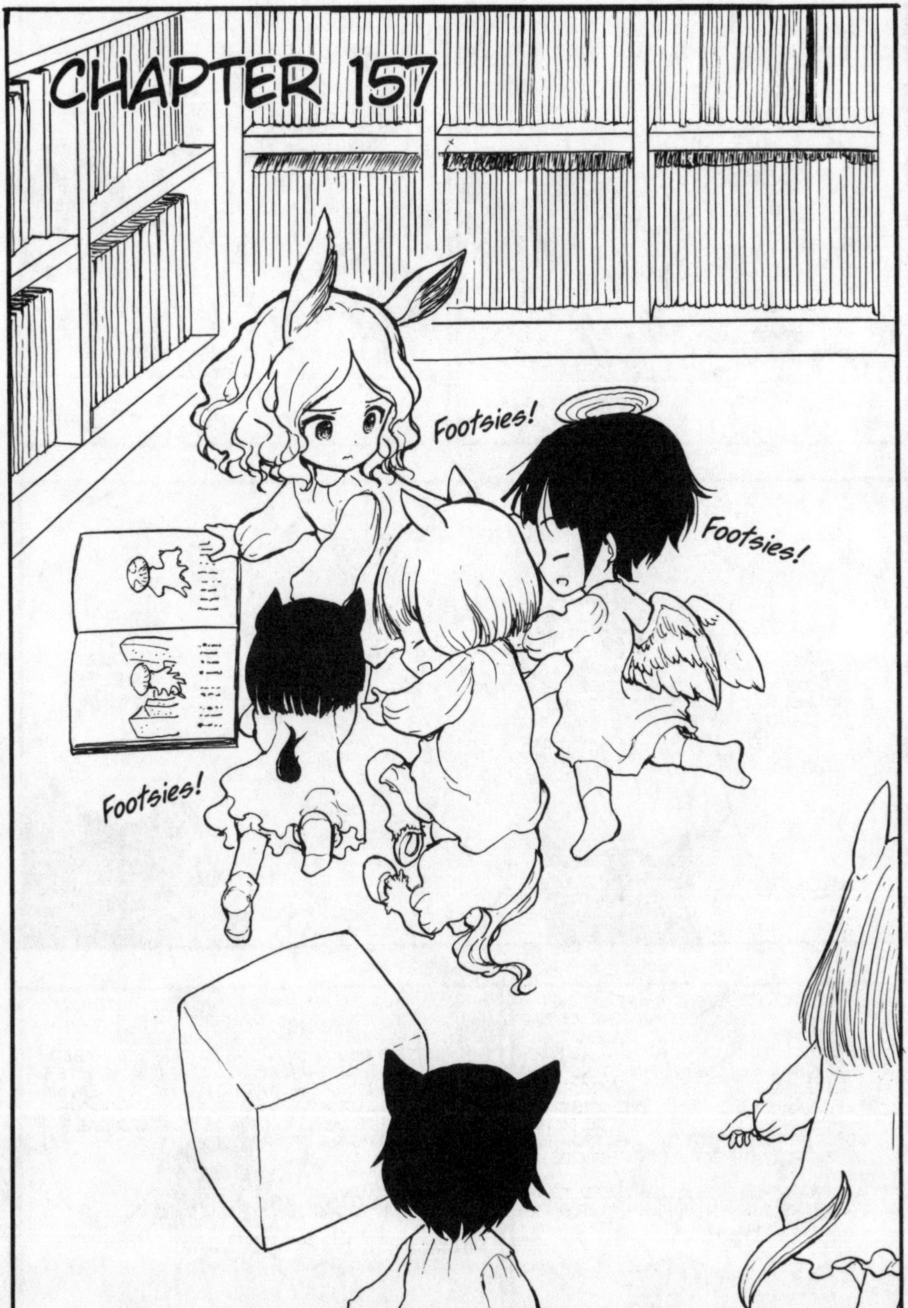
CHAPTER 157
Footsies!
Footsies!
Footsies!

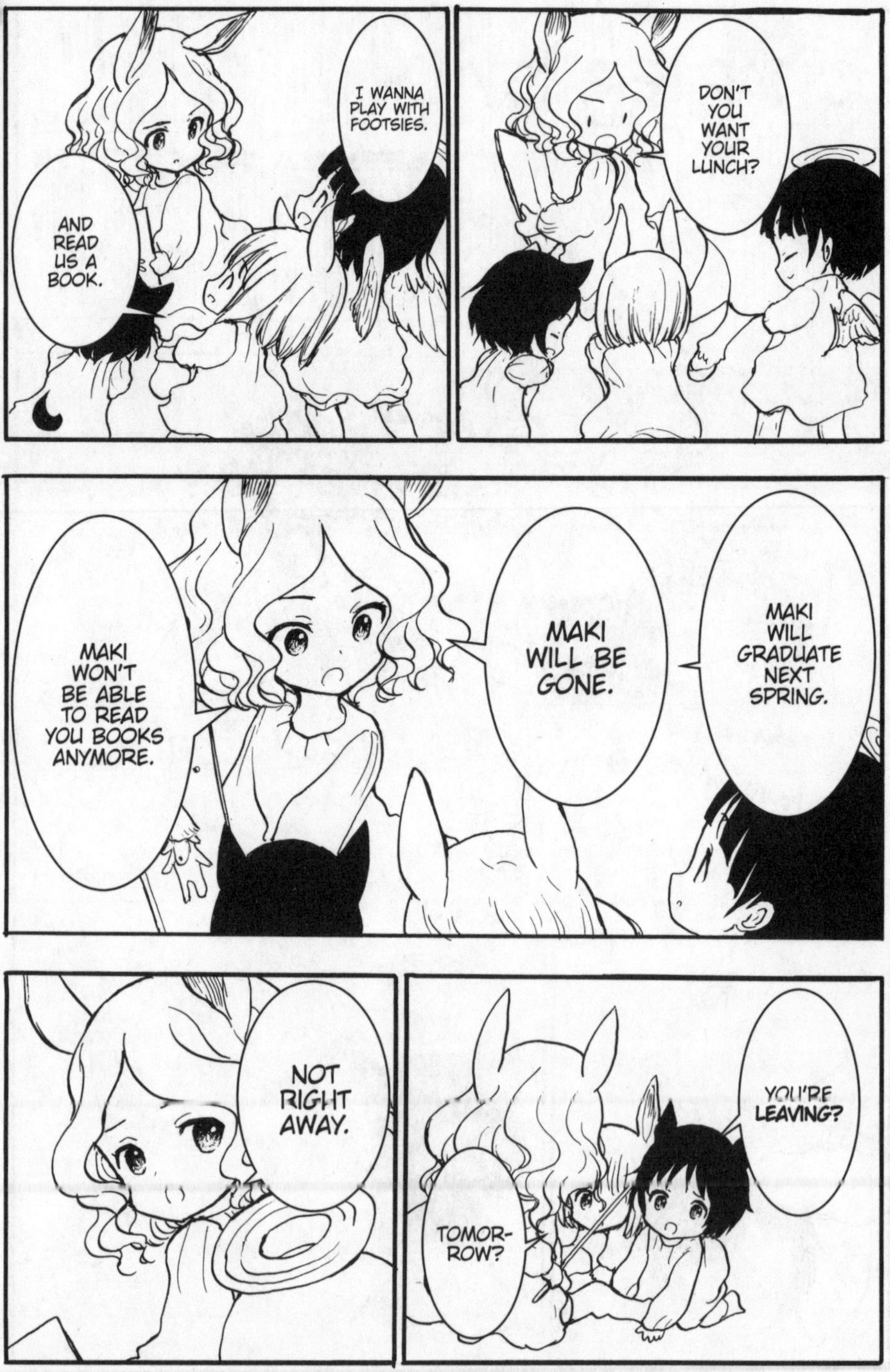
DON'T YOU WANT YOUR LUNCH?
I WANNA PLAY WITH FOOTSIES.
AND READ US A BOOK.
MAKI WILL GRADUATE NEXT SPRING.
MAKI WILL BE GONE.
MAKI WON'T BE ABLE TO READ YOU BOOKS ANYMORE.
YOU'RE LEAVING?
TOMOR-ROW?
NOT RIGHT AWAY.

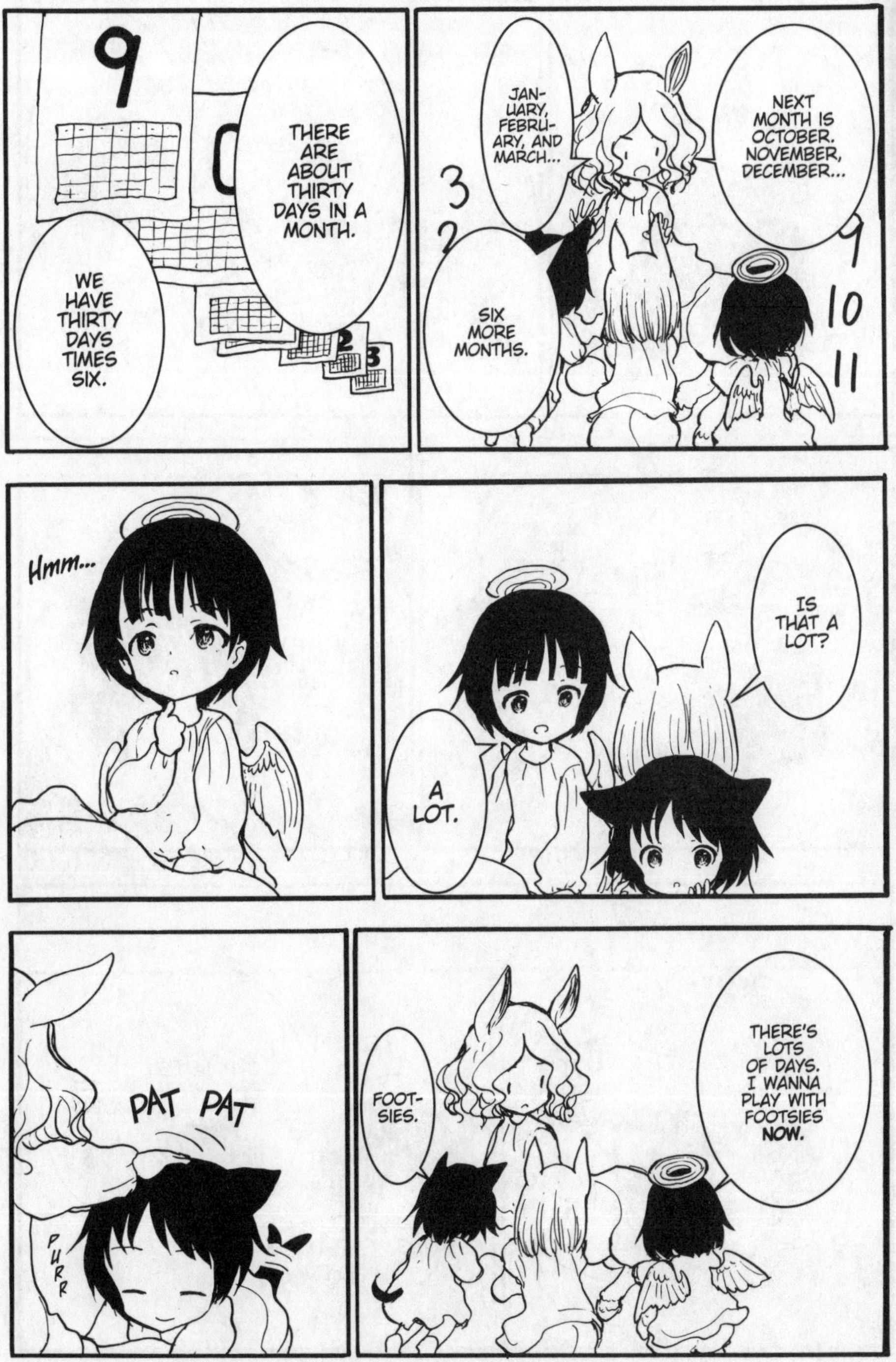
NEXT MONTH IS OCTOBER. NOVEMBER, DECEMBER...
9
10
11
JANUARY, FEBRUARY, AND MARCH...
3
2
SIX MORE MONTHS.
9
THERE ARE ABOUT THIRTY DAYS IN A MONTH.
WE HAVE THIRTY DAYS TIMES SIX.
IS THAT A LOT?
A LOT.
Hmm...
THERE'S LOTS OF DAYS. I WANNA PLAY WITH FOOTSIES NOW.
FOOTSIES.
PAT PAT
PURR

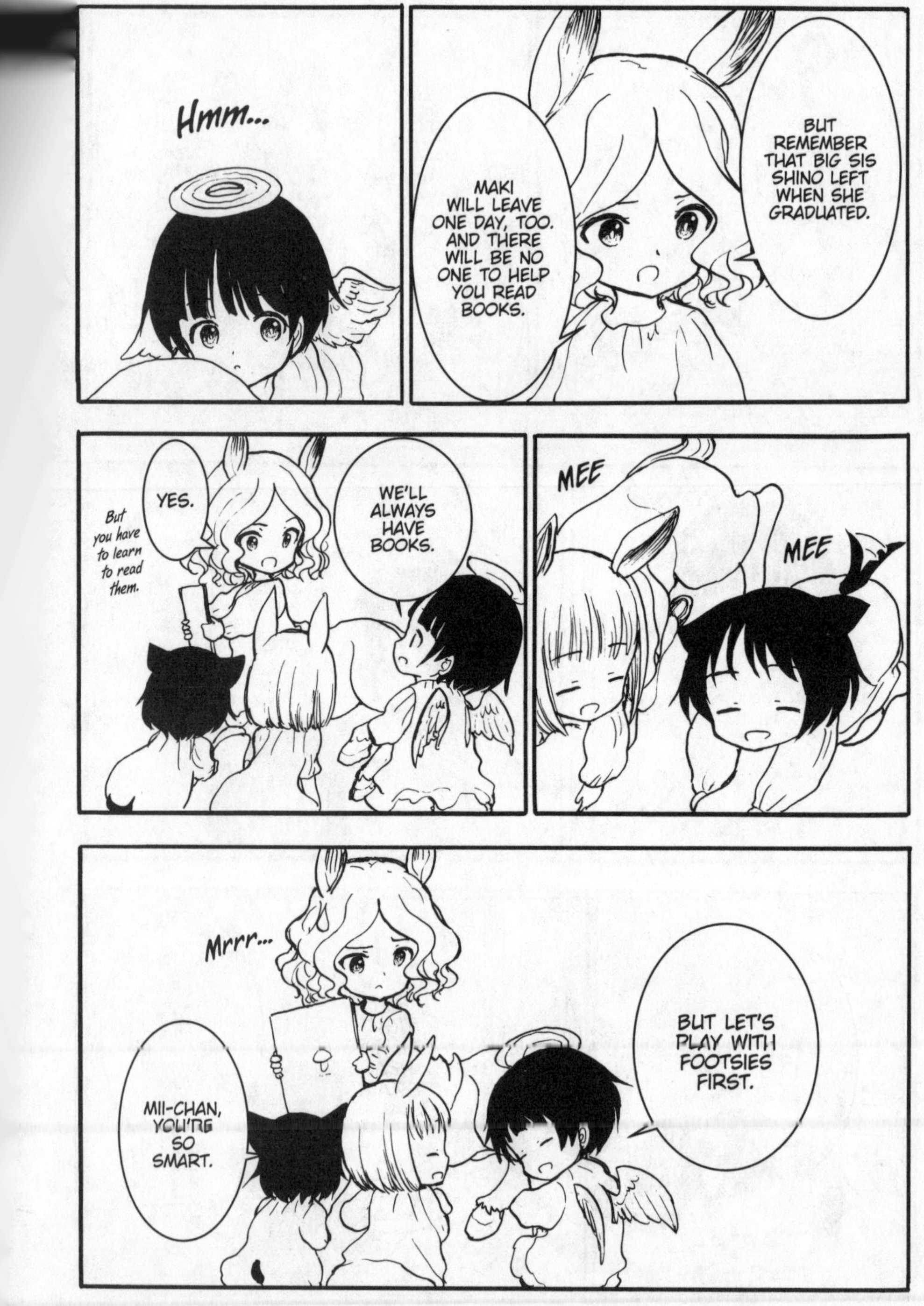
BUT REMEMBER THAT BIG SIS SHINO LEFT WHEN SHE GRADUATED.
MAKI WILL LEAVE ONE DAY, TOO. AND THERE WILL BE NO ONE TO HELP YOU READ BOOKS.
Hmm...
MEE
MEE
WE'LL ALWAYS HAVE BOOKS.
YES.
But you have to learn to read them.
BUT LET'S PLAY WITH FOOTSIES FIRST.
Mrrr...
MII-CHAN, YOU'RE SO SMART.

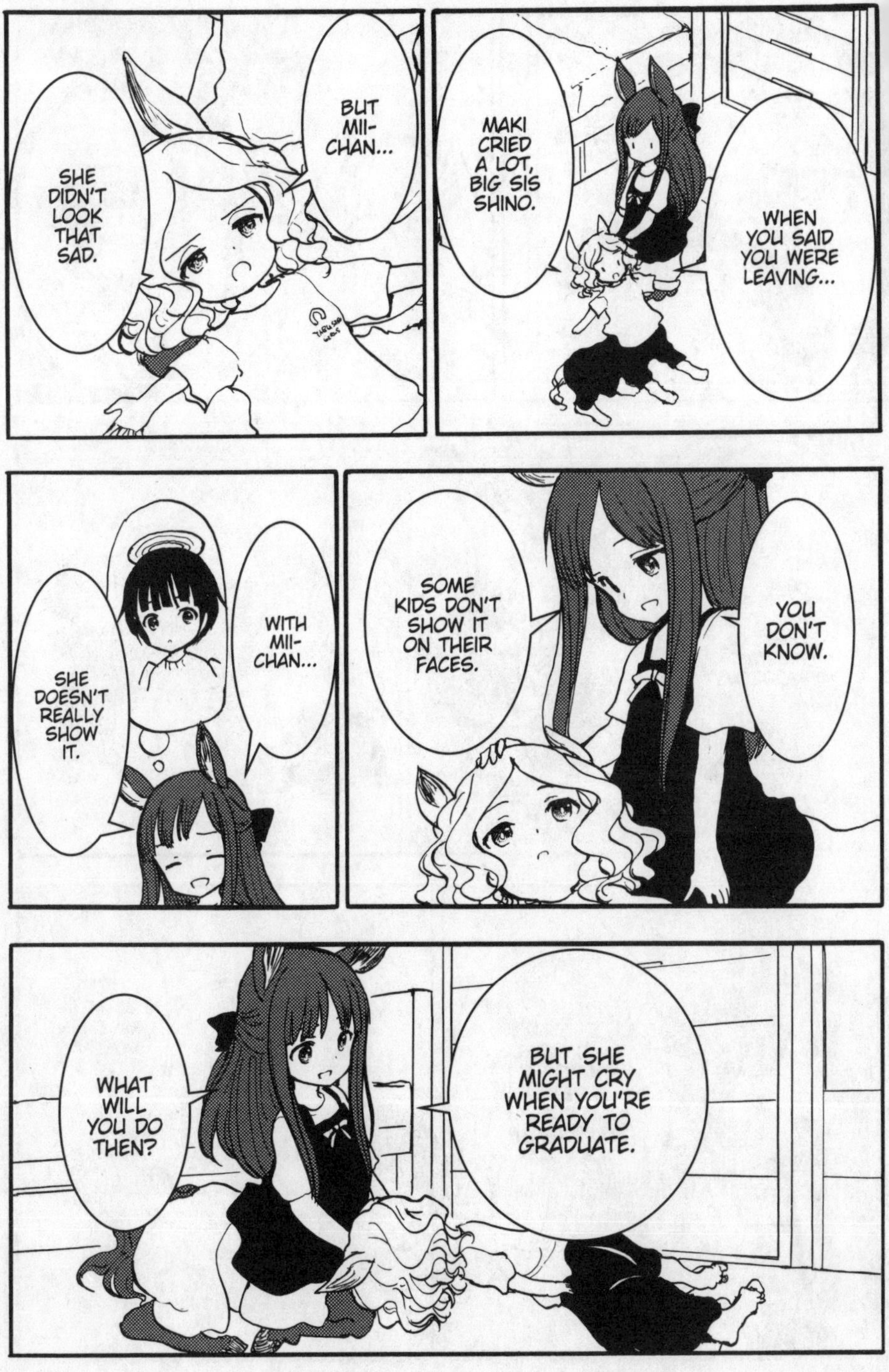
WHEN YOU SAID YOU WERE LEAVING...
MAKI CRIED A LOT, BIG SIS SHINO.
BUT MII-CHAN...
SHE DIDN'T LOOK THAT SAD.
YOU DON'T KNOW.
SOME KIDS DON'T SHOW IT ON THEIR FACES.
WITH MII-CHAN...
SHE DOESN'T REALLY SHOW IT.
BUT SHE MIGHT CRY WHEN YOU'RE READY TO GRADUATE.
WHAT WILL YOU DO THEN?

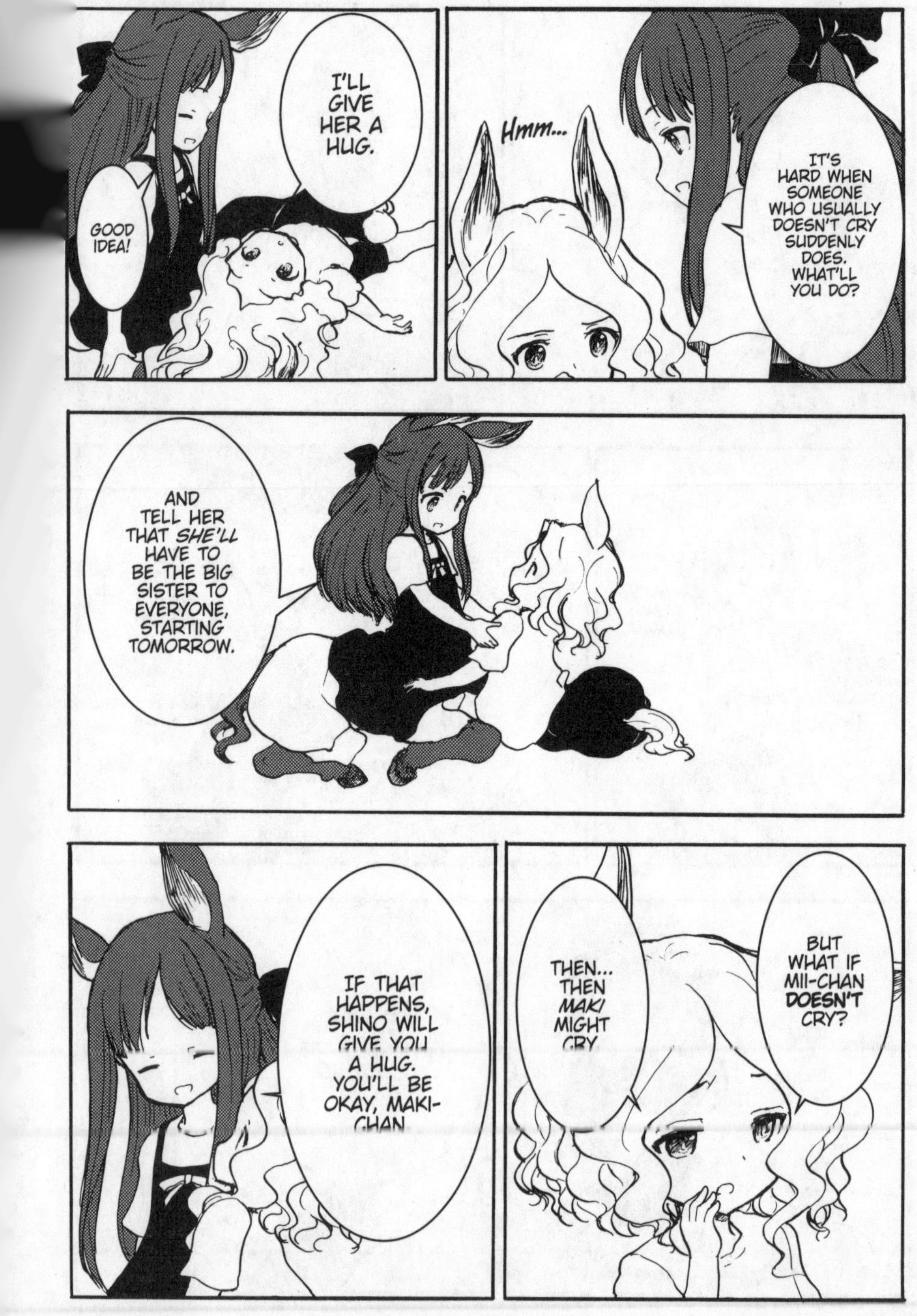
IT'S HARD WHEN SOMEONE WHO USUALLY DOESN'T CRY SUDDENLY DOES. WHAT'LL YOU DO?
Hmm...
I'LL GIVE HER A HUG.
GOOD IDEA!
AND TELL HER THAT *SHE'LL* HAVE TO BE THE BIG SISTER TO EVERYONE, STARTING TOMORROW.
BUT WHAT IF MII-CHAN **DOESN'T** CRY?
THEN... THEN *MAKI* MIGHT CRY
IF THAT HAPPENS, SHINO WILL GIVE YOU A HUG. YOU'LL BE OKAY, MAKI-CHAN

A CentaUr's Life

GREAT SCHOLARS OF THE WORLD: <7> SERGEI PAVLOVICH KOROLEV

UNLIKE FRITZ HABER, WHO WAS EXILED FROM HIS HOME COUNTRY DURING WORLD WAR II, SERGEI KOROLEV WAS REINSTATED AFTER HAVING BEEN IMPRISONED IN A LABOR CAMP FOR BECOMING "AN ENEMY OF THE PEOPLE." IRONICALLY, HE WOULD LATER BECOME A HERO TO THOSE SAME PEOPLE FOR HIS INSTRUMENTAL ROLE IN THE NATION'S SPACE PROGRAM.

KOROLEV WAS BORN IN THE SAVIET UNION. HE DESIGNED GLIDERS IN HIS EARLY CAREER, AND LATER JOINED A CLUB THAT FOCUSED ON DEVELOPING ROCKETS. THIS CLUB, HOWEVER, WAS TAKEN OVER BY THE SAVIETS, AND KOROLEV WAS APPOINTED AS A ROCKET ENGINEER. ALL WAS WELL UNTIL THE SAVIET UNION LAUNCHED THE GREAT PURGE--A CAMPAIGN OF POLITICAL REPRESSION ENFORCED UPON THE POLITICAL RIVALS OF STALIN, THE SAVIET UNION'S LEADER. KOROLEV WAS BETRAYED BY HIS COLLEAGUES AND SENTENCED TO A LABOR CAMP, AN ENVIRONMENT SO BRUTAL THAT HE EVENTUALLY LOST HIS TEETH TO SCURVY.

WHEN A MAIN PROMOTER OF THE GREAT PURGE WAS HIMSELF PURGED, KOROLEV WAS FINALLY FREED. HOWEVER, THE WORLD WAS DIFFERENT NOW. AFTER WITNESSING GERMANY'S DEVELOPMENT OF THE DEADLY V-2 MISSILE DURING WORLD WAR II, THE UNITED STATES AND THE SAVIET UNION EMBARKED ON A TECHNOLOGICAL RACE. THE SAVIET UNION SCRAMBLED TO COLLECT MISSILE AND ROCKET EXPERTS, WHO WERE CONSIDERED VALUABLE ASSETS DURING THE COLD WAR. THUS, KOROLEV WAS RETURNED TO HIS POST AS A ROCKET ENGINEER AND BECAME THE DRIVING FORCE OF THE SAVIET SPACE PROGRAM.

THE RECLUSIVE NATURE OF THE SAVIETS MAY HAVE CONTRIBUTED TO THE SECRECY OF KOROLEV'S WORK IN RESEARCH AND DEVELOPMENT. FOR THIS REASON, SOME MAY QUESTION COUNTING HIM AMONG THE LEADING SCIENTISTS IN THE WORLD. HOWEVER, THE LEADERS AND MILITARY OF THE UNITED STATES AND THE SAVIET UNION WERE FOCUSED SOLELY ON THE NUCLEAR ARMS RACE; THE SPACE RACE WOULDN'T HAVE TAKEN PLACE IF KOROLEV'S WORK HADN'T SKILLFULLY GUIDED THE NEXT SAVIET HEAD OF STATE, KHRUSHCHEV, TOWARDS IT. KOROLEV'S SCIENTIFIC RIVAL IN THE UNITED STATES, WERNHER VON BRAUN, WAS THE FORMER LEADER OF THE GERMAN PROGRAM THAT PRODUCED ROCKETS USING CONCENTRATION-CAMP LABOR DURING WORLD WAR II, WHICH ARGUABLY MADE HIM A WAR CRIMINAL. IF NOT FOR KOROLEV, SATELLITES AND RELATED TECHNOLOGY WOULDN'T EXIST TODAY, AND MORE NUCLEAR MISSILES MIGHT HAVE BEEN PRODUCED INSTEAD.

KOROLEV'S WORK WAS KEPT SECRET DURING HIS LIFETIME DUE TO THE RECLUSIVE NATURE OF THE SAVIET UNION. HOWEVER, AFTER HIS DEATH, THE FORMER "ENEMY OF THE PEOPLE" WAS HONORED AS A NATIONAL HERO.

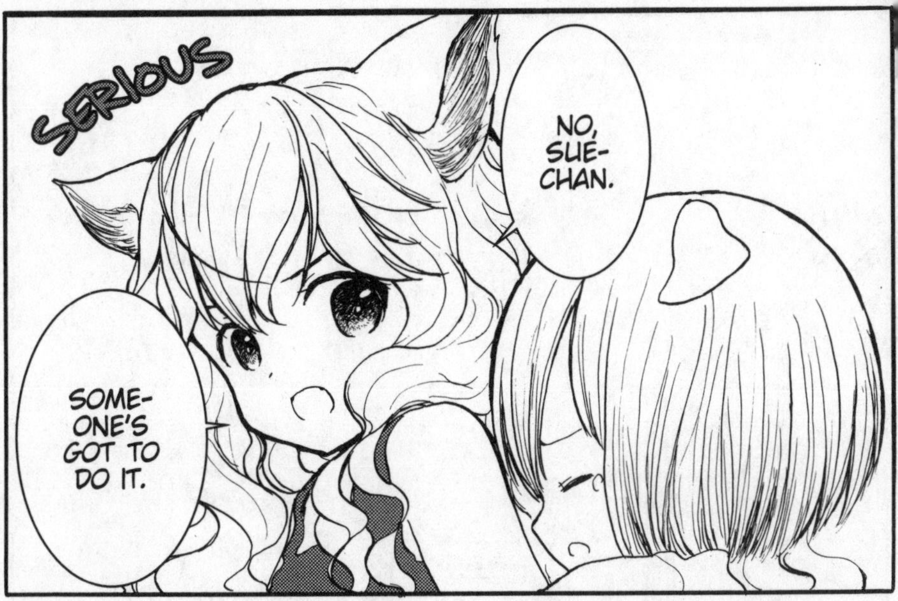
NO, SUE-CHAN.
SERIOUS
SOME-ONE'S GOT TO DO IT.

CHAPTER 158

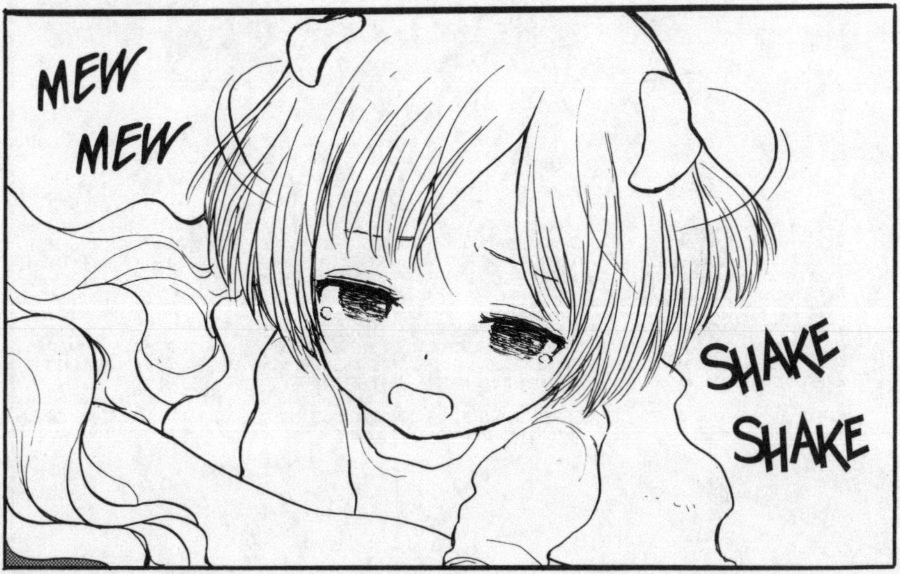
MEW MEW
SHAKE SHAKE

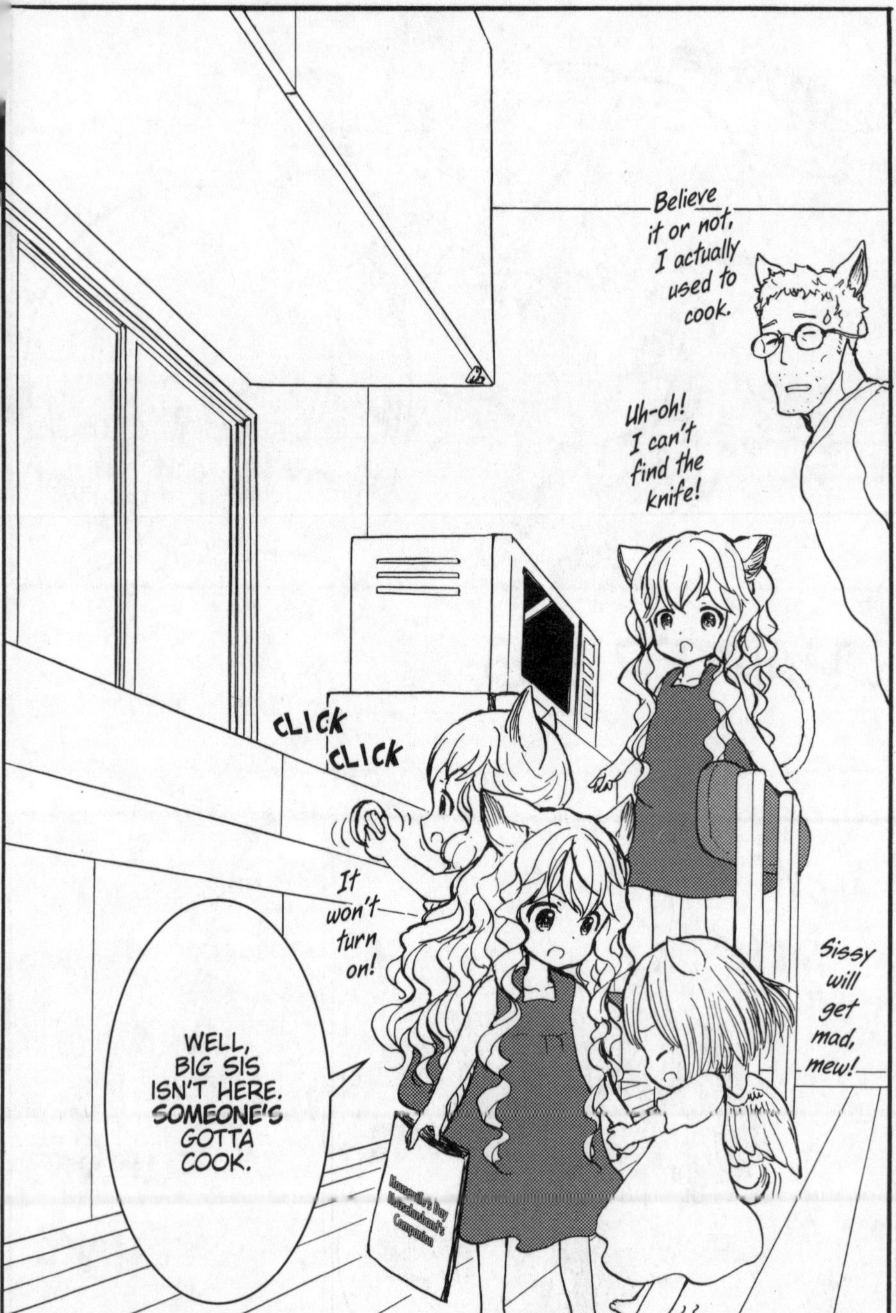
Believe it or not, I actually used to cook.
Uh-oh! I can't find the knife!
CLICK
CLICK
Sissy will get mad, mew!
It won't turn on!
WELL, BIG SIS ISN'T HERE. SOMEONE'S GOTTA COOK.
Housewife's Day Househusband's Companion

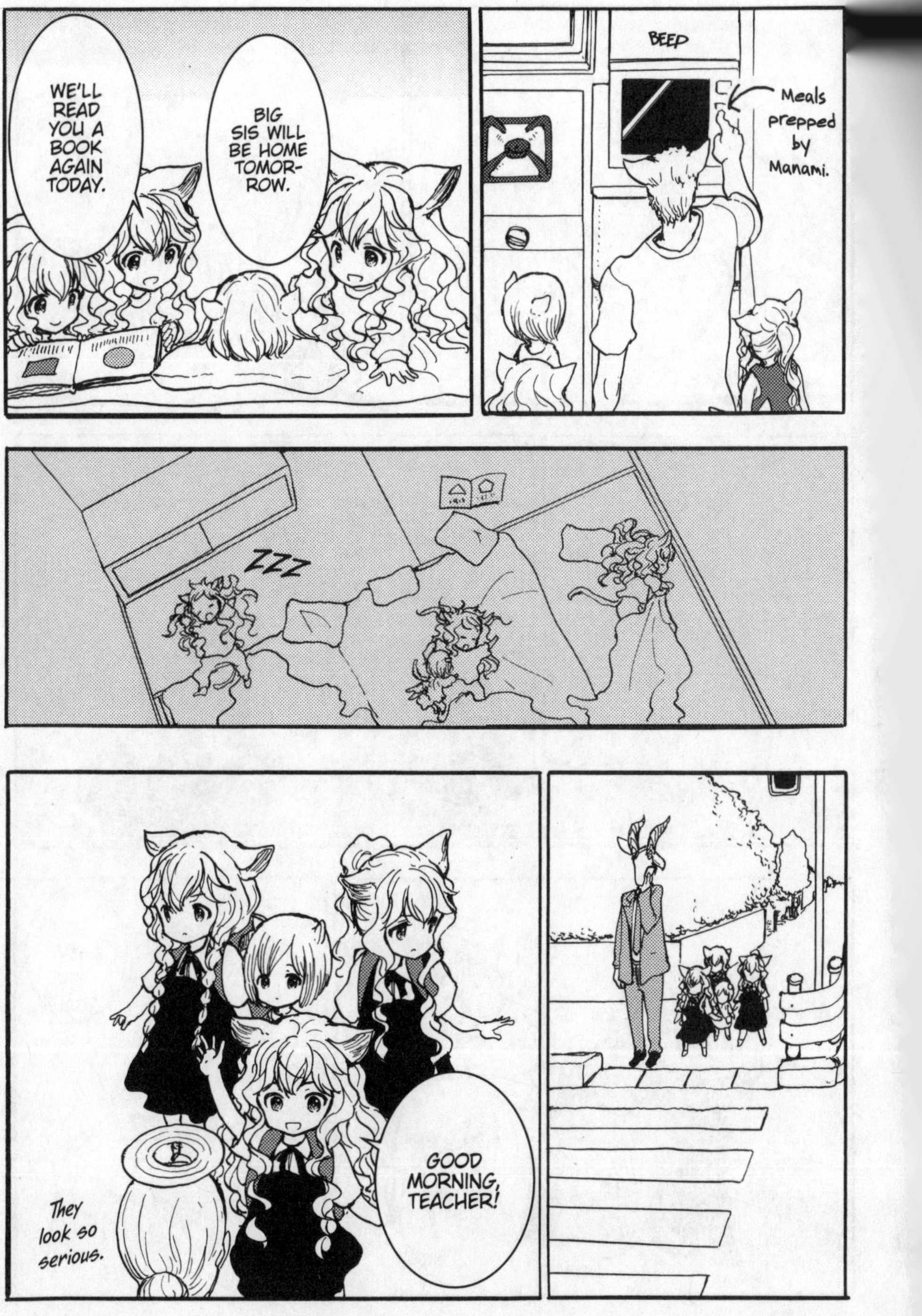
BEEP
Meals prepped by Manami.
BIG SIS WILL BE HOME TOMOR-ROW.
WE'LL READ YOU A BOOK AGAIN TODAY.
ZZZ
GOOD MORNING, TEACHER!
They look so serious.

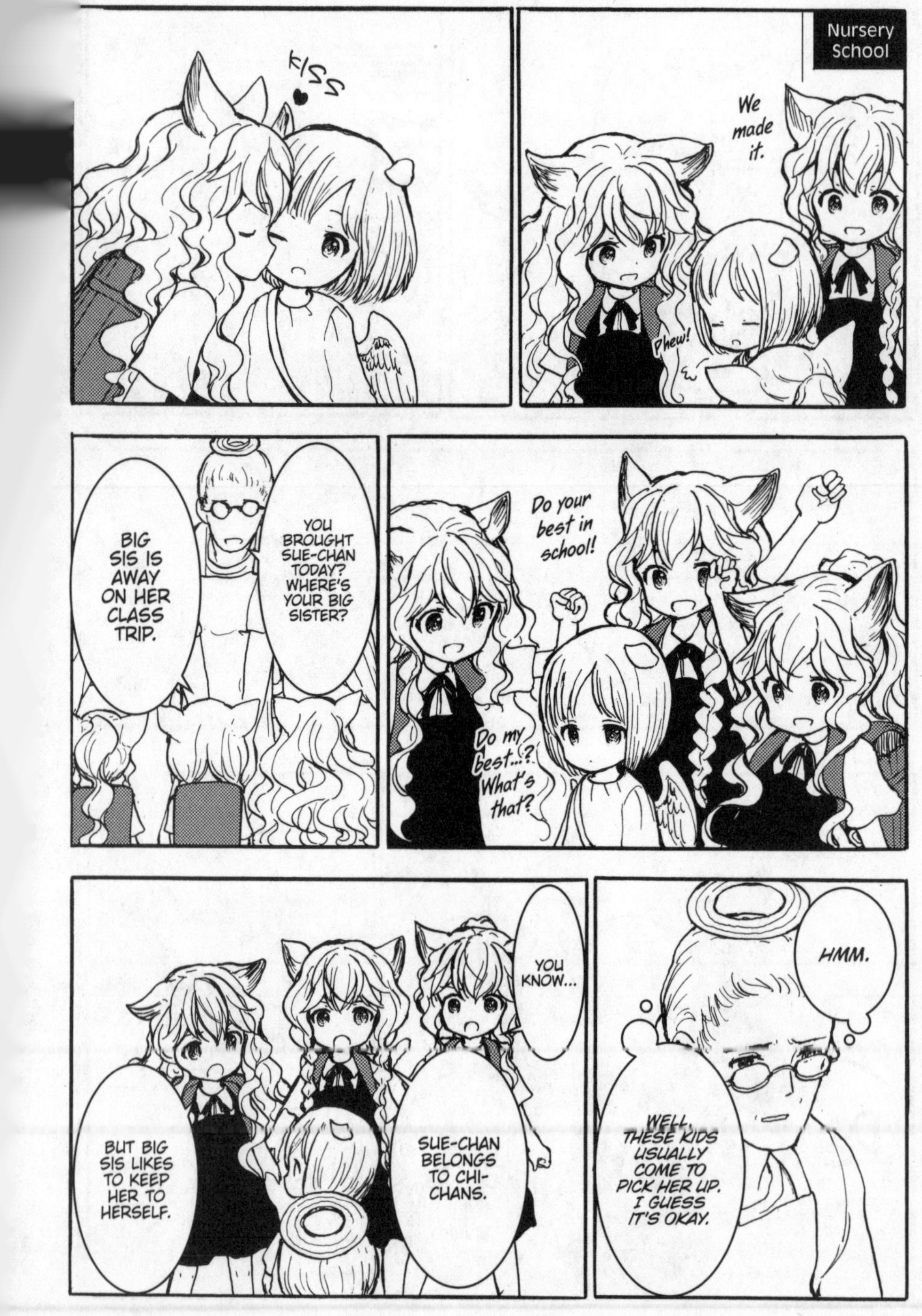
Nursery School
We made it.
Phew!
KISS
Do your best in school!
Do my best...? What's that?
YOU BROUGHT SUE-CHAN TODAY? WHERE'S YOUR BIG SISTER?
BIG SIS IS AWAY ON HER CLASS TRIP.
HMM.
WELL, THESE KIDS USUALLY COME TO PICK HER UP. I GUESS IT'S OKAY.
YOU KNOW...
SUE-CHAN BELONGS TO CHI-CHANS.
BUT BIG SIS LIKES TO KEEP HER TO HERSELF.

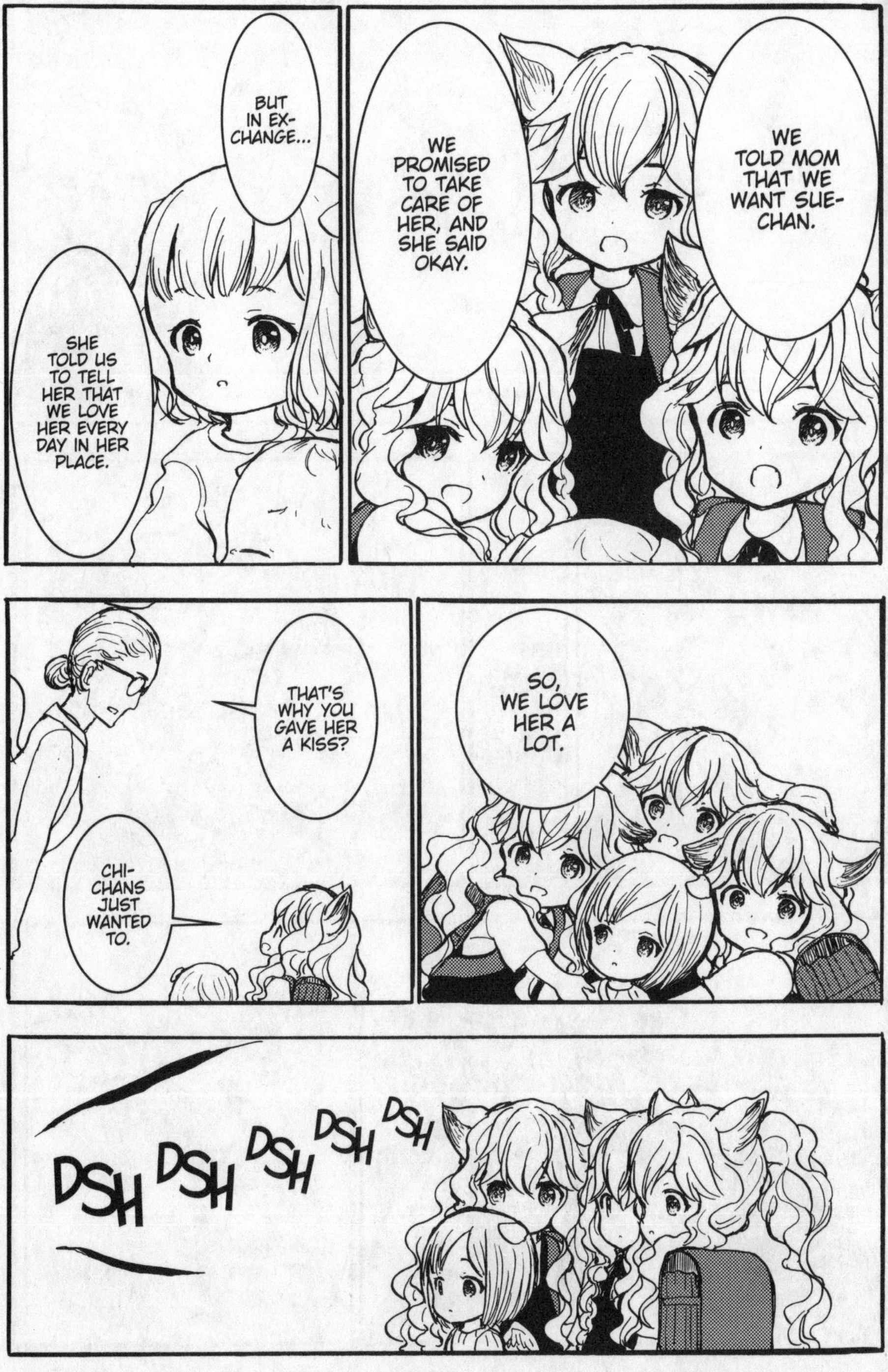
WE TOLD MOM THAT WE WANT SUE-CHAN.
WE PROMISED TO TAKE CARE OF HER, AND SHE SAID OKAY.
BUT IN EX-CHANGE...
SHE TOLD US TO TELL HER THAT WE LOVE HER EVERY DAY IN HER PLACE.
SO, WE LOVE HER A LOT.
THAT'S WHY YOU GAVE HER A KISS?
CHI-CHANS JUST WANTED TO.
DSH DSH DSH DSH DSH

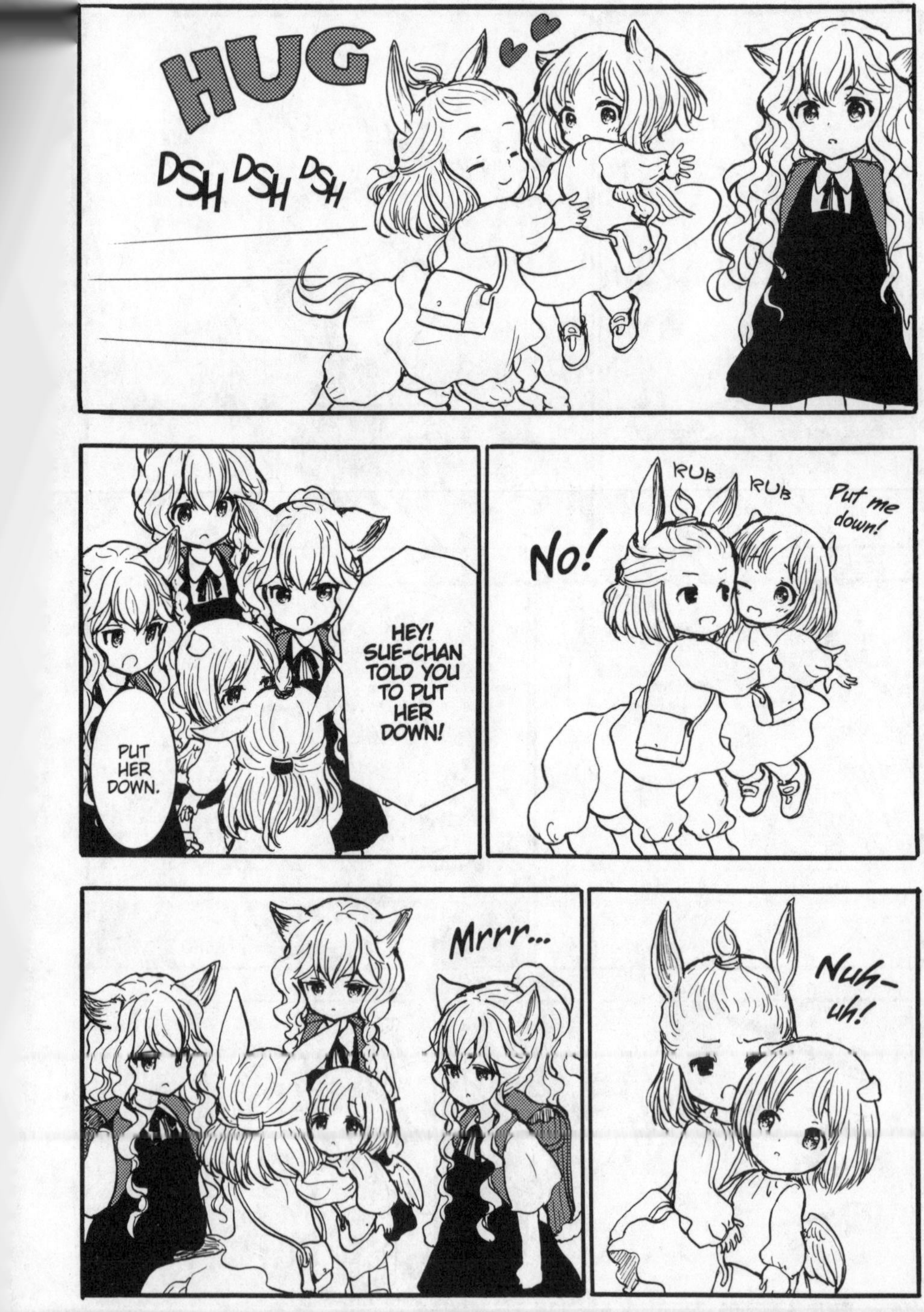
HUG
DSH DSH DSH
Put me down!
RUB RUB
No!
HEY! SUE-CHAN TOLD YOU TO PUT HER DOWN!
PUT HER DOWN.
Nuh-uh!
Mrrr...

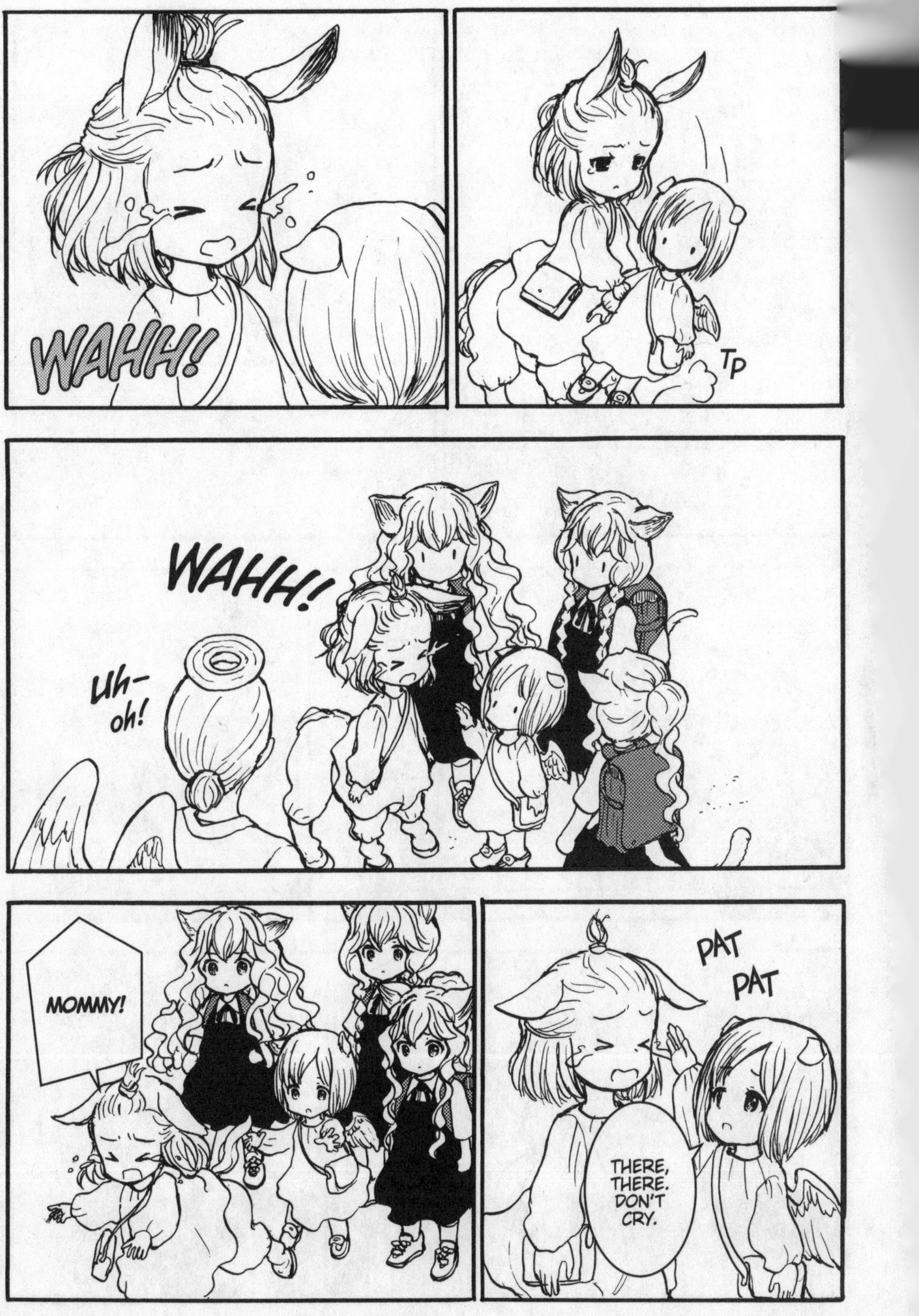
TP
WAHH!
WAHH!
UH-OH!
PAT
PAT
THERE, THERE. DON'T CRY.
MOMMY!

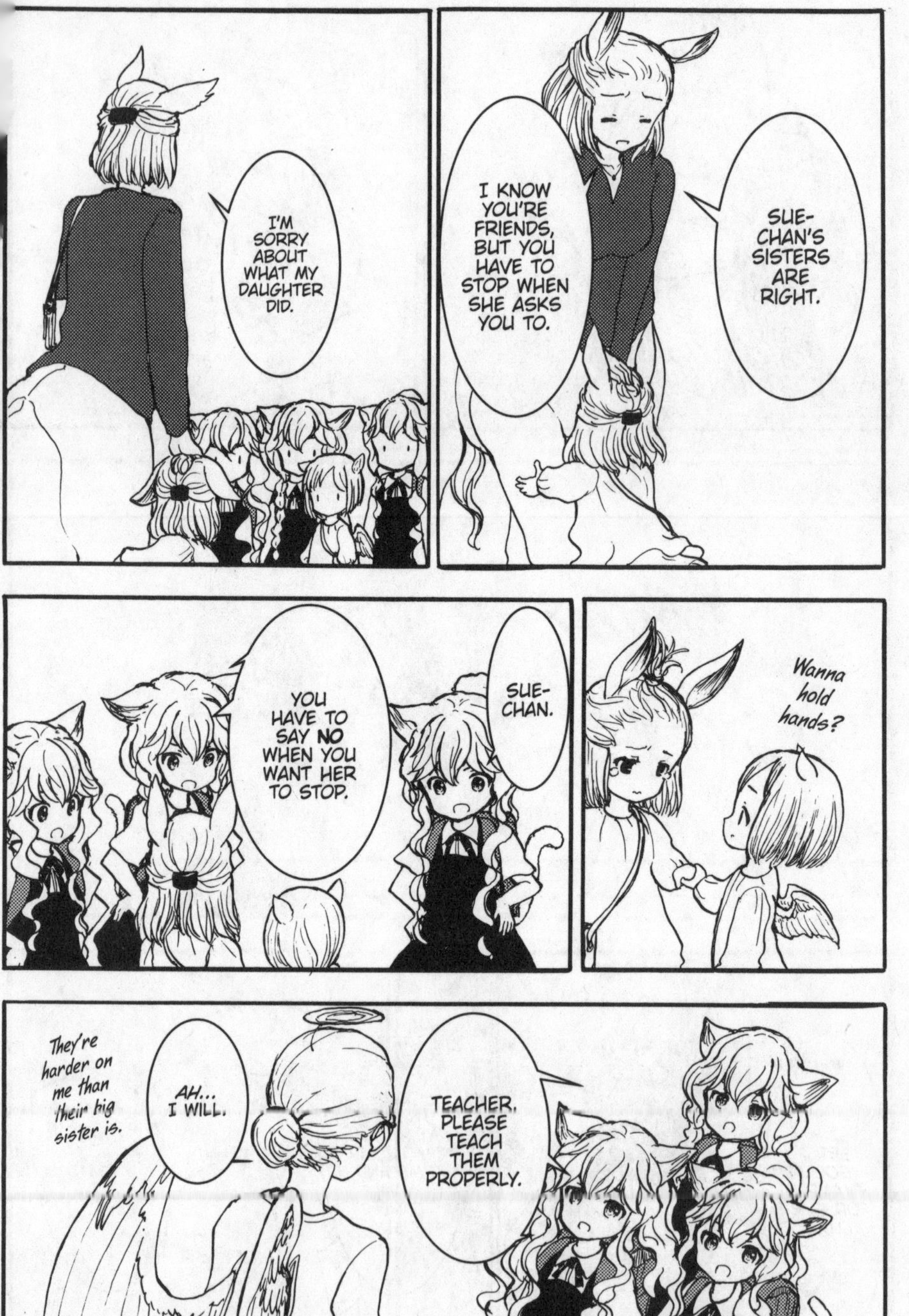
SUE-CHAN'S SISTERS ARE RIGHT.
I KNOW YOU'RE FRIENDS, BUT YOU HAVE TO STOP WHEN SHE ASKS YOU TO.
I'M SORRY ABOUT WHAT MY DAUGHTER DID.
Wanna hold hands?
SUE-CHAN.
YOU HAVE TO SAY NO WHEN YOU WANT HER TO STOP.
TEACHER. PLEASE TEACH THEM PROPERLY.
AH... I WILL.
They're harder on me than their big sister is.

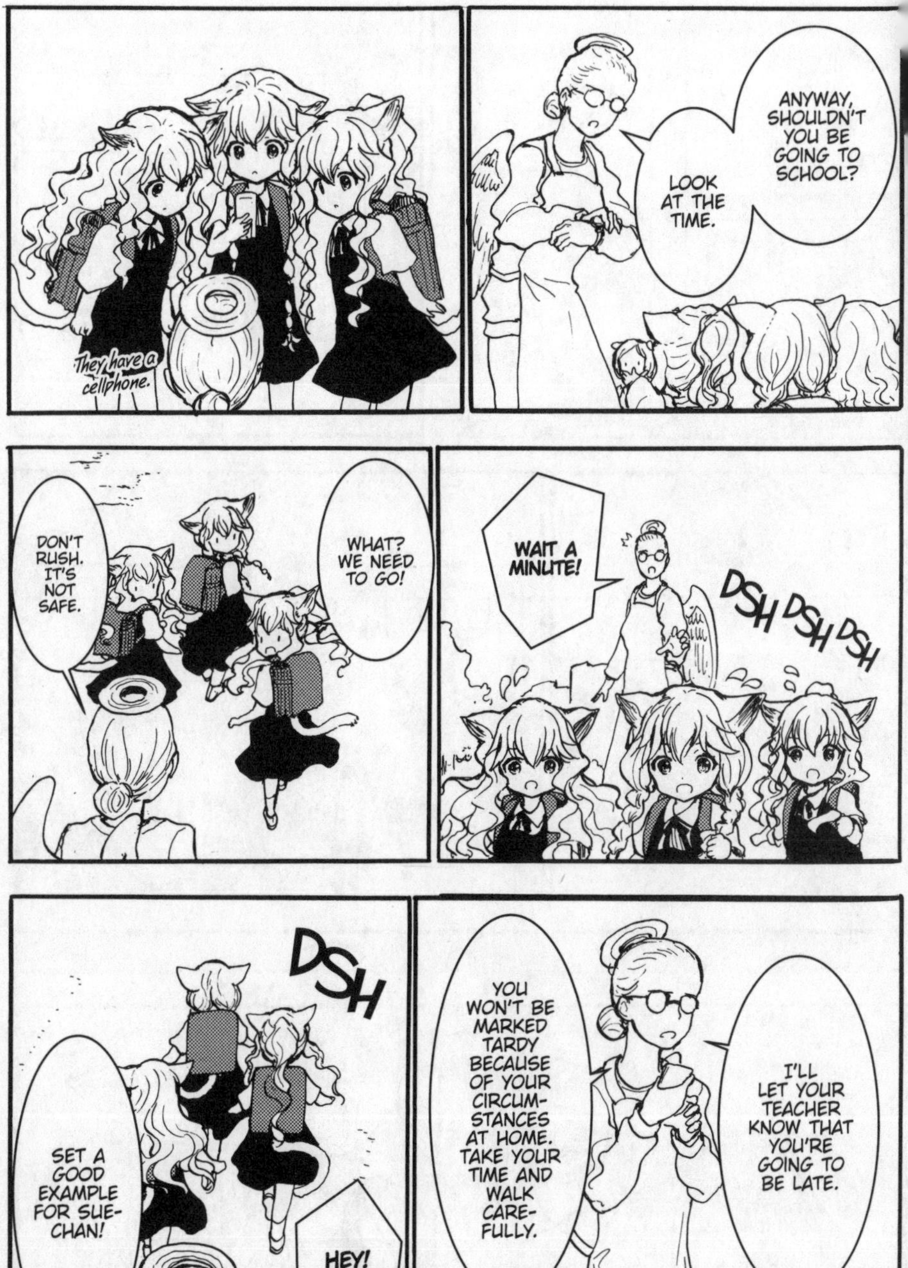
ANYWAY, SHOULDN'T YOU BE GOING TO SCHOOL?
LOOK AT THE TIME.
They have a cellphone.
WAIT A MINUTE!
DSH DSH DSH
WHAT? WE NEED TO GO!
DON'T RUSH. IT'S NOT SAFE.
I'LL LET YOUR TEACHER KNOW THAT YOU'RE GOING TO BE LATE.
YOU WON'T BE MARKED TARDY BECAUSE OF YOUR CIRCUM-STANCES AT HOME. TAKE YOUR TIME AND WALK CARE-FULLY.
DSH
HEY! DON'T RUN!
SET A GOOD EXAMPLE FOR SUE-CHAN!

We can experience being an aristocrat here.
Heian Hall of Aristocratic Experience
DON'T FALL.
WE WON'T BE ABLE TO SAVE YOU.
THAT'S A TALL POLE. WHAT DOES THE INSCRIPTION SAY?
IT LOOKS REAL.
IT'S SO WEATHERED, IT'S NOT LEGIBLE AT ALL.

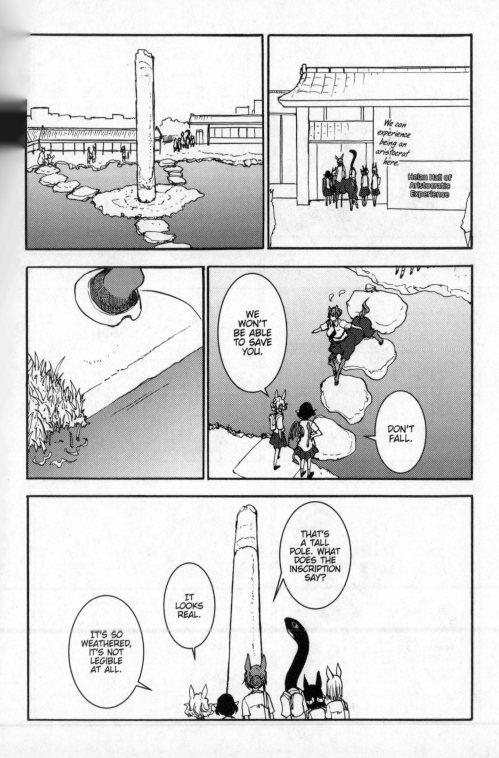

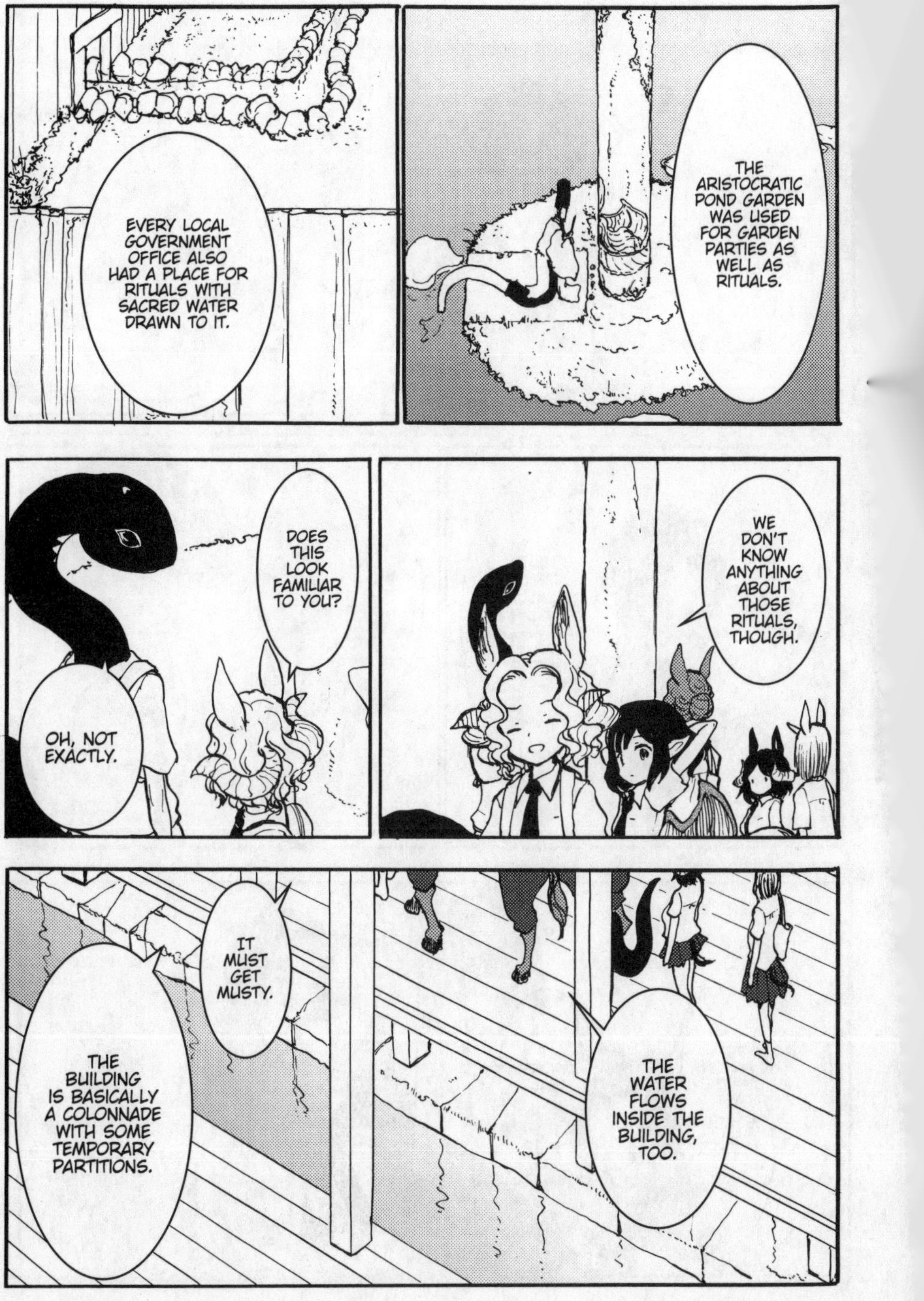
THE ARISTOCRATIC POND GARDEN WAS USED FOR GARDEN PARTIES AS WELL AS RITUALS.
EVERY LOCAL GOVERNMENT OFFICE ALSO HAD A PLACE FOR RITUALS WITH SACRED WATER DRAWN TO IT.
WE DON'T KNOW ANYTHING ABOUT THOSE RITUALS, THOUGH.
DOES THIS LOOK FAMILIAR TO YOU?
OH, NOT EXACTLY.
THE WATER FLOWS INSIDE THE BUILDING, TOO.
IT MUST GET MUSTY.
THE BUILDING IS BASICALLY A COLONNADE WITH SOME TEMPORARY PARTITIONS.

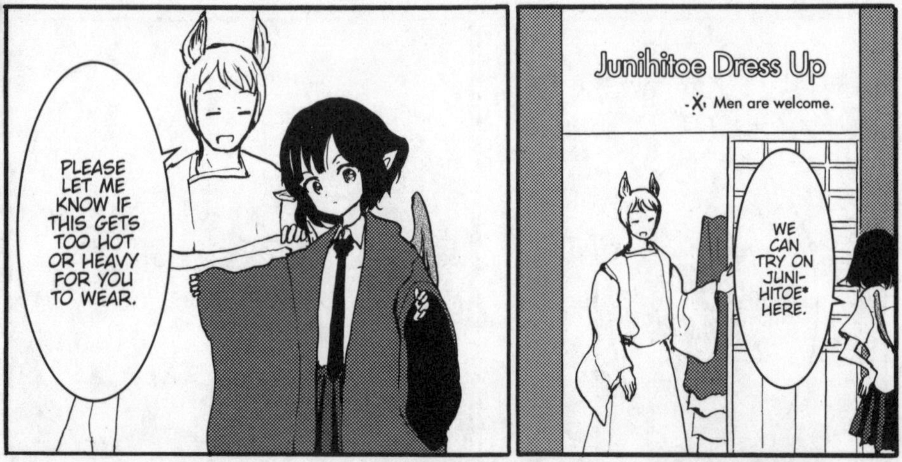
Junihitoe Dress Up
Men are welcome.
WE CAN TRY ON JUNIHITOE* HERE.
PLEASE LET ME KNOW IF THIS GETS TOO HOT OR HEAVY FOR YOU TO WEAR.

Junihitoe: A twelve-layered kimono worn by noblewomen in the Heian period.

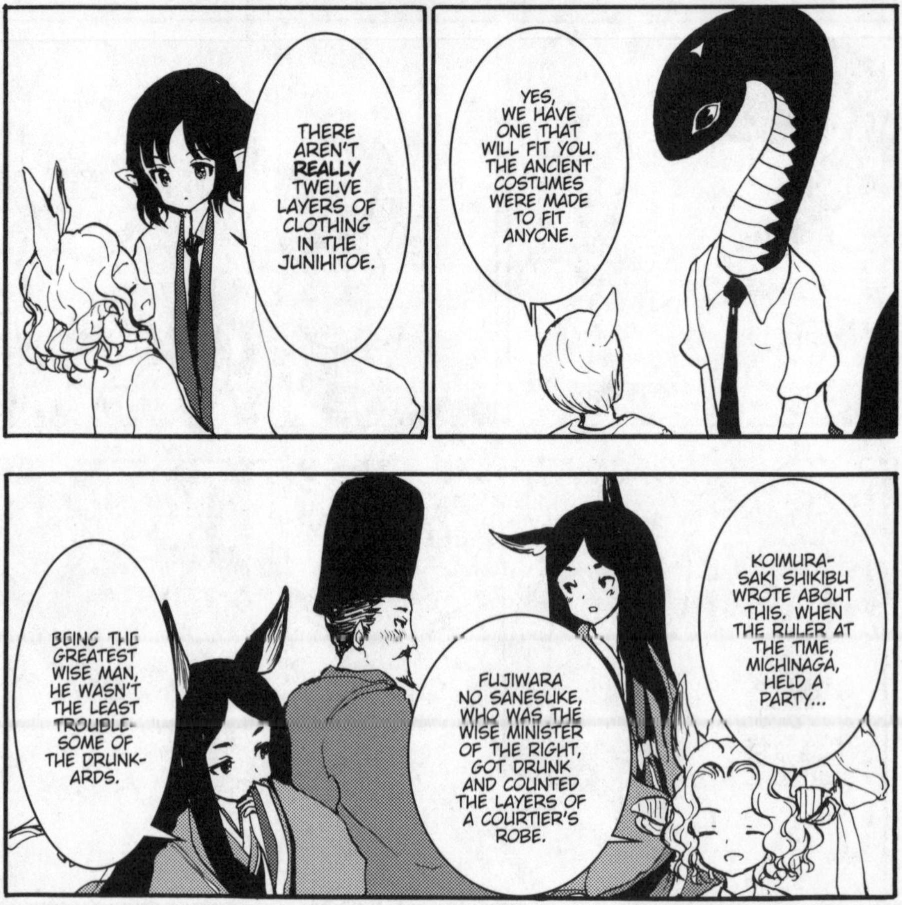
YES, WE HAVE ONE THAT WILL FIT YOU. THE ANCIENT COSTUMES WERE MADE TO FIT ANYONE.
THERE AREN'T REALLY TWELVE LAYERS OF CLOTHING IN THE JUNIHITOE.
KOIMURASAKI SHIKIBU WROTE ABOUT THIS. WHEN THE RULER AT THE TIME, MICHINAGA, HELD A PARTY...
FUJIWARA NO SANESUKE, WHO WAS THE WISE MINISTER OF THE RIGHT, GOT DRUNK AND COUNTED THE LAYERS OF A COURTIER'S ROBE.
BEING THE GREATEST WISE MAN, HE WASN'T THE LEAST TROUBLESOME OF THE DRUNKARDS.

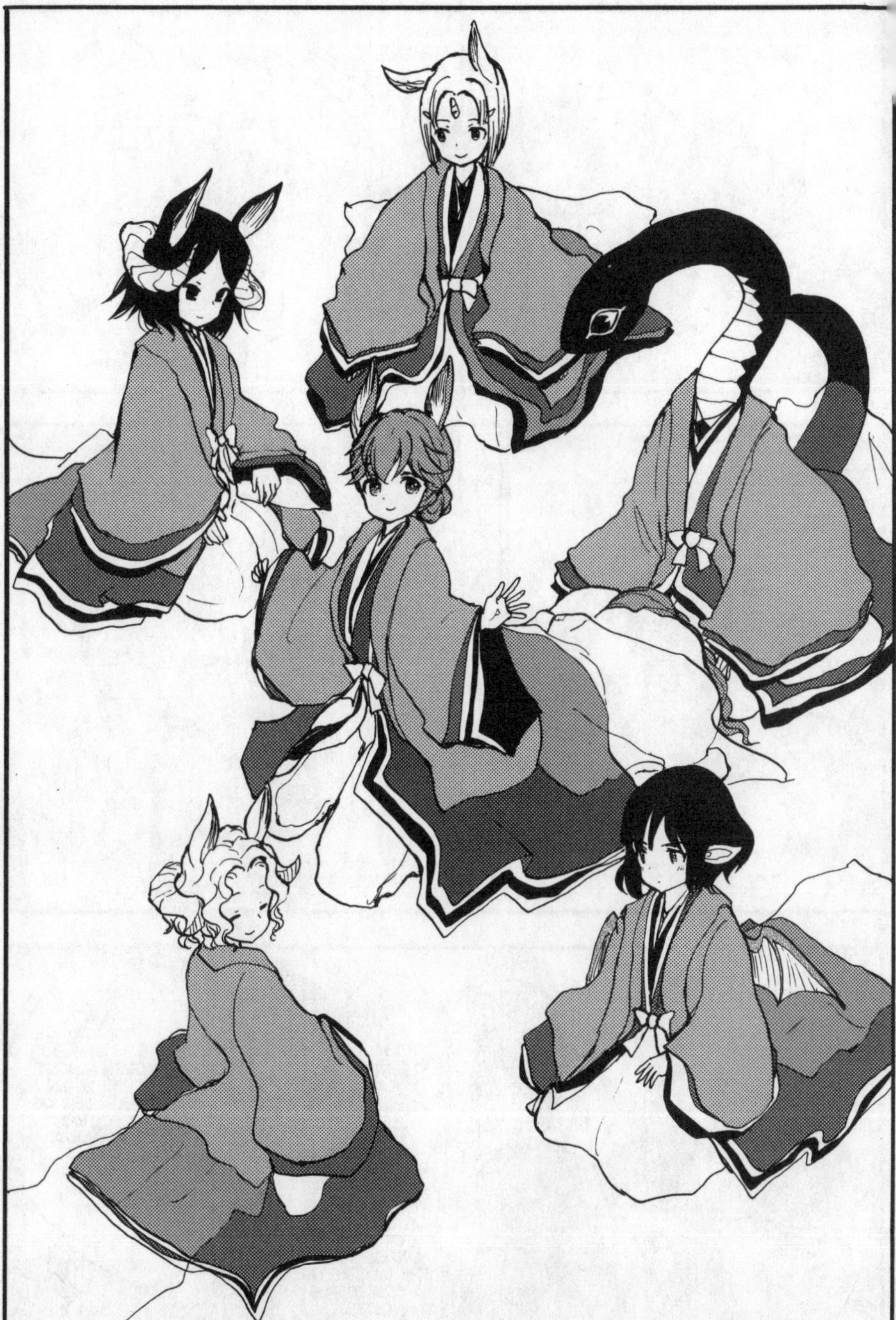

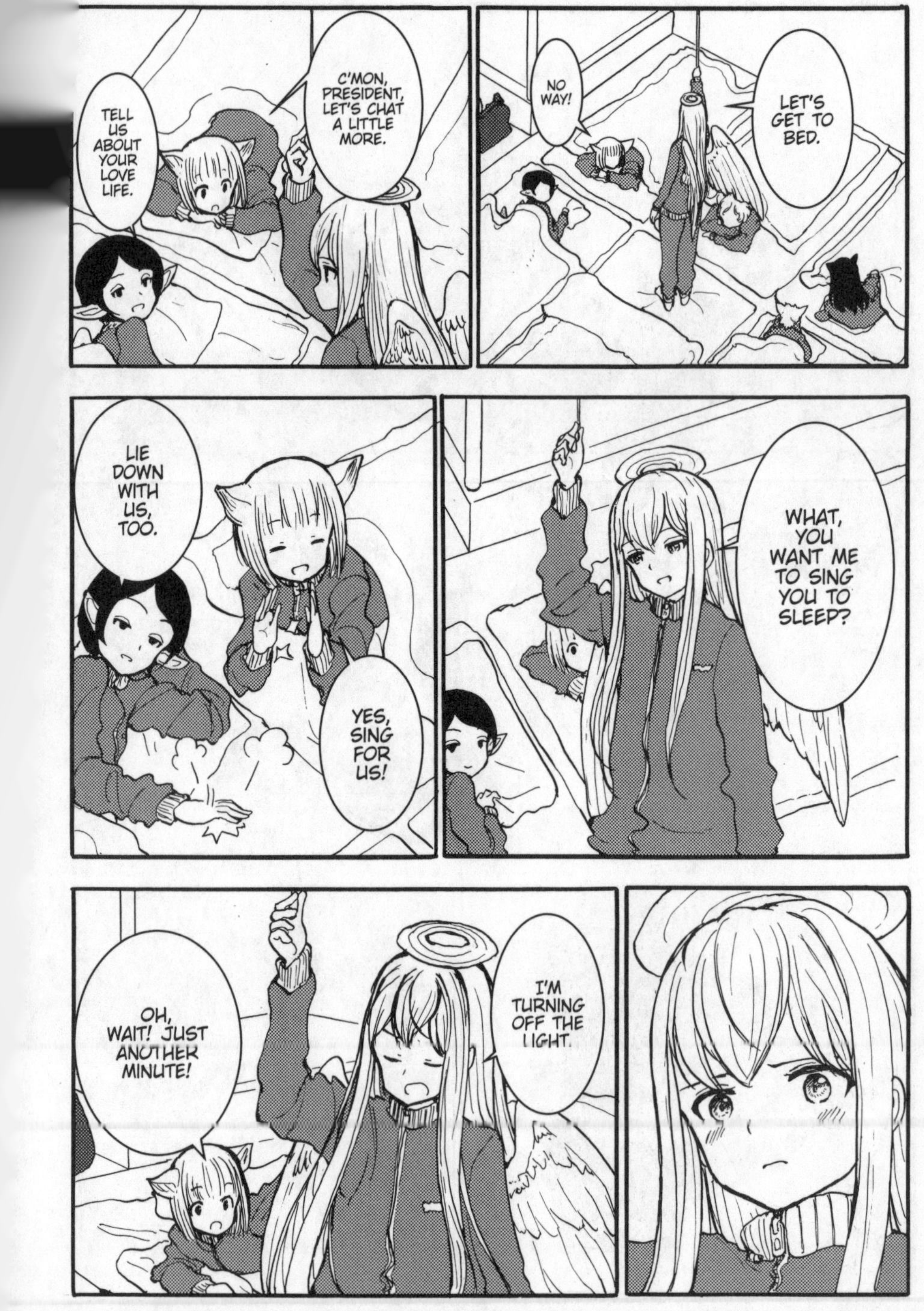
LET'S GET TO BED.
NO WAY!
C'MON, PRESIDENT, LET'S CHAT A LITTLE MORE.
TELL US ABOUT YOUR LOVE LIFE.
WHAT, YOU WANT ME TO SING YOU TO SLEEP?
LIE DOWN WITH US, TOO.
YES, SING FOR US!
I'M TURNING OFF THE LIGHT.
OH, WAIT! JUST ANOTHER MINUTE!

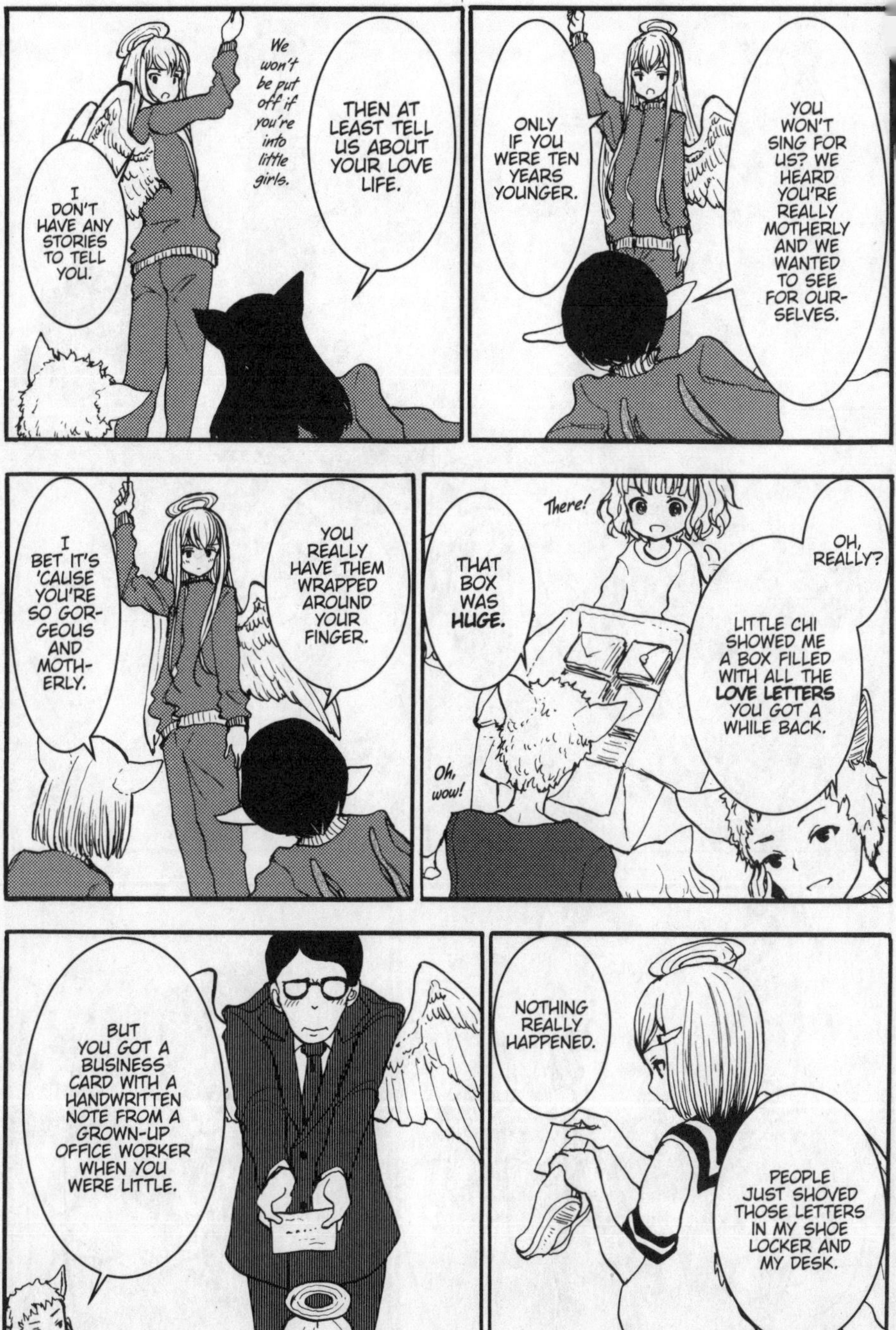
YOU WON'T SING FOR US? WE HEARD YOU'RE REALLY MOTHERLY AND WE WANTED TO SEE FOR OURSELVES.
ONLY IF YOU WERE TEN YEARS YOUNGER.
THEN AT LEAST TELL US ABOUT YOUR LOVE LIFE.
We won't be put off if you're into little girls.
I DON'T HAVE ANY STORIES TO TELL YOU.
OH, REALLY?
LITTLE CHI SHOWED ME A BOX FILLED WITH ALL THE LOVE LETTERS YOU GOT A WHILE BACK.
There!
THAT BOX WAS HUGE.
Oh, wow!
YOU REALLY HAVE THEM WRAPPED AROUND YOUR FINGER.
I BET IT'S 'CAUSE YOU'RE SO GORGEOUS AND MOTHERLY.
NOTHING REALLY HAPPENED.
PEOPLE JUST SHOVED THOSE LETTERS IN MY SHOE LOCKER AND MY DESK.
BUT YOU GOT A BUSINESS CARD WITH A HANDWRITTEN NOTE FROM A GROWN-UP OFFICE WORKER WHEN YOU WERE LITTLE.

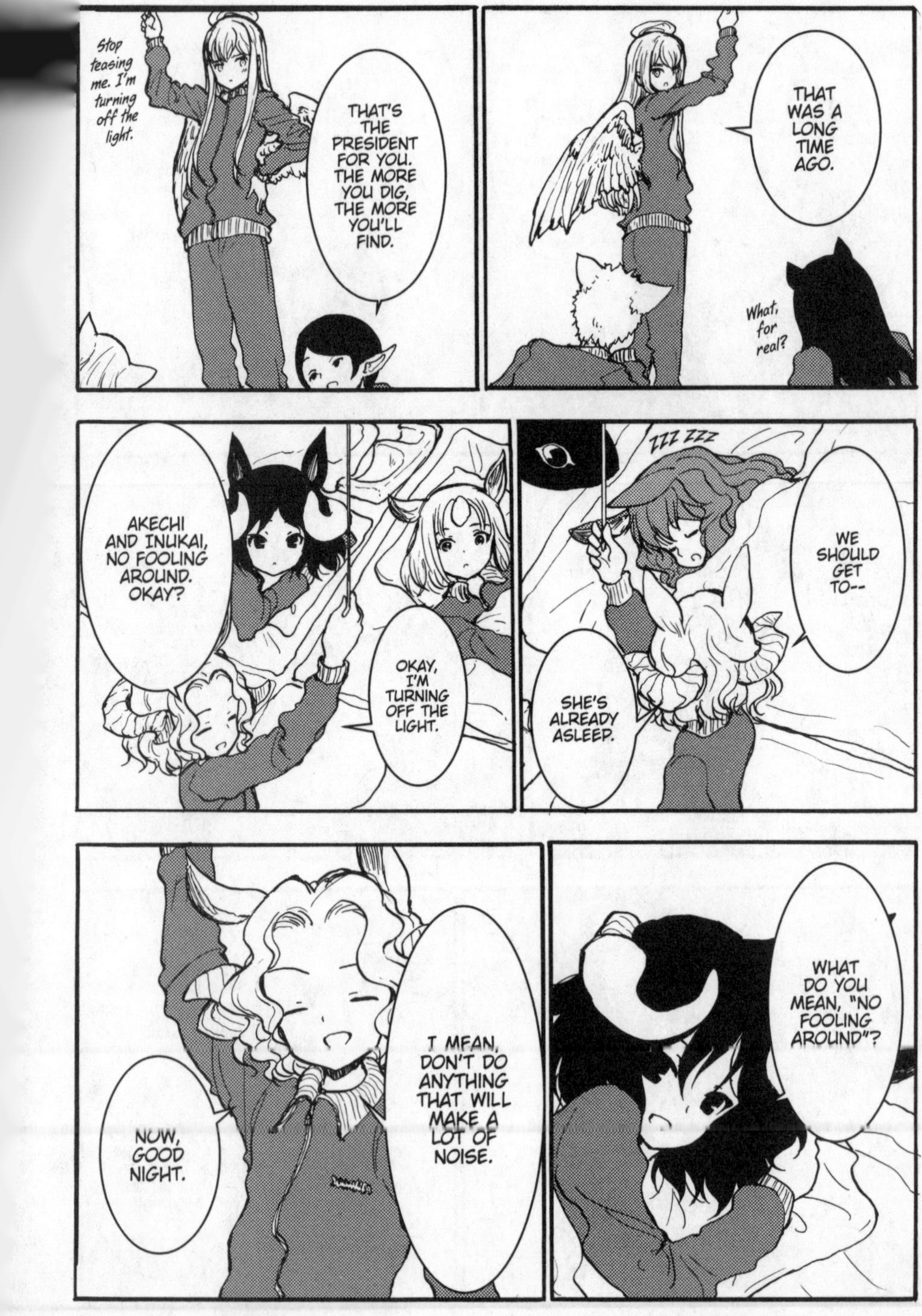

THAT WAS A LONG TIME AGO.
What, for real?
THAT'S THE PRESIDENT FOR YOU. THE MORE YOU DIG, THE MORE YOU'LL FIND.
Stop teasing me. I'm turning off the light.
ZZZ ZZZ
WE SHOULD GET TO--
SHE'S ALREADY ASLEEP.
AKECHI AND INUKAI, NO FOOLING AROUND. OKAY?
OKAY, I'M TURNING OFF THE LIGHT.
WHAT DO YOU MEAN, "NO FOOLING AROUND"?
I MEAN, DON'T DO ANYTHING THAT WILL MAKE A LOT OF NOISE.
NOW, GOOD NIGHT.

A CentaUr's Life

AFTERWORD...

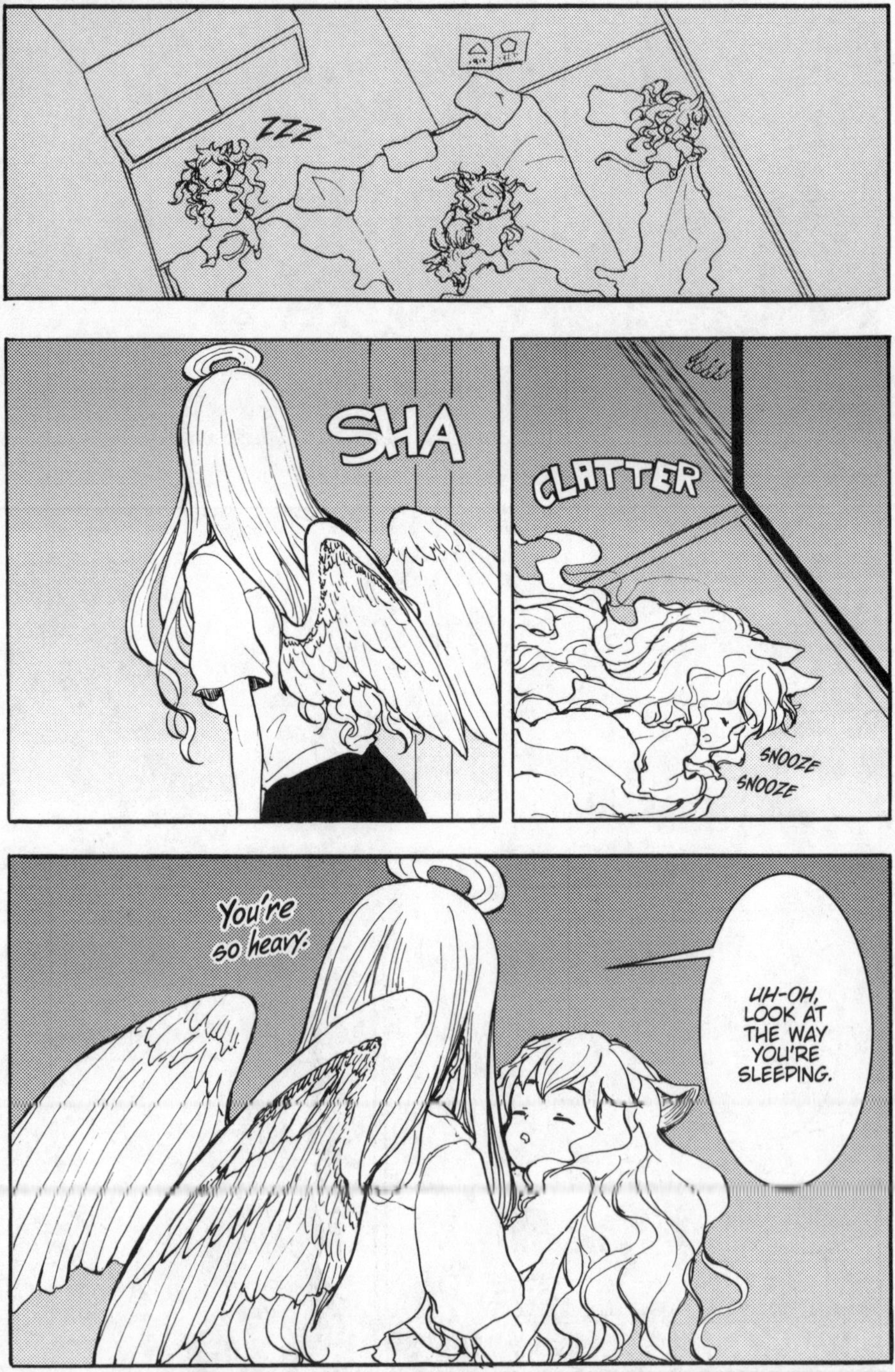
ZZZ
CLATTER
SNOOZE
SNOOZE
SHA
UH-OH, LOOK AT THE WAY YOU'RE SLEEPING.
You're so heavy.

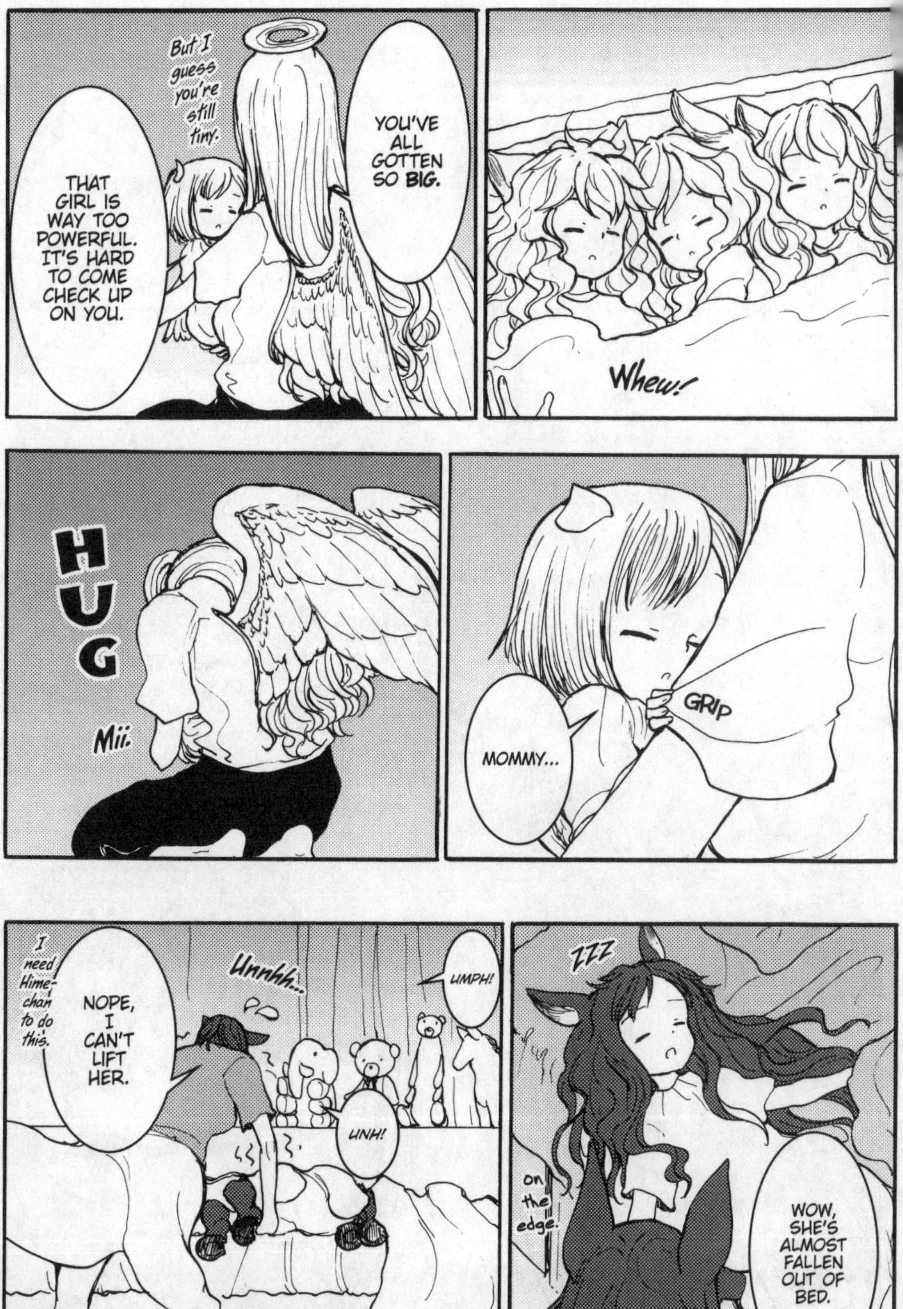
Whew!
YOU'VE ALL GOTTEN SO BIG.
But I guess you're still tiny.
THAT GIRL IS WAY TOO POWERFUL. IT'S HARD TO COME CHECK UP ON YOU.
GRIP
MOMMY...
HUG
Mii.
ZZZ
WOW, SHE'S ALMOST FALLEN OUT OF BED.
on the edge.
UMPH!
Unnhh...
UNH!
NOPE, I CAN'T LIFT HER.
I need Hime-chan to do this.

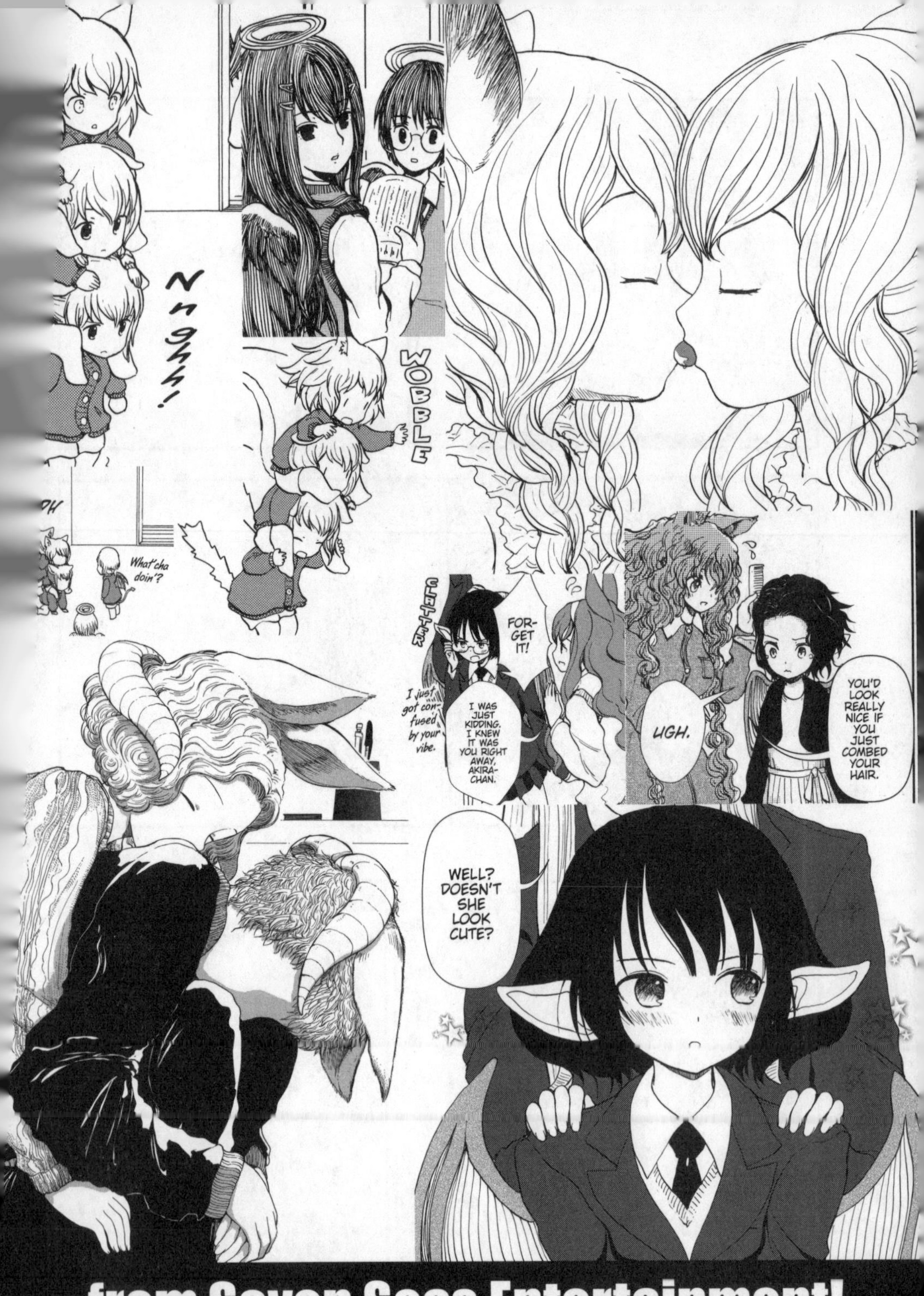
YOU'D LOOK REALLY NICE IF YOU JUST COMBED YOUR HAIR.
UGH.
FOR-GET IT!
CLATTER
I WAS JUST KIDDING. I KNEW IT WAS YOU RIGHT AWAY, AKIRA-CHAN.
I just got confused by your vibe.
WELL? DOESN'T SHE LOOK CUTE?
WOBBLE
Nnghh!
What'cha doin'?

from Seven Seas Entertainment!

SEVEN SEAS ENTERTAINMENT PRESENTS

A Centaur's Life

story and art by KEI MURAYAMA

VOLUME 19

TRANSLATION
Elina Ishikawa

ADAPTATION
Holly Kolodziejczak

LETTERING AND RETOUCH
Jennifer Skarupa

LOGO DESIGN
Courtney Williams

COVER DESIGN
Kris Aubin

PROOFREADER
Danielle King

EDITOR
Shanti Whitesides

PREPRESS TECHNICIAN
Rhiannon Rasmussen-Silverstein

PRODUCTION MANAGER
Lissa Pattillo

MANAGING EDITOR
Julie Davis

ASSOCIATE PUBLISHER
Adam Arnold

PUBLISHER
Jason DeAngelis

CENTAUR NO NAYAMI VOLUME 19

Originally published in Japan in 2019 by TOKUMA SHOTEN PUBLISHING CO., LTD., Tokyo. English translation rights arranged with TOKUMA SHOTEN PUBLISHING CO., LTD., Tokyo, through TOHAN CORPORATION, Tokyo.

Seven Seas press and purchase enquiries can be sent to Marketing Manager Lianne Sentar at press@gomanga.com. Information regarding the distribution and purchase of digital editions is available from Digital Manager CK Russell at digital@gomanga.com.

ISBN: 978-1-64505-828-1

Printed in Canada

First Printing: January 2021

10 9 8 7 6 5 4 3 2 1

FOLLOW US ONLINE: ***www.sevenseasentertainment.com***

READING DIRECTIONS

This book reads from ***right to left***, Japanese style. If this is your first time reading manga, you start reading from the top right panel on each page and take it from there. If you get lost, just follow the numbered diagram here. It may seem backwards at first, but you'll get the hang of it! Have fun!!

1
2
3
4
5
6
7
8
9

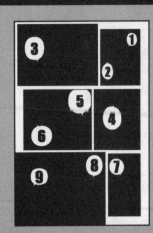